Korea since 1850

KOREA

SINCE 1850

STEWART LONE · GAVAN McCORMACK

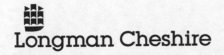

Longman Cheshire

St. Martin's Press
New York

Longman Cheshire Pty Limited
Longman House
Kings Gardens
95 Coventry Street
Melbourne 3205 Australia

Offices in Sydney, Brisbane, Adelaide and Perth. Associated
companies, branches and representatives throughout the world.

Copyright © Longman Cheshire 1993
First published 1993
For information write:
Scholarly and Reference Division,
St. Martin's Press, Inc., 175 Fifth Avenue,
New York, NY 10010
First published in the United States of America in 1993

Edited by Susan Jarvis
Designed by Tony Palmer
Set in 10.5pt New Baskerville
Produced by Longman Cheshire
Printed in Singapore

National Library of Australia
Cataloguing-in-Publication data

Lone, Stewart Peter 1960–
    Korea since 1850.

    Bibliography.
    Includes index.
    ISBN 0 582 87111 5 (cased)   ISBN 0 582 80138 9 (limp)

    1. Korea — History — 1864–1910. 2. Korea — History — 20th
    century. I. McCormack, Gavan. II. Title. (Series: Topics in
    Asian history, politics and international relations).

951.902

Library of Congress Cataloging-in-Publication Data
Lone, Stewart.
Korea since 1850 / Stewart Lone and Gavan McCormack.
p. cm.
Includes bibliographical references and index.
ISBN 0-312-09685-2 (cloth); ISBN 0-312-09686-0 (pbk.)
1. Korea—History—1864–1910. 2. Korea—History—20th century.
I. McCormack, Gavan. II. Title.
DS916.L66 1993
951.9'02—dc20 93-12490

CONTENTS

PREFACE

There are various systems for romanising Korean words: visitors to Pusan, for example, should not be surprised to see Busan commonly used, while Yi, Lee and Rhee are just three possible variants for the same surname. A helpful explanatory note on the language and its romanisation is provided in Donald Stone Macdonald, *The Koreans: Contemporary Politics and Society*, Boulder, Col., 1988 (pp. 281–86). The McCune–Reischauer style is generally accepted and broadly employed here, but exceptions are made for names which are already familiar, such as Seoul, Hyundai and Syngman Rhee, and Korean authors published in English are cited as in the original (e.g. Han Woo-keun). Japanese is romanised according to the modified Hepburn system, Chinese according to *pinyin*. In each of the three countries, the family name is paramount (hence the violent impact of colonial Japan's policy on Korean names — see Chapter 2). Thus, excepting Syngman Rhee and Korean scholars either resident in the West (e.g. Chong-sik Lee and Yur Bok Lee) or writing in the Western form (Hochin Choi), all East Asian names are given according to local custom (i.e. with the family name first). The bibliography and index will serve to clarify any uncertainty.

Stewart Lone and Gavan McCormack
Canberra, July 1992

The history of Korea (or, indeed, any state) from the mid-nineteenth to the late twentieth centuries is, among other things, the history of growing mechanisation in production and mobility, the expansion of communications, schooling and political participation, the growing links with societies hitherto separated by distance and ignorance — in short, the history of evolving nationalism. However, as Anthony Smith ruefully notes, under a strict definition of cultural and linguistic homogeneity coupled with demographic unity within recognised political borders, few states in the modern world can presently be identified as nations.[1] Instead, nationalism remains an ongoing and sometimes uncertain part of the modernisation process. Moreover, the tension between it and internationalisation in a world still dominated by former colonial powers is obvious in those societies to which modernity arrived in the guise of Westernisation — and often as the by-product of Western (or other) imperialism.

Definition of the term 'imperialism' itself remains a source of scholarly debate, yet the simple fact is that much of the twentieth-century world, not least the Korean people, continues to resent its modern history as a tale of foreign exploitation. This resentment is kept alive by the spread of education, literacy and communications, and thus the tools of the modern age are used to restrain that growing inter-connectedness of states which also is one of the fundamental trends of modernity.

There is a similar problem within nationalism. The British critic, J.A. Hobson, once described imperialism as the extension of nationality; however, nationalism itself, as portrayed in Eugen Weber's *Peasants into Frenchmen* (London, 1976), functions as a kind of domestic imperialism, eradicating regional differences and establishing dominance by the capital in language, learning, custom, atitudes to time and modes of production. Here also the process is hastened by the communications and mobilisational techniques of the modern world, not least through centralised control of education and the media. In this way, not only is national identity at odds with the internationalisation of society, but regional identity is also under threat from its domestic metropole.

If one accepts a basic similarity between imperialism and nationalism, then it will come as no surprise to find them both animated by history. In the nineteenth century, imperialism was often justified by its practitioners on the grounds that a state or people lacked 'world-historical' qualities: that they were without racial energy, the dynamism for cultural expansion, or scientific technology; indeed, that they were 'without' history in the case of Africa or, despite past greatness, had failed to keep up with the present — for example, in Egypt, India or China. As for Korea, the entire Yi period (1392–1910) was dismissed by Japanese and Western writers as being without any advance in agriculture or economy, enjoying the same production and consumption modes, ruled by the same people and the same ideology for 500 years.[2] Critics pointed to the socially static and anti-capitalist nature of Confucianism, and the weakness of a distinctly Korean historiography until the 1890s, by which point it was too late, meaning that there was no tangible body of native history to parade as the footsoldier of Korea's defence. Indeed, educated Koreans up to the 1890s learned history from Chinese texts and, according to the reformist noble, Prince Pak Yonghyo, the Korean literati were virtually ignorant about the record of their own people.

In traditional Korea, history served a direct political purpose: to legitimise the rule of kings. On the eve of annexation by Japan in 1910, and in direct response to the outside threat, Korean intellectuals had just begun to write a new historiography as part of the construction of nationalism. However, one of the mechanisms for controlling colonies was the accumulation, and in some senses the monopolisation, of knowledge. During the colonial period (1910–45), nationalistic histories could only be written and disseminated outside the country, and mainstream history within Korean schools and research were dominated by Japan. In terms of the power/knowledge relationship described by French thinker Michel Foucault, this left Koreans broadly powerless to define what was 'known' about themselves.

The unhappy corollary of this, as in other former colonies, is that post-independence Korean historians have confronted an enduring colonialism in knowledge, and have had to work to escape over-dependence on materials collected under the colonial regime. Insofar as the writing of history is a social act, created within and for a particular society, the colonial experience inevitably influences its presentation. In Korea, the repossession of history through publication of native newspapers, diaries and the collection of records on native political and social movements is itself a political act, and history functions less as something cold and academic than as a highly emotive and deeply politicised arena for nationalism.

The tradition of confrontationalism established in the 1900s has been maintained in both North and South Korea, producing, as Carter Eckert has written, 'a nationalistic view of history often quite impervious to facts'.[3] This ideological use of history is exacerbated by the division of Korea into heavily armed camps, each competing for the allegiance of the Korean people as a whole. Historians in both North and South Korea agree, however, when they place special emphasis on recurrent foreign interference as the main distorting factor in the country's modern fate: firstly Chinese cultural domination over many centuries; Japanese invasion in the sixteenth century and colonisation in the twentieth; and the Soviet–American division of the peninsula following the Second World War.

In the early 1990s, there was some reduction in political tensions between P'yongyang and Seoul, and in 1992 the South Korean education minister promised that school history books would be rewritten to downplay anti-communism from 1995. Insofar as the economic health of both states (especially were they to reunite) depends on foreign trade and improved contacts with the outside, this may signal a greater general diversity in Korean historiography. However, the forecast was uncertain: South Korea's rise in the global market during the 1980s appeared to sprout a history far more inclined towards an excluding nationalism than an embracing internationalism.

The bulk of foreign writing on Korea, not surprisingly, comes from Japan, and there are many Korean scholars either publishing directly or being translated into Japanese. For their part, Japanese scholars are generally critical of the imperialist past and sympathetic to the Korean interpretation. In the West, at the risk of waxing lyrical, Korean history resembles a white stallion galloping through a snow-clad forest: briefly visible, but mostly lost from sight. Thanks to the research efforts of several fine scholars working in the United States, this is now less true of the late Yi and colonial eras, but it remains a valid comment on the more distant past. Western studies of 'traditional' Korea are, in comparison to those on China or Japan, very much in their infancy; even in more modern works touching on East Asia, Korea is generally treated either as an addendum to China or Japan, or simply as a backdrop for international rivalries. Korea first impinged on the Western consciousness with the war of 1950, but there was no explosion of academic interest comparable to that surrounding the later Vietnam conflict. Consequently, while Keith McFarland's guide to the so-called Korean War (*The Korean War: An Annotated Bibliography*, NY, 1986) can run to more than 2000 histories, battlefield studies and memoirs by Western participants or observers, at the time of writing there is just a handful of scholarly general histories of Korea in the English language. The most recent are those by Andrew Nahm, *Korea: Tradition and Transformation* (1988) and the rewritten version of Ki-baik Lee's *A New History of Korea* appearing in 1990 under the title *Korea Old and New: A History*. The rest are largely dated translations from South Korean historians and bear a marked similarity in their approach. The present work aims to survey the modern period through all its vicissitudes of monarchy, colony and nation divided, and to reject mythology, whether of Korean or other origin. In its stead, it is hoped the reader will find, if not complete objectivity, at least an alternative perspective on some of the prevailing notions about Korea.

Our nominal point of departure is 1850. The Western calendar is alien to much of the world, and the series of stops and starts according to a change of dynasty produces a much more discordant and loosely linked historical line than the single band rising (perhaps falling?) from the birth of Christ. The habit of treating Korean history in terms of monarchical reign, however, suggests too great an authority at the centre, an authority which in practice would be hard to substantiate: of course, the same might be argued even for Showa Japan or for Victorian Britain. The starting point of 1850, however, has no special significance in Korea: it is intended here merely to indicate that we will deal primarily with events from the latter half of the nineteenth century. The half-century date is also used to evoke in the reader's mind a sense of matters unsettled, a halfway point from which anything might develop, and a rejection of the deterministic view that contact with Japan from 1875 inevitably led to the annexation of Korea in 1910. Moreover, the history of any state is more appropriately a kaleidoscope of images rather than a perfectly finished portrait and, whereas Western historians in the nineteenth century used to describe their subject through three clear stages of youth, growth and maturity (or decline), no such pleasant and complete resolution is applied here.

The following chapters divide Korea's modern history into three broad periods: to the fall of the Yi dynasty in 1910; the colonial era under Japan; and the post-1945 creation of separate republics. For much of the first of these periods, Korea was a nominal tributary of China, but there was an unprecedented variety and urgency about the foreign impacts washing on to its shores. For this reason, Chapter 1 unfolds in a basically chronological manner, charting the shifts in foreign relations, the rise of domestic political groups in competition with the traditional centre of authority (one torn apart by endemic factional rivalries) and surveying major socio-economic changes such as the spread of inter-national commerce and the first moves towards popular education. In the colonial era, Korea was far more subject to policies unilaterally decided by the Japanese government and the extent of foreign influences was commensurately foreshortened. Thus Chapter 2 is more topical than chronological, treating the colonial years through the dominant themes of agriculture, education, industry and political movements. The final period (Chapters 3 to 5) explores the tragedy of Korea's briefly restored autonomy and rapid division into war and rival governments. These chapters assess the post-1945 period from a diversity of viewpoints.

Finally, it should be noted that a work of this nature is inevitably indebted to the research of many individuals, even those with whom the authors are in complete disagreement. Care has been taken to provide an extensive, yet by no means comprehensive, English-language bibliography as acknowledgement of this debt. In the writing of this book, the burden has been shared as follows: Stewart Lone is responsible for the Introduction, and for Chapters 1, 2 and 4; Gavan McCormack has contributed Chapters 3 and 5. Each author bears absolute responsibility for the views, errors and omissions of his respective chapters.

Grateful thanks are expressed by Stewart Lone to the following colleagues for assistance and comments on the text: Dr Kenneth Wells for reading an earlier version of Chapters 1 and 2; Professor Colin Mackerras; Ron Harper, publisher at Longman Cheshire; and Drs John Caiger and Roger Thompson.

Notes

1   Anthony D. Smith, 'State-making and nation-building', in *States in History*, ed. John A. Hall, Oxford, 1986.
2   A representative view is Shikata Hiroshi, *Chosen Shakai Keizaishi*, 3 vols, reprinted Tokyo, 1976, vol. 3, pp. 150–51.
3   Eckert, 1991, p. 2. On Korean historiography, see Yong-Ho Ch'oe, 'Reinterpreting traditional history in North Korea', *Journal of Asian Studies*, vol. 11, no. 3, May 1981, pp. 503–21; also Kang Man'gil, 'How history is viewed in the North and in the South: Convergence and Divergence', *Korea Journal*, vol. 30, no. 2, February 1990, pp. 4–19.

Korea in the nineteenth century was a rice-based agrarian society, framed by mountains in the north, central south and along much of the the east coast, and with a population that was heaviest in the south-western plains. The style of government and social relations was Confucian, the political and ethical system long assimilated from neighbouring China. Designed to uphold a static agrarian and not a fluid commercial order, Confucianism was a paternalistic system of benevolent rule by civil bureaucrats acting in the name of a monarch who was technically absolute and the nominal possessor of all land in the kingdom. Its ethics were also highly patriarchal — in no relationship did women enjoy prestige except as mother to male child — and in preserving the *status quo*, it inhibited philosophical speculation or technological invention. This was to retard Korea's (and China's) response to the international challenges of the late nineteenth century. Instead, Confucianism offered stability through a clear social hierarchy and highly stratified social relations, a stratification upheld by distinctions in such matters as costume and grammatically explicit levels of honorific language. Social ranking, as in China and Japan, descended from scholar-bureaucrats (warrior-bureaucrats in Japan) to farmers, then artisans and finally merchants. In Korea, there was also an intermediate group of lower level officials with specialist skills known literally as 'middle men' (*chungin*), and these conducted much of the government's business as, among other things, scribes, accountants, translators and astronomer-astrologists. A variety of outcast professions existed, including butchers, tanners, entertainers, female shamans and — indicating Buddhism's degraded place in the Yi dynasty (1392–1910) — Buddhist priests and nuns.

The population of nineteenth-century Korea remains a matter for speculation. Sources are unreliable: the official figure in the 1880s was 28 million, but this is contradicted by a 1910 survey which showed a total of just 14.77 million. Most were farmers, mainly working tenanted land and cultivating rice or cereals in the southern rice bowl. Later observers thought Korean farmers even hardier than their Japanese counterparts, but agrarian technology was crude. Bullocks were used for ploughing, but much farmwork was manual. Villages were small, tight-knit communities, located within easy walking distance of a market town. There, frequently on every fifth day, farmers exchanged excess cereals and homemade wares for cotton goods, household items and foods brought from other regions by pedlars. Meat was expensive, so fish, caught in abundance on the east coast, salted, dried and carried inland by boat or pack-horse, provided the substance of a meal. Grass or wood faggots served as fuel for cooking and for the heated stone floors of Korean houses. Carts were few, and roads little more than bridle-paths. Railways, those arteries of imperialism and nationalism, were unknown until the 1900s, and domestic transport was limited either to river boats or land passage by hoof or foot. In the heavy summer rains, both tracks and rivers became virtually impassable and the flimsy makeshift bridges across streams were swept away.

Market day, Ulsan, late nineteenth century
Source: *Choson sidai* (The Chosen Period), vol. 1, pp. 10–11

The needs of the land circumscribed the farmer's geographical horizon, Confucianism determined his social relations and his religious view was dominated by animism, the belief in nature spirits inhabiting local trees, rocks and rivers, and pacified by the mediation of shamans. With low urbanisation, minimal inter-village contact, limited inter-regional commerce, and no entry to the élite, catalysts were lacking for peasant literacy or awareness of events elsewhere. There was, however, a vigorous folk culture of mask theatre, lively dance and song, and storytelling, often relating stories of nature in the manner of Aesop's fables. Given Korea's relatively small size and demographic congestion in the south, cultural and linguistic variation was not on the scale of China or even Japan, but differences in dialect were (and still are) keenly perceived.

Magisterially residing above the common herd and constituting some 10 per cent of the population was the hereditary élite: the *yangban*. The term originally denoted the civil and military authorities, but Confucian ideals were civil, not martial. (One nineteenth-century observer, British statesman George Curzon, noted acidly that Korea's standing army was more appropriately termed a standing joke.) Over time, and with no persistent military threat of any size to be engaged by a Korean army, the administration had become almost entirely civilian. The government structure, which survived basically intact to the end of the dynasty, was based on the Chinese model, with the king overseeing six ministries: Personnel, Revenue, Rites, War, Justice and Public Works. The offices of inspector-general and censor-general ensured official probity and both observed the court and advised the monarch. At the provincial level, a supervisor commanded authority as administrator, censor and military governor. At the lowest rung of central government were the district magistrates, whose duties were to promote agriculture, collect taxes, expand moral education and ensure social stability. This was carried out with advice from councils of local gentry, whose fortunes, as in China, depended on perpetuation of the established system, but also on ensuring a measure of justice for the peasantry and so preventing unrest harmful to their own positions.

The *yangban* were forbidden to participate in trade, an activity seen by Confucianism as self-serving and socially divisive. Their only skill was bureaucracy, and this led, as in China and Japan, to severe congestion for office, resulting in favouritism, corruption and over-staffing. Intense factional divisions within central government from the sixteenth century also caused endless personnel shifts. Many officials languished in unemployment, despite senior posts being rapidly rotated. For example, in the 1860s, 82 men served as Minister of Works in less than ten years, averaging just two months each. Supervisors and district magistrates were likewise quickly rotated to prevent them establishing any form of local power base. The unfortunate corollary of all this was a growing discontent within the élite, the very group with the education and resources to potentially challenge the government. It also forced provincial officals to rely for local knowledge on functionaries known as *ajon* who often controlled access to their superiors for personal gain. The result was that bureaucrats frequently squeezed dry a regional posting and paid only lip-service to the ideas of Confucian paternalism.

Unlike Western Europe, urban centres in Korea (and East Asia generally) were mainly administrative rather than economic in origin. Officials counted for over half the city population and artisans primarily supplied bureaucratic needs. This monochromatic urbanisation was a further impediment to social change, as was its concentration in the central south. Most *yangban* families resided in Seoul, with the majority

of 'local' or rustic *yangban* in the southern provinces of Ch'ungch'ong
and Kyongsang. Virtually none except those who had been demoted or
banished for one indiscretion or another were to be found in the north
or east. Consequently, the harsher mountainous regions which consti-
tute much of the Democratic People's Republic of Korea (DPRK) today
were historically known as 'the land of the exiles'. Gilbert Rozman, in
his *Urban Networks in Ch'ing China and Tokugawa Japan* (Princeton, 1973),
suggested that Japan modernised effectively in the nineteenth century
because it already had a large, widespread and dense urbanisation
(especially along the commercial roads such as the Tokaido), and that
China had taken longer because, however widespread, its cities remained
considerably smaller. Korea, neither in the nineteenth nor late in the
twentieth century, had anything like a balanced urban dispersal; instead,
the capital, Seoul, acted as a leviathan primate city, swallowing the bulk
of the country's economic, political and cultural product.

Chongo, Seoul, 1900
Source: *Choson sidai*, vol. 2, p. 71

Education for the élite commenced early. *Yangban* children memor-
ised Confucian ethics and the Chinese script at elementary primary
schools called *sodang*, similar in character to Chinese village schools or
the *tera-koya* (temple schools) of Tokugawa Japan. At the regional level,
there were both government-sponsored academies and private academies known as *sowon*. The latter were often founded by scholar-bureaucrats
excluded from office by political factionalism, and by the start of the
eighteenth century numbered more than 600, eventually virtually
supplanting the government institutions, which consequently declined
in quality. The Songgyun'gwan, or National Confucian Academy, in
Seoul was the highest institution of learning and trained its quota of 200
students for the civil exam. As in China, official appointment depended

on success in the district, provincial and metropolitan examinations, centred on approved interpretation of the Confucian classics and correct literary style. However, unlike China, where technically anyone might sit for the civil service, in Korea the original goal of public education and an open meritocracy had been unofficially abandoned with position restricted to sons of *yangban*. Indeed, high office became the monopoly of a small number of powerful *yangban* clans; this further heightened inter-élite factionalism, the perpetual bane of Korean politics.

At the apex of power, and determining the character of the state, was the king. In the Confucian system, the king mediated between heaven and earth to ensure continuation of the natural order of things and security for the people. His rule was sanctioned by the people's welfare and this could be achieved only by virtuous administration. The king was expected to conform to the accepted mould of the wise ruler rather than wield unquestioned authority — more than the divine kings of pre-modern Europe, he was in many ways merely the pre-eminent bureaucrat — and it was theoretically legitimate to remove by force a venal or corrupt monarch. In practice, however, the existence of established interests and the weakness of political opposition meant that less than perfect kings did retain power. Yet the question of legitimacy remained: the Confucian principle of remonstrance with the ruler was upheld and Confucian academies took on the role of an inspectorate of monarchical behaviour. In the face of these multiple constraints, a truly despotic monarch was unlikely, but so was one with the authority to institute radical change when necessary. This was to be discovered by the penultimate of the Yi monarchs, Kojong (r. 1873–1907), treated by

Emperor Kojong, in full regalia as Great Han Emperor Kojong (1852–1919)
Source: Tongnip undong (Independence Movement Through Pictures), vol. 1, 1987, p. 42

historians — perhaps unfairly — as a helplessly weak and venal ruler, but who, in his youth, appeared an exemplary Confucian monarch.[1]

The Korean system began to unravel in the seventeenth century in the wake of foreign invasion and the collapse of central land tax revenue. Indicative of change was the spread of commerce as the government minted more coinage in an attempt to pay its way out of difficulties. The British historian of the Roman empire, Edward Gibbon, asserted in the eighteenth century that the spread of a cash economy was a prime indicator of 'civilisation'. Confucianism, in stark contrast to the West, placed tight regulations on unbridled commerce and gave scant respect to businessmen. In Korea, foreign trade was a state monopoly, while the Yi's domestic economy declined relative to the earlier Koryo dynasty (918–1392). The court in Seoul was the country's major consumer, but it originally dealt only with government-sanctioned suppliers. Internal trade was carried out mainly by itinerant pedlars: long distance shipping was prohibited and water transport was designed mainly for provincial grain taxes to Seoul. However, new commercial players arose in the seventeenth century from among the commission agents (*kaekchu*) and brokers (*yogak*) who unloaded goods on Seoul's Han River. As money became more widely used, these men accumulated higher profits, gradually developing a business relationship with regional producers through loans to control and ensure supply, and ultimately challenging the accredited merchants by setting up their own wholesale and retail stores in the outlying areas of Seoul.

Observing these commercial developments, postwar Korean scholars have refuted the Japanese colonial view that Korean capitalism developed only as the product of nineteenth-century Japanese influence. Instead, they point to the sprouts of capitalist relations well before the 1870s, citing persistent agrarian hardship resulting in land and labour becoming accepted market commodities, the existence of manufacturing industries such as brassware production in P'yongan and Kyonggi, a system whereby rich farmers employed weaving girls for wages, and the development of inland market towns like Taegu in central southern Korea, and ports such as Wonsan in the central north-east. It is generally accepted that the decline in government authority allowed some merchants to amass considerable wealth — notably the Kaesong traders of Hwanghae province in the north-west, well placed to benefit from trade with China — and that there were *yangban* who quietly participated in commerce for personal gain. However, the 'sprouts of capitalism' theory is firmly rejected by Carter Eckert in his landmark study *Offspring of Empire,* and whatever developments did take place were undeniably small in scale, inhibited by the lack of internal communications and the limited consumer market.[2] Moreover, the Korean élite was hereditary, and businessmen were not given the incentive enjoyed in China (albeit one essentially designed to blunt commercialism) of admission to the élite through purchase of a scholar's degree.

Historians have queried the impact of a general world crisis following global climatic changes in the seventeenth century. Certainly, for whatever reason, the regimes of Korea, China and Japan were all confronted by rising disorder in the social hierarchy and heightened agrarian unrest in the late eighteenth century. The Yi dynasty was the single longest monarchy enjoying direct power in East Asia, but its continued authority depended on mollifying the peasantry and maintaining stability. Compared with Japan, the Korean peninsula is relatively free of earthquakes, but there are natural calamities enough: between 1782 and 1840, Korea recorded on average a famine or epidemic once every two years, followed by twelve major floods betwen 1841 and 1860. The court had allowed large tracts of land to slip from the tax register into the hands of officials or Confucian academies, and so had little money to deal with catastrophes, while moves to increase taxation only exacerbated peasant immiseration. Mass uprisings occured during 1811 in P'yongan, and in 1862 across the southern provinces. Fifty years apart, and without sufficient arms to seriously endanger the government, the significance of these revolts should not be overestimated, but the many-layered nature of the protests is important: they were led by discontented or politically fallen *yangban* and included not only peasants, but also rich farmers and merchants. The decline in government authority offered some compensatory freedoms for merchants and the better-off farmers, whose participation in revolt was thus qualified. This left poor peasants with an unenviable choice: they could abandon their fields and try to evade taxation by farming hill lands outside government purview; they could become tenant-farmers; or they could offer themselves as agrarian wage labour. Many chose the first option but, discovered by the authorities or failing to eke out an existence, increasingly turned to banditry. Others crossed the border into Manchuria or, from the 1860s, into the bleak Russian maritime province: in 1869 alone some 7000 Koreans entered Russian territory, laying the seeds of a community unofficially estimated at 750 000 in the 1980s (but one centred in Soviet Central Asia and Kazakhstan after forcible relocation by Stalin in the 1930s).

Among the Korean élite, imaginative (i.e. radical) solutions to Korea's difficulties came only from the scholar-officials known generally as the Silhak (or Sirhak) 'school'. Their philosophy was influenced by trends in China, where the seventeenth-century collapse of the Ming dynasty had produced a re-evaluation of Confucian beliefs, and which also suffered from official congestion, the rise of commercialism and shifts in the rural population. Some Silhak scholars visiting Beijing on official missions were also converted to Catholicism by Western missionaries. These scholars, however, were not simply recipients of Chinese or Western learning and their attempt to go beyond the acceptable tinkering of 'change within tradition' by promoting study of native history, geography, language and society is credited with preparing the ground for modern Korean nationalism. Some of the solutions they proposed had extraordinary implications. Pak Chega (1750–1805), a leading Silhak figure, compared the economy to a well which only flows naturally with constant use: to achieve this, he urged the government openly to promote business and inspire the *yangban* to muddy their hands by plunging into trade. In the end, however, the unorthodoxy of Silhak views, the links of some with Christianity, and their lack of weight in court factionalism led to their political decline from the turn of the nineteenth century. Nonetheless, their ideas established a native tradition for later progressives.

In the wake of the 1862 southern rising, a conservative approach to reform was undertaken by the Taewon'gun, regent from 1866 to the juvenile King Kojong. The Taewon'gun aimed at stability in administration and revenue, appointing men of talent to improve efficiency and employing secret inspectors to report on provincial administration. He also abolished many quarrelsome *sowon* academies, both to limit criticism of the government and to restore the valuable lands in their possession to the throne. However, despite the Taewon'gun's attempt to re-empower the monarchy, bureaucratic congestion and corruption remained essentially unchecked, and the Taewon'gun's plan to enhance royal prestige through large-scale palace construction produced limited gains while consuming vital funds. Revenue was further diverted by defence needs following the appearance of foreign ships off Korea's coast in the 1860s. With the monarchy and centralised Confucian bureaucracy incapable of dealing with social change, an outside force was now, for good or ill, to break the impasse.

'The Hermit Kingdom'

As noted in the introduction, Korean historians give particular emphasis to the role of foreign actions in distorting the country's modern fate. In an age before steam transport, geographical proximity inevitably left neighbouring China and Japan the most important external influences, and one result of this is a too frequent dismissal in the West of Korea as a cultural subdivision of either China or Japan. This misconception may derive from Korea's relatively low level of interaction with the West up to the 1940s, and from its traditional diplomacy of *sadae kyorin*: attendance on the great (China) and goodwill to one's neighbour (Japan). However, the practices of the élite should not blind us to Korea's individuality. The Yi enjoyed high status (and relative largesse in presents) as China's most faithful tributary, but Korean historians rightly protest exaggerated claims of Korea's dependence on Beijing: pre-twentieth century Korea was an independent entity; in the very basics of everyday life — language, clothing and food — Koreans were quite distinct from their northern neighbours. Actual contact was limited to the periodic reciprocal missions of Korean and Chinese envoys. That Korea's élite was educated in Chinese thought, script and culture is beyond doubt. For the ordinary people, however, China was an entity without meaning in their daily lives, and the literate amongst them read not in the scholar's tortuous Chinese but in their own phonetic *han'gul* script, created by order of King Sejong in the mid-fifteenth century.

While the relationship with China was largely voluntary (tiny Korea had little choice but to accept Chinese suzerainty) and in many ways beneficial, that with Japan was much more volatile. During the Yi dynasty, and indeed up to the present, Koreans took pride in the fact that Japan's initial understanding of the Chinese script and Buddhism was obtained from Korean travellers in earlier centuries. Into the seventeenth and eighteenth centuries, Japanese intellectuals continued to esteem Korean scholarship, and some Koreans were employed in domain schools. However, the single event to embitter Korean–Japanese relations for all time to come was Hideyoshi's bloody and extended invasion of Korea en route to China in the 1590s. The six years of war were intensely destructive of Korean life and property, and only Hideyoshi's death in 1598 enabled the succeeding *shogun*, Tokugawa Ieyasu (whose family was to retain control of Japan until 1868), to restore a semblance of goodwill in the 1600s. Subsequently, Korean diplomatic missions visited Tokyo, and Japanese trade on Korean soil was permitted, but only with specified merchants. It was also limited to Pusan on Korea's southern coast (just as Japan limited foreign trade to Nagasaki and China confined Western merchants to Canton). Yet the fact is that Korea and Japan, immediately prior to the modern period, enjoyed over 250 years of peace, and with Western vessels arriving in East Asian waters at the start of the nineteenth century, the needs of mutual security momentarily brought them even closer through exchanges of intelligence.

Both Korea and Japan had adopted policies of exclusion towards the West from the mid-seventeenth century. Of the two, Korea was the most rigid as the early nineteenth century progressed, and arguably the most under threat as Western economic and missionary interests began looking to expand up the China coast. However, Western traders in the nineteenth century were preoccupied with the supposed El Dorado of China and, from mid-century, with their fancy of 'lotus-land' Japan. British and Russian ships sniffed at Korea's coast from the 1830s, but Korea, visibly smaller and poorer than its neighbours, rested on the periphery of Western consciousness. The first English-language history, compiled by William Eliot Griffis from Japanese sources, was *Corea The Hermit Nation* (1868), a title overlooking the clearly non-hermitic links to China and Japan. The dominant Western interest in Korea, even into the twentieth century, was religious: Catholicism, as noted with members of the Silhak, had entered Korea through contacts in Beijing, and Catholic missionaries infiltrated Korea's northern border in the mid-nineteenth century. The doctrines of Catholicism, perhaps especially the belief in equality before God, appealed across social classes and the rising number of Koreans converting to this foreign religion provoked a government backlash from 1866 — 8000 Korean Catholics and nine

French missionaries were executed. Late in 1866, a French gunboat arrived in search of reparation, but the mission was half-hearted and retreated before Korean coastal defences. A distressed United States vessel which arrived the same year was treated kindly and its crew assisted to China, but a second American ship in 1871, in search of loot, was violently rebuffed. Western commercial indifference continued but, in 1875, there came a new power whose vital economic and strategic interests lay precisely in Korea: Meiji Japan.

Japan's own isolation policy had been ended in 1854 by the United States. A series of unequal treaties ensued with the Western powers and the Tokugawa fell in civil war during 1868. A coalition of regional domains took over government with the Emperor Meiji harnessed as the focus of a modern nationalism. The Meiji government did not come to power on a groundswell of popular support: it had in its favour only the figurehead of the emperor, its own limited military force and the promise of general improvement for the infant Japanese nation. In the age of 'new imperialism', commencing about 1870, states were judged less by conditions at home than by their global influence. In the imperial Charter Oath of 1868, Japan embraced Western methods for self-strengthening, and for overseas expansion the immediate avenues were the southern Pacific and Korea. Of the two, the pick was Korea, with its promise of a doorway to Manchuria and north China.

Korea has never been inclined or able to interfere in the politics of its neighbours. Seoul treated the ascension of the Meiji regime as a domestic Japanese matter and merely anticipated the resumption of equal relations. Tokyo, instead, unilaterally changed the format of diplomatic documents, placing the Japanese emperor in a position of superiority to the Korean king. In literal terms, this was correct, as Japan did not accept the suzerainty of China. It was not, however, accepted diplomatic practice and was rejected by the Taewon'gun in 1869. Thereafter, the problem festered without resolution, and provoked in Japan a debate which was to continue for the rest of the century: whether to give precedence to economic or armed development — that is, in which order to interpret the official Meiji slogan of 'rich nation, strong army'. In 1873, advocates of 'Sei Kan-ron' (invade Korea), under acting head of government Saigo Takamori, considered Korea an easy prize to strengthen Japan both internally and internationally. Other ministers in the Iwakura mission, then touring the West in search of treaty revision and observing first-hand the Occident's industrial and military strength, realised the danger of becoming embroiled in war at this time and managed to outmanoeuvre the militants. The Sei-Kan group angrily resigned from office, only to ignite mounting discontent with the Meiji leaders in those very regions which formed the base of government support. The idea that Japan could ease its internal political troubles by expanding into Korea was to be resurrected in future years, however.

A new era began in Korean politics with King Kojong's coming of age in 1873. Kojong was aware of events beyond Korea's borders and knew that China had begun its own search for 'wealth and strength' based on imported Western science and technology. He also knew that Korea, lacking an effective military or military ethos, could not defend itself against a modern invader, especially when armed support from Beijing was so uncertain. With the demonstrated use of violence in international dealings by the Western powers, and their insistence on treaties both written in unfamiliar legal terms and heavily imbalanced against the states of East Asia, only a tiny minority of Koreans actively wanted better links to the outside. They were mainly the inheritors of Silhak thought and those with diplomatic experience in China, but they were also joined by Kojong. Yet the weakness of the Korean throne and interference from politically powerful royal in-laws caused matters with Japan to lie in abeyance for much of 1875, and the Japanese foreign office, revealing its insensitivity to Korean memory, even considered despatching warships to intimidate Kojong's opponents. Late in 1875, the Korean government finally agreed to a new relationship with Japan, but local officials at Pusan deliberately let the Japanese negotiator there depart in ignorance. At that very moment, in September 1875, the *Unyo-kan*, a Japanese warship, found itself in convenient hostilities with a Korean battery on Kanghwa island, guardian of the main waterway to Seoul and the same spot at which French and American vessels had appeared in earlier years. Shore batteries attacked a small boat from the Japanese vessel, purportedly intending to request fresh water. The *Unyo-kan* responded in kind, marines landed and 35 Korean soldiers were killed.

This was Korea's first military humiliation in the modern age and came from the one state which could best serve Korean adaptation to the changing world. For Japan, it was a callous blunder, undermining Kojong's goodwill and resuscitating anti-Japanese sentiment. Had Japan been confident in its economic and military position, the affair might have served as a *casus belli*, but in fact it was no better placed for a continental war than in 1873. Fortunately for Tokyo, faced with Japanese sabre-rattling and personally favouring agreement, Kojong accepted a treaty of friendship, commerce and navigation, which was signed at Kanghwa on 26 February 1876. There were still those, not least the Taewon'gun, who rejected all dealings with Japan, but the sense of general crisis gave Kojong an authority at home which he was rarely to enjoy. The treaty preamble defined the international legal position of Korea *vis-a-vis* China, explaining that Korea, 'being an independent State, enjoys the same sovereign rights as does Japan'. The treaty included provision for exchange of diplomatic representatives in the respective capitals, and stationing of Japanese consuls in specific Korean ports which were to be opened to direct trade. Clause 10 is the most contentious to historians, granting Japanese citizens in the open ports extraterritorial rights — that is, the right to be tried for any offence by officers of their own country. Enforcing the unequal nature of the agreement, further details were negotiated in August 1876, giving tariff exemption on Japan's exports to Korea and permitting Japanese to use their own currency in the open ports.

The opening of international trade was to bring profit and loss to the Korean people. Domestic commerce was expanded and foreign goods became more readily available, but not everyone was enriched equally and some local producers found their wares uncompetitive. There was to be a mass of information and technology more readily available for inspection, but disagreement over what should be assimilated and by whom. However, insofar as modern diplomacy worked at an ever-increasing pace and served as a spotlight on the capitals of the world, the fate of Korea now rested heavily on the activities of the king and his court. Whereas Meiji Japan preserved an umbrella for stability through its essentially supra-political monarchy, even increasing its pre-modern religious power, complaints in Korea from foreigners and natives alike fell on the more orthodox bureaucrat-king, frequently with unsatisfactory results. This constantly served to erode both the king's authority and, with it, that of Korea as an independent state.

The Korea market

The 'scramble' for Korea was slow to start and sedate in its development. It took several years for other powers to conclude trade treaties with Korea: first came the United States in May 1882, followed by Britain and Germany the following month, Russia in 1884 and France in 1886. China encoded its relationship with Korea in internationally recognisable terms through a commercial agreement in 1882, but one explicitly noting Korea's tributary status *vis-a-vis* China. By this time, Pusan had been open as an international port since October 1876, the north-eastern port of Wonsan from April 1880, and Inch'on from January 1883. Only two additional ports were subsequently opened to international trade before the Sino-Japanese War of 1894–95.

At Pusan, individual relations between Japanese and Koreans did not start amicably, but this was partly the result of Korean officials who attacked imports as unwanted luxuries and inimical to existing social values. At Wonsan, the reception was warmer, but low peasant incomes meant slow business for Japanese traders whose confidence only rose with the arrival of home financial institutions; a branch of the Dai-Ichi Bank opened at Pusan in 1878, with offices at Wonsan and Inch'on from 1880–82. Despite the financial weakness of Korean traders and con-sumers, and official abuses in inflating purchase prices to the Japanese, mutual trade expanded from a total of 0.2 million yen in 1876 to 2.5 million yen in 1883. Japan purchased mainly food — rice, wheat and beans — with a considerable trade in cow hides which were then cured, repacked and shipped on to Europe. After an early emphasis on grains, cotton piece goods (largely British manufactures) made up 75.3 per cent of all Japanese exports to Korea between 1877 and 1882. This policy of exporting British cottons for Korean grain continued and expanded into the 1880s.

As others entered the Korea market, the value of Japan's trade dropped rapidly, falling in 1883 to one-quarter that of the previous year. Throughout the 1880s, however, Western commercial interest remained fixed on China and Japan. The powerful British company Jardine & Matheson made a tentative incursion into Korea, opening a branch for imports and mineral exploration at Inch'on in July 1883, but withdrew at the end of 1884 after losing faith in the unsubstantiated promises of the Korean government and incurring heavy losses. The first American businessman arrived hot foot on the heels of the Korean–United States treaty, but was in the country no more than a few days before he collapsed and died. Up until 1894, there was no United States investment in Korea, and of global United States exports of $921 million in 1895, only $111 803, or 0.013 per cent, went to Korea.[3] Americans were later to develop a key missionary presence, but the level of economic activity was never sufficient to justify Washington's overt involvement in Korean affairs.

The new trading players were Chinese merchants based in Seoul, and especially in Inch'on after 1883. Like their Japanese counterparts, they bought Korean rice and cow hides, as well as seafood and the highly prized (because of its reputedly aphrodisiac qualities) ginseng root, and in return sold cotton goods of Western origin. According to Korean customs records, goods from China rose sharply against those from Japan in the 1880s and 1890s; by 1893, the two had roughly 50 per cent apiece of total Korean imports. The export trade, however, was very different: the vast Chinese empire was far more self-sufficient than Japan and at no point between 1885 and 1893 did Japan take less than 90 per cent of Korea's exports.[4]

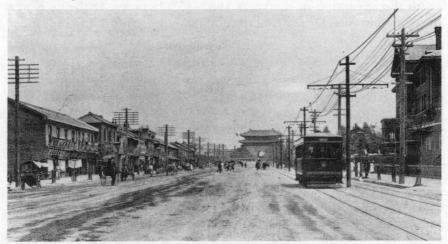

Seoul, from Railroad Station towards Namdaemun, 1900s.
Source: Kundae Hanguk (Modern Korea), vol. 1

The relative sophistication of Chinese or Japanese traders put some Koreans out of business. The *kaekchu* merchants, however, had earlier proved the benefits of flexibility in competition with the government-accredited suppliers, and they now flocked to the open ports and Seoul, which thus became the centres of a new Korean economic dynamism. The expanded rice export trade also made rich men of many Korean landlords, and it was principally they who were to fund the establishment of industries in the 1920s. Thus international trade, and especially that with Japan, forced rapid modernisation on the Korean economy and prepared the way for Korean capitalism.

Sino-Japanese competition lowered retail prices, allowing the market in foreign goods to expand throughout the 1880s and early 1890s. Chinese and Japanese traders also attuned themselves to Korean manners and tastes, something ignored by British traders, who seemed indifferent to Korea as an individual market. Korean consumers were not compelled to purchase foreign wares: they did so because of better price, quality or easier access. It was the *kaekchu* acting as middlemen who bought Korean peasant crops for export and who conducted foreign goods into the agricultural village markets, yet their own profits depended on the response of rural consumers. This opens to doubt the claim by Korean historian Lee Ki-baik that Japanese traders were mostly from the lawless or depressed elements of Japan's society, and were unscrupulous in exploiting the Korean peasantry.[5] Moreover, until the Sino-Japanese War, most Japanese in Korea were artisans or ran small businesses in the open ports: an 1895 survey of Pusan listed, among others, 87 carpenters, 41 confectioners, 23 tobacco sellers, 3 watch-makers, and 9 ladies' hairdressers.[6] It should also be noted that, while Korean and Japanese scholars have often emphasised pursuit of the Korea market as Japan's motive for war with China in 1894, modern Japan's primary economic interest has in fact always been in the West (with the exception of the years 1937–45): between 1886–95, Korea accounted for just 1.7 per cent of total Japanese exports and only 3 per cent of its total imports.[7]

For Koreans to regain control of trade, and the state's political future, it was essential to import advanced technology. This was the tangible base of the West's superiority, the nuts and bolts foundation which supported ideologies of racial hierarchy contemptuous of East Asia. That East Asia had not formerly been technologically backward was obvious from the achievements of China, not least in the discovery of gunpowder, and in Korea's own printing arts. Yet so great was the disparity in mechanical strength by the mid-nineteenth century that each of the East Asian states was forced to adopt elements of Western culture. Where they differed was in the degree to which central authority could enforce this 'modernisation', and the extent to which they modified the social apparatus to accommodate new approaches to time, production, movement, even life itself. Japan succeeded most visibly, but only at the cost of destroying traditional social divisions and instituting systems of mass compulsory education and military service. China, after a second defeat by Anglo-French forces in 1860, and much in line with its policy in the 1980s, sought 'wealth and strength' based on Western technology, but without socio-political reconstruction.

In its lack of structural alteration, Korean policy followed the Chinese example. Superficial modernisation began with a diplomatic mission to Japan in August 1880. The leader of the mission was Kim Hongjip, a young official who was to devote a lifetime to reform, but who was to meet his death in 1896 at the hands of a Seoul mob after being branded a Japanese collaborator by Kojong. His first contact with Japan, therefore, is worthy of mention. In Tokyo, Kim's hosts outlined a strategy for Korea: follow China and Japan's lead by improving defences and importing technology, then Japan and Korea could unite against Western, and especially Russian, imperialism (this appeal to East Asian solidarity would continue to attract support even into the 1940s). At the Chinese legation in Tokyo, one Huang Tsun-hsien reinforced Kim's fears with a memorandum:

> If Russia is to swallow the Far East, it will start with Korea. Russia is ambitious and has used force over three centuries to control affairs beyond its borders. Its invasion began in Europe, moved through Central Asia, and is marching on the Far East. Korea is at the centre of that invasion. Korea must now defend itself and the only way is through close relations with China, linking with Japan, and establishing friendly ties with the United States.[8]

Kim returned to Seoul obviously impressed by Japan's modernisation to date and by the uniformity of Sino–Japanese warnings on Russia. At his urging, Kojong instituted a number of political and military changes between 1880 and 1881. These included the appointment of new and talented men to important positions, the establishment of a special military unit under Japanese tutelage and the creation of an additional government office, the *T'ongni Kimu Amun* (Office for the Management of State Affairs), dealing (amongst other things) with foreign trade, border defence, weaponry, machinery, ships and foreign languages. Crucially, the education system was not modified and there was no reduction in *yangban* élite privilege. Yet even limited change provoked a backlash: Kim was denounced by conservatives as a traitor, and a plot against the throne revealed the fragility of Kojong's authority as a Confucian monarch.

While Korea sought Western knowledge, its understanding arrived secondhand through the filter of Chinese and Japanese interpretation. There were some benefits to this: use of the Chinese script and an overlap in cultural norms facilitated transmission of ideas, while sending students to neighbouring China or Japan was considerably cheaper and easier than sending them to the West. In January 1881, 38 Koreans went to China to study science, particularly the techniques of naval and armaments production. As a forecast of things to come, the mission to Tianjin was starved of funds, suffered language difficulties and was ultimately withdrawn following troubles within Korea during 1882. The students returned with Chinese translations on Western science and understood something of weapons technology, chemistry and physics, but it was not until 1887 that a Korean arsenal, the Pukch'ang munitions factory, was established (initially with Chinese help) and this succeeded no better in producing modern rifles than China's own earlier attempts at Shanghai.

In the summer of 1881, another party of Korean officials visited Japan. In a condensed Korean version of the Iwakura mission, they viewed shipyards, railways, factories, hospitals and schools, all the panoply of modern society, and discussed with Japanese authorities every aspect of modern social organisation. On this, and a subsequent mission led by Prince Pak Yonghyo in 1882, a total of about 50 Korean students enrolled in Japanese schools, most of them at the famous Keio School (modern Keio University) founded by newspaper editor and pioneer of modernisation, Fukuzawa Yukichi. The students included two future leaders in Korean reform politics: the 17-year-old Yun Ch'iho, who entered the Japanese Christian school, Doojinsha, and So Chaep'il (Philip Jaisohn), who joined the Toyama Military School.

One avenue which Korean reformers were determined to explore was journalism, the closest thing to the traditional scholar's art. In the dissemination of knowledge and the formation of opinion, newspapers were the most significant mechanism of the modern age. Partisan newspapers began early in Japan, and it was a Japanese newspaper at Pusan — the *Chosen Shimpo* — which in December 1881 introduced journalism to Korea. The first native publication, the thrice-monthly official gazette, *Hansong Sunbo*, began in October 1883 under the direction of Pak Yonghyo and with assistance from Fukuzawa disciple, Inoue Kakugoro. It carried articles on Western science and technology, with summaries of foreign reports culled from Chinese sources. The original aim was to extend the audience by including some measure of the native *han'gul* script, but conservative obstruction from the family of Queen Min restricted the gazette to Chinese letters and thus made it largely inaccessible outside the élite, an élite whose Confucian education basically conflicted with the nascent reforms. The *Hansong Sunbo* folded after less than one year, but resurfaced in January 1886 (ironically at a time of direct Chinese domination of Korea), renamed *Hansong Chubo*, and finally using a mixture of *han'gul* and Chinese. The habit of reading and the ability to interpret newspapers required modern schools but, while the government set up a small program in Seoul for training interpreters, it was left to businessmen at Wonsan in 1883 to organise locally the first modern school for science, technology and the English language. Yet this could achieve little in the absence of broad social support, qualified teachers or the opportunity to achieve high office with a non-Confucian education.

Opponents and proponents of reform: The Imo and Kapsin incidents

The gradual suffocation of Korean-directed reform began with the 1882 Imo incident. Imports of finer and cheaper textiles had undercut artisans working for the urban market, and exports of rice had inflated the price paid in towns for this most basic of Korean foods. Preferential treatment for the Japanese-trained army unit angered ordinary soldiers, who endured late wages and sub-standard rations. On 23 July 1882, the common soldiery rose and murdered the Japanese military advisor, razed the Japanese legation, killed senior members of the dominant Min family, and went hunting for the Queen Min. Unrest spread to some Korean towns but stopped short of the villages.[9] Antipathy towards Japan was easily roused, but the underlying discontent lay squarely with the Korean government, and was heightened by a millenarian belief of imminent social collapse. During the chaos, the reassuring figure of the Taewon'gun seized authority as regent and undid many of Kojong's reforms. Under popular assault and outwitted by the Taewon'gun, the Min family appealed for Chinese aid and China, nervous of a weak Korea at its back door, duly sent troops under the pretext of its traditional right to intervene in tributary unrest. A Chinese guard forcibly escorted the Taewon'gun from the country, while Chinese forces and government advisors remained in Seoul.

Japan's official response was outrage at the violence to its nationals and property, but it ignored calls for draconian measures from such as Fukuzawa. Instead, China's leading statesman, Li Hongzhang, assisted Korean–Japanese negotiations to a peaceful conclusion in the Treaty of Chemulp'o (Inch'on) on 30 August 1882. This gave Japan an indemnity of 500 000 yen, the right to station guards at its (rebuilt) legation, and the satisfaction of seeing the main rioters punished. Additional agreements also produced the opening of commerce at Yanghwajin in Seoul, and the freedom of inland travel for Japanese consular staff. In this push–pull fashion, typical of imperialism generally, each rejection of the outside brought foreign interests ever more deeply into the Korean social fabric.

Following the Imo revolt, Kojong rephrased his policies, announcing a new start under the slogan 'Eastern ethics, Western technology' (tongdo sogi). In effect, this merely gave a more broadly acceptable name to precisely what had been happening since 1880. A maritime customs service and modern foreign ministry were now established but, as inspector of customs and diplomatic advisor, Korea was obliged to accept Li Hongzhang's nominee, a former German diplomat called Paul Georg von Mollendorff. Kojong did try to escape over-reliance on Chinese aid, and turned particularly to newly arrived United States minister Lucius Foote for American experts in diplomacy, defence, education and agriculture. Foote was agreeable, but his State Department at no time in the nineteenth century approved a more prominent role in Korea.

Kojong's authority was also being diminished by the royal in-laws. After the Imo rising, Queen Min and her relatives were determined to avoid further unrest and, backed by Chinese officials, they gradually pushed Kojong into the political background. They were pragmatic enough to recognise the need for change, but the train of reform moved only slowly forward. Trade was promoted, commercial taxes lifted and traditional monopolies ended; a start was made on a Korean steamship industry and systems of post and banking; a Machine Hall *(Kigiguk)* was opened in June 1883 to house machinery purchased from China; Western companies appeared with the opening of Inch'on; and an easing of the ban on Christianity allowed foreign missionaries access to the country. The Min family employed gradualist progressives such as Kim Hongjip (Foreign Minister in 1884), but the reliance on minting coinage was no solution to the difficulties confronting the government and only added to inflation. The catalyst for the next uprising, however, was the political and military presence of China at the capital, a presence which to some élite reformers known as the Kaehwadang threatened Korea with an imperialism far more regressive and destructive than anything from the West or Japan.

The Kaehwadang progressive reform group was a tiny band of nobles and officials, influenced by Silhak ideas, actively seeking the assistance of foreign states, and in particular Japan, for the improvement of Korean politics and society along Western contemporary lines between 1881 and 1884. In December 1884, they attempted to seize power in a bloody palace coup, known as the Kapsin incident, but were crushed after only three days by local Chinese forces.

Although never clarified and never implemented, some historians see the Kaehwadang vision of social reform and independence from China as the origin of modern Korean nationalism. In North Korea, Kim Okkyun, descendant of the once-powerful Andong Kim family and popularly identified as leader of the coup, has been hailed as the pioneering first bourgeois reformer in the Marxist scheme whereby bourgeois revolution leads ultimately to communism.[10] In relying on Japanese aid and inspiration, however, the members of the Kaehwadang are frequently criticised for trusting Japanese who ultimately, and by implication inevitably, betrayed them. Yet Korean officials at the capital had minimal contact with their provincial countrymen — Kim's biography implies that he rarely travelled away from Seoul, and then only to the immediately neighbouring region. Indeed, in a rigidly stratified society, there was no social plane on which Korean nobles could meet with their countrymen to build a non-élite base for reform. Thus the reform group remained a small, conspiratorial clique, tied firmly to the capital.

In a society which equated age with respect, the reformers were distinguished by their youth: in 1884, Pak Yonghyo (1861–1939) was 23,

So Chaep'il (1864–1951), returned from Japan, was just 20, while Kim (1851–94), described by contemporaries as headstrong and impulsive, was by comparison an elderly 31. Although the group had coalesced before 1876, it was Japan's success in social reconstruction, and standing up to China in international disputes over Taiwan and the Ryukyu Islands which inspired and guided their ambitions. Between 1881 and 1884, Kim Okkyun visited Japan three times, on each occasion strengthening his contacts with Fukuzawa Yukichi. Controversy exists concerning Fukuzawa's real intentions towards Korea, but he undoubtedly supported Korean reform, whether for its own sake or merely to improve Japan's position by acting as Korea's tutor. The reformers, however, were never mere pupils of Fukuzawa, nor besotted Japanisers. Their overriding goals were to release Korea from Chinese domination and end the *yangban* monopoly of power. By instituting a meritocracy at home, they intended to improve government, stabilise taxation and payment, provide incentives to develop capital accumulation and alleviate peasant distress. In common with many revolutionaries, they were commited to social order and planned to safeguard commercial and agricultural production through modern police and military systems. In cultural terms, the Kyujanggak or Palace Library, with its repository of Chinese-script volumes, was to be abolished so as to make way for a purer Korean culture, using native script and professing modern ideas in a modern school system.[11] Ideas such as these were later to figure heavily in the 1894 Kabo reform, also with Japanese advice, and subsequently in the 1896–99 Independence Club movement under So Chaep'il.

The actual timing of the 1884 coup was decided by events elsewhere. Hostilities between China and France over Vietnam led to the withdrawal of half the 3000 Chinese troops in Seoul. The Kaehwadang feared Korea might be drawn into the war as China's tributary, yet at the same time the partial troop withdrawal weakened the authority of the Min family. By mid-1884, the reformers had concluded that real progress and true independence were impossible under the basically self-serving and conservative Min, and by October that year they resolved on a *coup d'etat*. Acknowledging Korea's new position in the international system, their covert search for approval was directed to the foreign powers. Neither the American nor British ministers would sanction violence, and the Japanese government, uncertain of China's present (or future) weakness, hesitated to challenge Beijing's influence in Seoul. However, on an individual level, Fukuzawa and his followers appeared supportive; in November 1884, the Japanese minister to Seoul, Takezoe Shinichiro, appeared to modify his earlier caution, privately (if ambiguously) urging Koreans to stand up for their independence. From this, one author concludes that Japan's new policy of 'direct intervention' was crucial in bringing about the coup.[12] This is ingenuous: the reformers had already decided to strike before Takezoe's vague indication of Japanese aid, aid which must have seemed particularly unreliable given the Japanese foreign minister's coldness to Kim on his most recent visit to Tokyo.

The coup took place on the evening of 4 December 1884 at a banquet to celebrate the opening of a Korean postal office. It was a bloody affair: seven officials, including senior Min family members, were murdered, but Kim Okkyun managed to convince Kojong that this was the work of China and have him appeal for Japanese protection. Without instruction from Tokyo, Takezoe independently ordered legation guards to the palace. However, on 6 December, under assault from the superior Chinese troops of Yuan Shikai, Takezoe withdrew his forces to Inch'on. The reformers were thus abandoned: many were killed in the Chinese attack, some escaped; Kim and Pak Yonghyo fled to Japan, while So Chaep'il and Yun Ch'iho ended up in the United States.

The reformers had assumed that possession of the king's person would legitimise their actions and give them popular support for modernisation and nation-building. To ordinary Koreans, however, this seemed merely another Seoul power-play. The Kaehwadang was excessively parochial: it looked only to Seoul, a narrow political hive from which the mass of the population was physically and emotionally estranged. The reformers did not question their ability to lead in the creation of a new Korea; this was their traditional right by virtue of birth and education. Their tactics, however, were naive and the appeal of these civilian nobles to foreign troops rather than the domestic military only cost them metropolitan support. Paradoxically, the absence of a strong Korean army was to prolong factionalism at Seoul and drag international rivalries ever deeper into the peninsula.

In the wake of the coup, China and Japan negotiated a mutual troop withdrawal (the Tianjin Treaty of April 1885), but reserved for themselves the right to send forces back into Korea in the event of further unrest. This satisfied China more than Japan: China had more territory than it could handle, remained economically self-sufficient, and Korea offered nothing but a cushion on the northern border. Yet Kojong, proving the Kapsin reformers correct, now took steps to escape Chinese domination. Influenced by von Mollendorff, whose own faith in his Chinese patrons had waned and who recognised America's disinterest in Korea, the king approved secret talks for a Russian protectorate. This was merely the first of many occasions on which he was to seek Russian help and clearly the earlier warnings about Russian imperialism no longer seemed relevant with Chinese forces already encamped in Seoul. The Russian government, however, not unlike Washington, was wary of involvement in a Korean quagmire but there was, and would remain, considerable ambivalence in its Korean policy. Cultural and military rebuffs in Europe had fostered a belief that Russia's national future lay in the East, an area in which, physically straddling both Europe and Asia, it could claim a peculiar right to dominate. Yet, in April 1885, even before rumours broke of the protectorate talks, British ships tried to grab the Korean island of Komundo (Port Hamilton) to pre-empt any Russian gain. Both Britain and Japan preferred to see China exert greater control over Seoul than to see Russia expand its influence, and with Russia backing away, Kojong's position was further undermined. Mollendorff, abandoned by the king, quit Korea at the end of 1885.

Defeat in Indochina prompted Beijing to take a harder line in Seoul. In October 1885, an initially reluctant Yuan Shikai returned as Chinese resident and de facto Governor-General. In the face of continued attempts by Kojong to enlist foreign aid against China, Yuan, much to the disgust of twentieth-century Korean historians, concluded the tributary monarch had forfeited his right to the throne and should be replaced. In the 1880s, however, traditional relations could have unforeseen international consequences and Yuan's superiors rejected this advice. The notion of Sino-Korean harmony, however, was trampled underfoot as Yuan forced Kojong to purge officials he considered anti-Chinese, and Kojong retaliated by purging others he believed too close to Yuan. The result was to exclude men like Kim Hongjip from senior posts until after 1894. Li Hongzhang tried to install neutral outsiders and arranged for an old American friend, Judge Owen Denny, to become advisor at the Korean foreign ministry; However, as with Mollendorff, Denny took up the cudgel on Korea's behalf, attacking Yuan publicly in his book, *China and Korea* (Shanghai, 1888).

Beyond Seoul, however, Korean *yangban* and peasants were generally indifferent to Yuan's new control of affairs. Chinese and Japanese merchants were rarely seen in Korean villages until about 1890, when their increasing food purchases and their imports of cheaper textiles began disrupting peasant markets. By and large, Japanese traders also kept out of Seoul until the late 1880s. When some did appear in 1887, Korean merchant guilds offered a peaceful, orderly response, requesting all Korean businesses in the capital to temporarily close their doors, and sending a large delegation to the Korean Foreign Ministry to seek stricter enforcement of regulations.[13] This civic action, however, was not matched by strong Korean government and the protests went unheeded.

Although China dominated Korean politics and Sino-Japanese merchants monopolised Korea's foreign trade, there was still progress at home. It was men of business who led the way, tightening their organisation, forming modern commercial associations and starting new ventures, including photography, brewing and book publishing. In the field of diplomacy, the Korean government overcame Yuan's attempt to restrict its overseas representation, managing to appoint its first ministers to Japan (July 1887) and the United States (August 1887). A second mission to the United States in 1889 was led by Yi Wanyong (1858–1926), a recent graduate of the Royal College (*Yukyong Kongwon*) as well as future prime minister, and a man unjustly infamous in history as Korea's Quisling.

The Royal College, designed to train young *yangban* men as official translators, opened in May 1886. It had three American teachers, including the Methodist Reverend Homer Hulbert, and it was American Protestant missionaries in the late 1880s who pumped new energy into Korean education. It was they who, in 1886, founded the Paejae School for men in Seoul (one of whose future students was Yi Sungman, better known as Syngman Rhee) and the Ehwa School, the first school for girls in Korean history and forerunner of the present Ehwa Women's University.[14] Missionaries also took modern education to the neglected north, establishing secondary schools for boys and girls in P'yongan province in 1894. Problems obviously remained. Ehwa offered free food, clothing and lodging, but parents mistrusted Christianity: only twenty years earlier it had been the object of government purges, and rumours in the 1880s still depicted Westerners as cannibals.[15] Ehwa's first student in May 1886 was the concubine of a high official who aspired to work as the queen's interpreter, but she stayed only three months. Others followed, however, and a few women even took the momentous decision to leave Korea for study in the United States.

It was here, in education and religion, that the United States influence was greatest and most enduring. Missionaries from North America, including Canadians such as James Scarth Gale, saw Korea as fertile land for the gospel — by 1900 there were at least 150 missionaries active in the country — and perhaps nowhere else in Asia, with the exception of the Philippines, was Christianity to play such a major social and political role. Even more than in China (which had a more varied foreign community), the missionaries were the ones to interpret Korea to the outside world through Gale's *Korean Sketches* (NY, 1898), Hulbert's *The History of Korea* (Seoul, 1905) and innumerable articles on contemporary society, history and culture in *The Korean Repository* and Hulbert's own *Korea Review.* Yet evangelism had to compromise with local tradition. Christian tracts expanded the use of *han'gul,* but Christian doctrine was explained using Confucian concepts. In women's education — with the power to alter the family sytem and potentially the most explosive change in a Confucian order — the missionaries realised that zeal could not be allowed to make social pariahs of their students. As one teacher wrote in 1892:

> Whatever may be the private opinion of anyone concerning woman's sphere and proper occupation we must, for the present, at least, act under the supposition that in Korea domestic life is her sphere and destiny . . . We want to make better Koreans and not foreigners of our girls.[16]

Such compromises were to continue at least into the 1920s with, for example, missionaries in rural areas preaching to congregations where the sexes were separated by a screen.

In the final analysis, the greatest obstacle to modernisation was money. Though customs revenues trebled under efficient Western administrators seconded from the Chinese Maritime Customs, exorbitant salaries for foreign officials ate into the profits, and Yuan prevented indiscriminate foreign loans for deficit financing. Reforms consequently died for lack of assured funds: in one instance, Kojong asked time and again for American military advisors and a military training school with four United States instructors opened in 1888, but their salaries came irregularly and the quality of teaching swiftly declined.[17]

The employment of foreign advisors, rising international trade and the piecemeal reforms multiplied the opportunities for offical abuse and the overall costs devolved ultimately on the peasants. Irregular taxes were common, while the revenue-starved government overlooked corruption and maladministration. With authority slipping from the court and government, Koreans in the worst hit area of the south looked to a new religion and protest movement — the Tonghak.

The Tonghak and peasant nationalism

Nationalism is most easily identified when it appears as anti-internationalism. Digging for the earliest traces of nationalism in Korea, historians generally emphasise the anti-foreign, and particularly anti-Japanese, element in Tonghak pronouncements, and point to the very name itself — Tonghak or Eastern Learning — being distinct from and in opposition to Sohak or Western Learning, that is, Catholicism. While acknowledging the elements of national consciousness, it is important to distinguish the foundation of Tonghak popular support, and to note that in 1894 there were two Tonghak risings, quite different in character and leadership, and taking place in quite distinct circumstances. Thus, in considering the Tonghak and its nationalist credentials, one must be aware of the differences between the broader religious movement and the armed rebel group in 1894, and their conjoining in a patriotic struggle against Japanese control during the war with China. Moreover, from the mid-1920s, it took Chinese Communists considerable effort over several years, and fortunate political conditions — the impact of Japanese invasion — to mobilise the Chinese peasantry. There is no convincing evidence that Korean peasants in the nineteenth century were unusually politicised, and the mixed character and background of those presenting themselves as Tonghak members results in a confusion of tongues. Rather than nationalism or xenophobia, the Tonghak in general were concerned with more limited aims: better local government by the existing authority; relief from excessive taxation; and freedom for their beliefs.

Tonghak thought originated in April 1860 with Ch'oe Cheu (1824–64), a native of Cholla province in the south-west, and in conditions of broad social distress similar to those generating the Taiping Rebellion in China during the 1850s. Ch'oe's inspiration for Tonghak was a religious vision, familiar in Korean shamanistic practices, but also not unlike the mental collapse of Taiping leader Hung Hsiu-chuan. As the son of a failed *yangban*, Ch'oe had both reason for discontent with the prevailing system and the erudition to inspire followers. He was also aware of international trends in East Asia and the threat of Western imperialism to Korea. As for xenophobia in Tonghak thought, one should note that, in 1860, the raids by French and American ships on Korea were some years distant, and though Ch'oe saw the spectre of Hideyoshi behind modern Japan, the Tokugawa had co-existed with Korea for over two and a half centuries of peace.

Tonghak thought was an eclectic mix, with erudite elements to appeal to the scholarly mind and a ritualistic incantation promising relief from suffering which drew illiterate commoners. The ethics of mutual respect and egalitarianism were noble, but the litany of Tonghak was extremely simple and easily recited. Ch'oe explained his doctrine as similar in part to Confucianism, which mollified interested Confucians, while Tonghak practices such as building mountain altars were adopted from shamanism. The crux of the theory was that man and God were spiritually one and the same, that man could develop his character through faith and sincerity, and that all men should live as equals for the common good. Insofar as all men were potentially god-like, Tonghak egalitarianism implicitly contradicted the Confucian order. However, loyalty to the throne remained a cardinal principle, as did Tonghak support for the basic Confucian relationships between people. Tonghak appeals to the king for rectification of local conditions were also in the true spirit of the Confucian system.

Geomantic prophecies of the Yi dynasty's collapse after five centuries (i.e. some time around the 1890s) prepared the way for an alternative religion. The year 1864 was also expected to be one of decision, and this prediction was confirmed by the government itself: with the southern uprising just two years earlier, the authorities decided to crush any spark of popular resistance and in that year executed Ch'oe Cheu as a rebel. The Tonghak mantle then passed to a gradualist, Ch'oe Sihyon of Ch'ungch'ong province, who strove to avoid conflict either within the movement or with the government. By 1892, however, the Tonghak contained so many disparate elements — *yangban* ruined by factionalism, disaffected Confucianists, impoverished peasants and political opportunists — that the movement as a coherent whole seemed unlikely to survive. To hasten its demise, officials in Ch'ungch'ong, one of the areas hardest hit by social unrest, increased their repression of believers. Showing they still enjoyed a high level of support and organisation, the Tonghak convened a mass protest at Cholla that December and Ch'oe Sihyong petitioned Kojong to recognise Tonghak loyalism:

> We, as ordinary subjects of His Majesty's benevolent reign, after having read the Confucian writings, living on His Majesty's soil, are determined to follow this new doctrine only because we want people to reform themselves, to be loyal to their king, to show filial piety to their parents, to respect their teachers, and to show friendship to their fellow men.[18]

The king, however, failed to address Tonghak appeals and, in February 1894, abuses by the governor of Kobu in Cholla province finally led to an armed uprising of Tonghak and peasants. This was led by Chon Pongjun of the Tonghak Southern District (Cholla and South Ch'ungch'ong). The Northern District (Kyongsan, Kangwon, North Ch'ungch'ong, Hwanghae and P'yongan) took no part in the rising, instead remaining faithful to Ch'oe Sihyong, who later denounced Chon as both a rebel to the throne, despite the latter's own Confucian loyalist proclamations, and an heretic to the Tonghak faith.

After taking Kobu, Chon spent three months stabilising his authority, abolishing exploitative taxes, redistributing grain from government stores and using word of mouth and handbills to reassure would-be followers he opposed only the parasitic *yangban* and its supporters, not the throne. He made no particular use of xenophobia, and the march on Seoul from May 1894 had mainly domestic goals. These included the reform of maladministration, an end to excessive taxation, employment of talented officials and better treatment for the lower classes, especially in the equitable distribution of farmland and the cancellation of existing public and private debt. On international trade, he asked only that foreign merchants be restricted to the treaty ports, that their covert forays into the interior be prohibited, and that the government place limits on the increasing outflow of rice.[19] Chon's order before the march on Seoul is similar to that of China's Communist army in the 1930s: unnecessary bloodshed was forbidden, the ordinary people were to be protected, and towns famed for virtue or loyalty were to go untouched; corrupt officials or scholars, however, were to be shown no mercy.[20] This mix of fealty and populism, upholding the existing political order (the power of the king) but attacking the corrupt social order, had precisely the right taste for many reluctant revolutionaries who trusted in the king, once freed from corrupt advisors, to restore social harmony. Recruits were gathered from all the surrounding region and, by 31 May 1894, Chon's popular army had seized the capital of Cholla, with risings following also in neighbouring Ch'ungch'ong and Kyongsang. The Tonghak leadership in North Ch'ungch'ong, however, threatened forcibly to block any march on Seoul; as for Kojong, seeing government forces repulsed by the rebels, he once more looked for help outside his borders, fatefully requesting Chinese military aid on 4 June.

Korea and the Sino-Japanese War

In 1894, the Japanese government used the Chon uprising as an excuse to provoke war with China. It did this for two reasons: to silence its domestic critics, increasingly vocal since the opening of a parliament in 1890; but more importantly, to establish a bridgehead within Korea before Russia completed its Trans-Siberian Railway and with it the potential to dominate all of East Asia. For Korea, the conflict was to prove a fundamental turning point, heralding the final cessation of the tributary relationship with China, and bringing about the start of a new, and vastly more complex, relationship with Japan. During the war itself, Koreans were exposed to massive dislocation: hostilities between China and Japan were confined largely to the north-west, but the south experienced an even bloodier conflict as Tonghak fought with Japanese forces; while the government's dizzying reform program, known generally as the Kabo reforms, threatened entirely to overturn the established social order.

China's despatch of troops in response to Kojong's appeal gave Japan the right under the 1885 Tianjin Treaty to send its own forces into the peninsula. Once there, the government in Tokyo made a great play of defending Korean reform and, put bluntly, China was challenged either to fight or withdraw. The wider peril of backing down to the much smaller Japanese forces, however, was unambiguous in the age of late imperialism. Instead, both China and Korea sought international mediation to prevent Japan going to war. Belatedly realising the forces he had unleashed, Kojong also arranged a truce with the Tonghak. His demands for Japanese troops to leave, however, were ignored. Although the Western powers roundly condemned Japan for provoking war, none was ready to intervene on Korea's behalf. On 1 August 1894, Korea became, not for the first or last time, the battlefield of alien ambitions.

Even before the start of war, Japan had taken control of Seoul. On 23 July, an incident between Korean royal guards and Japanese troops was used to justify occupation of the Kyongbok palace. The queen and her children were taken to the Japanese legation as virtual hostages. However, Japan presented itself to the world as the defender of Korean independence and did not intend a complete usurpation of royal authority. Instead, the occupiers looked for a native statesman with the prestige to maintain order but without the means to challenge them — their surprising choice was the Taewon'gun. Yet Korean reformers themselves, perhaps ignoring his conservatism and acknowledging his patriotism, had urged Japan to appoint the Taewon'gun as regent. He undoubtedly accepted because he felt best able to defend Korean interests from within the occupation camp. Late in July, a new administration under Kim Hongjip was set up, publicly reaffirming Korea's legal independence, terminating the tributary relation with China and calling on Japan to expel Chinese forces from the peninsula. The new Korea–Japan relationship was sealed in a treaty alliance on 26 August 1894. Recognising the limits of the Taewon'gun's commitment to change, a Deliberative Council (Kunguk Kimuch'o) was created on 27 July as the supreme state organ: it was this body which directed internal reform until its abolition in December 1894. Its authority, however, was diluted by its mutually antagonistic composition of progressives, centrists and Taewon'gun supporters.

The Kabo reforms began almost from the moment the new government was established. That Korea needed reform was generally accepted, but scholarly opinion is divided over Japan's underlying motives and about Korean input in the reform program. A leading authority, Lew Young Ick, argues the Kabo reforms were originated by Koreans, and this is accepted, at least with regard to the initial stage, by some historians in North and South Korea. Others, Han Woo-keun included, see the program as wholly directed by Japan and 'devised primarily to destroy the traditional Korean society and establish capitalistic institutions which the Japanese could exploit'.[21] This latter view ignores the role of progressives such as Kim Hongjip and the inheritance of Kapsin ideas. The reforms were Korean in spirit, but obviously modelled on those of Japan, and, in their formulation and implementation, heavily influenced by the many Japanese advisors in Seoul. Where Japan's influence proved critical, however, was in forcing the pace of change in order to head off Western intervention in its war with China. The result was a blitzkrieg assault on the traditional order, causing widespread unrest and anger towards those Japanese and Koreans behind the reforms.

A foretaste of what was to come was already on hand by 30 July 1894. Within one week of its foundation, the Deliberative Council announced a complete overhaul of Korea's political structure. The royal household was separated from government and a prime ministerial cabinet system introduced. Eight modern ministries were created (Internal Affairs, Diplomacy, Finance, Law, Education, Industry, Military and Agriculture/ Commerce), with the brief to impose order on national finances, improve official records on population and production, enhance welfare and public works, clarify and enforce regulations for the legal and nationwide police systems, establish central control of national defence and promote new advances in industry, agriculture and commerce.[22] The key for Korea's future was education based on expanded use of the native script. Textbooks in *han'gul* were readied by the Education Ministry for a modern school system, and government documents began preparing to include Korean letters. The new official gazette, founded on 23 July 1894, was printed from January 1895 in a mix of Chinese and Korean, and a royal pronouncement on independence and social reconstruction, also in January 1895, was similarly published in the mixed script.

Expanded literacy had enormous potential for change, but this could only be realised by opening education to the masses. In this, the Kim administration followed Japan's example: priority was given to the base through primary and middle schools, with those at the higher level to follow in due course. Announced in July 1895, the new primary school curriculum stressed reading, writing and calculation with, at the higher level, history and geography of Korea and other countries, plus sciences and an optional foreign language. In line with a global trend towards physical education, sport was emphasised along with morals to give youth the intellectual, ethical and physical capacity for participation in the new mobile Korea. The curriculum also made explicit allowance for girls, providing additional tuition in what would now be called domestic science or, more prosaically, sewing.[23]

Taken as a whole, the reforms between July 1894 and December 1895 covered every aspect of society: traditional social classes were abolished and *yangban* allowed to participate in commerce; official appointment was decided on merit, and avenues to government broadened by replacing the Confucian civil examination with one testing subjects such as Korean, Chinese, mathematics, political science and international relations; local administrative boundaries were redrawn, changing the official map of Korea; slavery was proscribed, widows were freed to remarry and child marriage was prohibited (the minimum age becoming 20 for men and 16 for women).

Given time, the reform program would have bundled Korea into the modern world, and there were merchants, entrepreneurs and urban residents who supported the changes. Yet, in the midst of war and widespread rumours of Kojong being held captive by the Japanese, refusal to heed orders from the 'puppets' in Seoul was seen as an act of patriotism. Arguably, this was to confuse *patria* with the person of the monarch. However, the dislocations of war and uprising in the south left Seoul politically estranged from the provinces and unable to enforce its directives until well into 1895, by which time both the feasibility of the reform program and Japan's position in Korea had radically altered.

A state of war continued in Korea until early 1895. Hostilities between China and Japan on Korean soil were fortunately brief. The first and only major land battle took place at P'yongyang on 15 September 1894. This resulted in defeat for China and the squandering of local sympathies as Chinese troops abused and robbed friendly Koreans. One Korean observer described the sense of outrage:

> Where once there was confidence and respect now there is nothing but loathing and hatred. It is so to this day. Not that Pyeng Yang [sic] loves the Japanese more but she hates the Chinese with greater hatred.[24]

Northern Koreans lived temporarily under threat from the disorder of Chinese troops in retreat, but it was in the populous southern provinces that the violence was most widespread. Here the fighting was between Tonghak and Japanese. Tokyo had tried to limit conflict by issuing strict orders on army discipline and payment for all goods, and by limiting the activity of Japanese soldiers in the Tonghak heartland. However, these efforts were undermined by its insensitive treatment of Kojong; indicative of the king's desperation was his secret request to Britain on 3 September 1894 to provide 1000 troops as palace guards to protect him from Japan.[25]

The Tonghak had consistently expressed their loyalty to the king, but they also had reasons of their own for battling Japan. In August 1894, Ch'oe Sihyong had complained of the decline in Tonghak morale, in which 'strong parishes threaten weak parishes and the evil dominate the good'.[26] However, the Japanese occupation improved their support; as a senior Korean official noted; 'the term Tonghak can now be applied to the whole population of Korea outside the capital with the exception of the three northern provinces, where the influence of the Society has not yet reached'.[27] In October, with failed harvests in Kyongsang, Chon Pongjun planned to use the general unrest to launch a second rising, aimed at rescuing the king and opposing Japan. After some discussion, Ch'oe Sihyong pledged the backing of his Northern District and, later that month, Chon took command of 100 000 men in Cholla. This first truly representative Tonghak army quickly seized control of the southern provinces, cutting off revenue and tribute rice for Seoul, and eliminating safety for Japanese outside their army bases.

The strength of the Tonghak exposed the weakness of Japan's claims in Korea, and it replied with violence and an acceleration of the reform schedule. In November 1894, Japanese and Korean troops moved in force against the Tonghak, using superior training and arms to inflict heavy casualties. Despite their numbers, the Tonghak, lacking money and support from merchants or the Confucian élite, quickly lost heart. Chon was betrayed at the start of 1895 and later executed in Seoul. Japanese repression, however, continued until all trace of Tonghak resistance had been erased.

To balance the repression, and improve its position both internationally and within Korea, Japan needed to show tangible results from the many reforms announced on paper. In October 1894, it had already sent a new, and highly prestigious, representative to hasten this process. This was Inoue Kaoru, the former Japanese foreign minister. Modelling himself on Lord Cromer, Britain's minister to Cairo and *de facto* regent of Egypt, Inoue tried to utilise the throne by improving relations with Kojong and forcing the Taewon'gun into retirement. Confronted by evidence of his earlier collusion with Chinese forces at P'yongyang and continuing aid to the Tonghak, the Taewon'gun stepped down, but characteristically refused to fade away. Inoue's improved relations with Kojong, however, were undercut by the need to strengthen the Korean progressives in government. Under Japanese pressure, Kojong reluctantly pardoned two of the leaders of the 1884 coup, Pak Yonghyo and So Kwangbom. Returning from exile in Japan, they became respectively Home and Justice Ministers in the second Kim cabinet formed on 17 December 1894. Inoue also had a large body of Japanese advisors appointed to the Korean government, but the increasing openness of Japanese intervention only aroused the suspicions of Koreans and foreigners alike. As Britain's consul in Seoul reported, his Russian, German and American counterparts made no secret of their dissatisfaction with Japan:

> The sentiments expressed by my colleagues are echoed by every foreigner in this city. The American missionaries in particular, who were inclined at first to welcome the Japanese as the agents of providence for the regeneration of Korea, and to regard the war with China as a species of crusade, have now, almost without exception, completely changed their views.[28]

At the start of 1895, the power of the throne was conscripted for reform. On 7 January, Kojong publicly went to the Confucian shrine of the Yi kings to declare his support for progress. The royal declaration fused tradition and modernity in a manner evocative of Japan's 1868 Charter Oath and, as on that occasion, the pursuit overseas of scientific and technological understanding was made a priority. The immediate source of this knowledge was Japan and, in May 1895, 114 young Korean men arrived at Fukuzawa's Keio School; as so often, however, pursuit of reform was undermined by political shifts in Seoul and the students were quickly forgotten. This forced them to look after themselves, and future Koreans studying in Japan, from the 1900s through the colonial period, were notable for their high level of self-organisation and mutual support.

The Sino-Japanese War ended in April 1895. Western intervention in the peace terms, however, forced Japan into a humiliating backdown in Manchuria. In Korea the following month, international pressure against Japanese domination and its attempt to monopolise rail concessions also brought a diplomatic retreat. Japan remained the most influential foreign power in Seoul, but its failure to use that influence for Korean improvement soured relations with the reform party. Kim Hongjip resigned on 19 May, but Pak Yonghyo, who became acting prime minister, was discovered plotting against the still powerful queen, and soon found himself once more on a ship heading for refuge in Japan. Kim resumed the premiership in August 1895, but his support had been dissipated by relentless factionalism. The Jacobean interruption to this political impasse came on 8 October when Japanese and Korean activists, in collusion with members of the Japanese legation, stormed the Kyongbok palace and brutally murdered the queen.

As with her contemporary, Empress Dowager Cixi in China, Queen Min had used her ability to wield power in a purely masculine political system. In the process, she made bitter enemies, such as the Taewon'gun, who did not mourn her demise, and it is possible Kim's government might have reasserted its authority despite its links to the disgraced Japanese. However, on that same 8 October, progressive ministers Yi Wanyong and Yi Pomjin, fearing assassination, deserted the cabinet and went into hiding (Yi Wanyong taking sanctuary in the United States legation). An official statement demeaning the murdered queen compounded public anger with the government, but it was the reckless decision to surge ahead with reform and attack the traditional badge of Korean manhood, the top-knot hairstyle, that reignited violent protest. As monarch, Kojong was made to set an example by having his top-knot cut off. However, so emotive was this issue, so central to the Korean male's conception of himself, that those in Seoul who followed the king's lead did not dare to leave the city. One provincial governor trying to enforce the ordinance was murdered by local people who seized control of the town, and a new *uibyong* or 'righteous army' movement, led by orthodox Confucians defending this most powerful of Korean traditions, spread across the southern and central regions.

To sum up, the various impacts of the Sino-Japanese War included the fusing of a new Tonghak unity, but also its near annihilation at the hands of Japanese and Korean arms; the misuse by Japan of the royal person and further decline in the monarchy's prestige; the linking of moderate Korean progressives with 'collaboration' and, as noted below, their subsequent expulsion from power; and the breathless rise and fall, but not complete disappearance, of Japanese domination of Korean politics. However, all this effectively cleared the domestic stage for new forces.

The Independence Club and nationalism

In February 1896, with help from his officials, including Yi Pomjin and Yi Wanyong, Kojong was spirited away from the palace where he lived virtually as a prisoner of Japan, and went into refuge at the Russian legation. His first act was to denounce the cabinet as traitors and Kim Hongjip with others ended their lives at the hands of a Seoul mob. Pro-Russian and pro-American officials formed a new cabinet, with Yi Pomjin taking the Justice portfolio and Yi Wanyong becoming the Minister for Education. The Russian government, however, only accommodated Kojong in the belief Japan intended him some harm. Convinced of a future Anglo-Japanese naval clash, St Petersburg desired better relations with Tokyo and initially played down its new influence in Seoul. At the coronation of Tzar Nicholas II in mid-1896, Russo-Japanese concerns in Korea were stabilised by the Yamagata–Lobanov protocol which, in a secret article, agreed in the event of unrest requiring Russian and Japanese troops to divide Korea north and south of a neutral zone. This concept, of course, was unconsciously to be resurrected in 1945.

At the Tzar's coronation, Russia found itself besieged by East Asian emissaries seeking its favour. In addition to the Japanese negotiations, China purchased a secret anti-Japanese alliance with rail concessions in southern Manchuria, thus drawing Russia deeper into the region, while Korea's envoy, Prince Min Yonghwan, a relative of the murdered queen, persuaded Russia to send military and financial advisors to Seoul. Russian support for Korea, however, remained equivocal in view of its greater concerns elsewhere. In Korea itself, with China gone and Japan on the defensive, a momentary vacuum appeared, offering new opportunity for independent reform.

The *Tongnip Hyophoe* or Independence Club (1896–99) was founded in July 1896 under the guidance of So Chaep'il, returning from exile in 1895 as a naturalised American and with a doctorate in medicine from what is now Georgetown University. Its goal was to oversee two projects: an Independence Arch and Independence Park, both in the capital on sites formerly used to demonstrate Korea's subservience to China, and now to act as manifest symbols of the new independent Korea.

The Independence Club was the first reform movement in Korea acting in peacetime and testing its proposals through public debate. It was also the first movement to establish branches around the country and seek broad geographical and social support for its aims. One of its weaknesses, however, was the diverse and unco-ordinated nature of its activities — a diversity and ad hoc spontaneity which enabled various groups to function temporarily under the same general flag but ultimately weakened its base. The club's genesis and collapse have been examined by Vipan Chandra, and may be viewed through the largely English-language diary of one of its leaders, Yun Ch'iho (1865–1946). That Yun came to write in English indicates one of the major inspirations, and weaknesses, of the Independence Club: the impact of Western, primarily American, social, political and religious beliefs. This has caused some critics in north and south Korea to denounce club leaders as 'running dogs' of American or even Japanese imperialism.[29] However, Western theories alone could not have attracted the range or level of club support. Shin Yongha, a leading South Korean scholar of the movement, believes traditional reform Confucians constituted the majority of members, and that its policies faithfully represented the socio-economic condition of Korea at that time. Certainly, loyalty to the throne and the widespread belief that Kojong was sympathetic to its aims ensured the club's early success, while its emphasis on national independence was a goal which all could support. Continued success, however, depended on balancing the conflicting forces of national independence and the inevitable dependence on foreign advice, training and investment for Korean self-strengthening. Just as the later success of Marxism in China would depend to some degree on its naturalisation by Mao, so, in the same way, Western-educated members of the Independence Club acknowledged that a modification of Western political ideals was essential in Korea: this same position was to be adopted by President Park in South Korea during the 1960s.

As graduate students in the United States, So and Yun had become firm believers in American democracy, individual rights and Christianity. It was these values and beliefs which they brought to the Independence Club and their voices dominated its newspapers, *Tongnip Sinmun* and, in English, *The Independent*. Other members also had experience of the United States, not least Yi Wanyong who, becoming Foreign Minister, was to spearhead in cabinet the club's rejection of economic concessions to Russia. The reform Confucians included Chang Chiyon and Pak Unsik, both of whom were to play leading roles in the campaign for national consciousness in the 1900s, while among younger members was the future president of South Korea, Syngman Rhee.

The maiden issue of *The Independent* (7 April 1896) clearly defined Club goals:

> Korea for Koreans, clean politics, the cementing of foreign friendships, the gradual though steady development of Korean resources with Korean capital, as far as possible under foreign tutelage, the speedy translation of foreign text-books into Korean that the youth may have access to the great things of history, science, art and religion, without having to acquire a foreign language, and LONG LIFE TO HIS MAJESTY.[30]

The prerequisite for development was a modern sense of nationalism. In its domestic context, this meant the creation of a public opinion, bringing all sections of society under the gaze of debate and eradicating the dark corners in which élites could act with impunity. Public opinion was to be horizontal and free of class restriction, in contrast to Confucian tradition which in practice limited debate to the educated élite. The creation of public opinion depended on building the sense of involvement in the nation and this, in nineteenth-century thought, was predicated on disseminating among the people a unified consciousness of language and history. The *Tongnip Sinmun* was the first newspaper to use pure *han'gul* and, with official support from the Education and Home Ministries, managed to reach a circulation of 3000 by 1898. In its wake came other newspapers solely in *han'gul* script, including the missionary *Choson Kurisutoin Hoebo* and *Kurisuto Sinmun*, the *Hyopsonghoe Hoebo* run by Paejae School students, and Korea's first commercial newspaper, *Kyongsung Sinmun*, edited by Yun Ch'iho. Neglected by scholars, the orthography of *han'gul* was in disorder and it was the *Tongnip Sinmun* editor, Chu Sigyong (1876–1914), who pioneered a standard spelling, a program continued by his disciples in later years. Reformist Confucians in the Independence Club also worked to replace the dominant Chinese histories with a new Korea-centred historiography and, in 1896, produced the five-volume *Taedong Yoksa* (History of the Great East).

Given minimal literacy, however, newspapers and histories were directly accessible only to a Chinese-educated élite with a vested interest in preserving traditional ways, and works such as the *Taedong Yoksa* were forbidden by Education Minister Sin Kison, self-styled defender of orthodox Confucianism. Sin reversed many of the reforms instituted earlier by Yi Wanyong and publicly flailed against Catholicism, the West and the use of *han'gul*. So Chaep'il's reply to this attack appeared in *The Independent* of 29 September 1896 and incidentally exposes the degree to which the outside world had already infiltrated Korea unannounced:

> Mr. Sin has a fine contempt for Europe and Europeans but . . . He wears cotton pants which were probably woven in Manchester. The watch he wears was perhaps made in Switzerland. He lights his pipe with matches from Vienna unless he prefers the cheaper Japanese product. He reads by the light of American kerosene oil. He probably wears a piece of amber from the Baltic in his top-knot; if it were not for European glass he would not be able to look out of his windows in winter; his friends the insurgents [*uibyong*] in the country are armed with weapons from Europe; and his sovereign is the guest of one of those 'low-down, bird chirping' Europeans.[31]

To lay the bedrock of popular nationalism, the club looked to the Independence Arch and Park as concrete symbols. Public support began strongly, with 6000 *won* being collected in donations between July 1896 and July 1897. In November 1896, the Arch's foundation stone was laid with much fanfare and speeches on patriotism and progress before a crowd of several thousand. Construction was on a modified design of the Arc de Triomphe and erected, ironically, with the participation of Chinese labourers. Given the low level of Seoul, it was a striking feature of the metropolitan landscape. Yet, beyond the capital it was invisible and public enthusiasm waned before adequate funds were collected for the Independence Park. The Independence Club, however, continued to build symbols for popular nationalism, including a Korean national flag and a national anthem, and it supported Kojong when, in August 1897, he promoted himself to emperor (thus equal to the Chinese ruler) and gave the country the grand new title *Taehan Cheguk* (Empire of Korea).

Above all, the club aimed to win public support by the immediately practical measures of administrative and economic reform. The *Tongnip Sinmun* repeatedly attacked official corruption and proposed national development, both through universal education for male and female alike, and through Korean industry, based initially on cotton spinning but progressing into heavier industries as resources expanded. The club restated much of the Kabo program, not least in tax reform, appointment of officials based on merit, and change in social attitudes such as accepting outcast professions and eliminating early marriage. Under So and Yun, however, it went even further in promoting female equality, and this radicalism arguably forfeited more support than it attracted. Yet Korean women did respond to the offer of new respect, forming their own social and political groups. At the club's political height in 1898, an unprecedented memorial to the throne was drafted by several hundred women in the capital seeking girls' schools and endorsing Independence Club policies.[32]

Substantive socio-economic change depended in large measure on imported technology such as steam engines and railways, and this required better foreign relations. The Independence Club, unsurprisingly, wanted Korea to stand independent from overt interference by any one state, but was ready to extend an equal welcome to all with peaceful interests in the peninsula. At this point, however, the previously agreed Russian military and financial advisors appeared in Seoul.

Shortly before Kojong remodelled himself emperor in October 1897, the new (and most impolitic) Russian minister, Alexis de Speyer, arrived in Seoul. Within days, Korea once more took on the complexion of a client state. Russian advisors began training Korean troops, in November the Russian financial advisor replaced Britain's John McLeavy Brown as inspector of Korean maritime customs and, on 18 February 1898, de Speyer brusquely requested a coaling station at Chollyong-do near Pusan. London and Tokyo, a decade earlier, had welcomed Chinese authority in Korea if this meant the reduction of Russian influence, and they were now alarmed by the changes: British warships sailed into Inch'on to protest McCleavy Brown's dismissal, while Japan instantly set about buying the very land on Chollyong-do sought by de Speyer. The real fight, however, was shouldered by the Independence Club. On 20 February 1898, a memorandum from 2000 club supporters went to Emperor Kojong urging on him the need for true Korean independence. Thereafter, the club organised daily meetings to demonstrate public anger and frustration. De Speyer demanded the protests be suppressed, but Kojong on this occasion stood with his people: on 12 March, Yun Ch'iho proudly informed his diary that a royal letter was on its way to St Petersburg, thanking the Tzar for his advisors but explaining the Korean government and people preferred henceforth to manage their own affairs.[33]

All Russian advisors were soon withdrawn, the Russo-Korean Bank was closed virtually before its doors were open, and de Speyer found his talents redeployed to Brazil. It was a victory for the Independence Club and civic protest, albeit a victory eased by Russia's change of priorities after just acquiring from China a lease on south Manchuria. Russia's foreign minister had already approached Japan for a new accord over Korea, resulting in the Nishi–Rosen Protocol in Tokyo on 25 April 1898. This restricted either state from interfering in Korean domestic affairs and, without prior consultation, from sending military or financial advisors. In addition, Russia agreed not to obstruct Japan's commercial or industrial interests in Korea. Their simmering rivalry over Korea continued well into 1899, as both chased land rights in the southern port of Masan, and there was brooding talk of a coming war. For the present, however, Russia was preoccupied in south Manchuria while Japan's policy was to hold the line in Korea and expand through its Taiwanese colony into southern China and the South Seas.

Emboldened by its victory over Russia, the Independence Club began pressing for moves towards democracy at home. Its momentum as a group, however, was in doubt. Some members had resigned as the club became politically active, but this was balanced by the opening of the first regional branch early in 1898, and growing public interest in the wide-ranging metropolitan debates which started late in 1897. Between April and July 1898, it increasingly promoted discussion of parliamentary democracy and, on 3 July, memorialised Kojong directly to explain the benefits for Korea of such a system. As with Western missionaries, however, the Independence Club diluted the foreign nature of its message by employing traditional terms and quoting in support of democracy the statement by Mencius: 'if all the people of the nation say he is wise, use him; if all the people say he is no good, leave him'.[34] The first step in democratising Korean politics, as they saw it, was to arrange for popular election of local officials and so erect barriers to regional corruption. At this crucial moment, however, discord within the club and personality conflicts resulted in So Chaep'il quitting Korea.

Leadership fell to Yun, but he was hard-pressed to restrain younger and more radical members. Although the club sought partial representation in government, it steered away from anything smacking of republicanism: for Yun, the Korean people were politically inexperienced and the monarchy, albeit in a modified constitutional form akin to the British system, remained the linchpin of national unity (and community support for the club). Once the Russian threat was withdrawn, however, the stresses within the club and between it and the authorities came quickly to the fore. In October, several hundred members launched a traditional three-day protest outside the palace to force the sacking of certain notorious ministers. The public donated money to the protesters, merchants closed their shops in sympathy and, as noted above, a delegation of women dramatically petitioned Kojong in their support. 'It was such a demonstration as Korea has never seen before,' remarked United States Minister Horace Allen, but it was also the club's swansong.[35] Although Kojong acceded to this demonstration of public opinion, and a new cabinet was formed, the government resented the direct challenge, and rumours of underlying republicanism in the club were used to justify the arrest of its leaders on 5 November. In the face of renewed peaceful mass protest against the arrests, government conservatives turned to the pedlars, traditional defenders of the state in times of crisis, and it was they who, with simple, incontestable violence, late in November physically brought the Independence Club to an end.

Chong-sik Lee and Vipan Chandra have argued that nothing short of revolution could have brought fundamental change in Korea at this time. Revolution, however, was premature and could not have succeeded without an organised urban industrial base. It was in part to build the economy and establish such a base that the Independence Club sought peaceful reform. For the majority of peasants and officials, however, the definition of nation remained tied to the king's person rather than abstract symbols of flag and anthem. Thus both the Tonghak and Independence Club were at the mercy of one man's whim: in the patriotic fight against Japanese or Russian expansion, they enjoyed support, but in the nationalistic restructuring of Korea, that support disappeared. In time, some Korean nationalists were to consider removing the monarch and, in the absence of native revolutionary forces, some even turned to Japan for the task.

The Yi's last decade, 1900–1910

At the beginning of the twentieth century, Western onlookers, purblind from the *fin de siecle* pessimism of advanced industrial societies, saw Korean decline as irreversible. Britain's Minister to Seoul, John Jordan, noted privately: 'One is always inclined to wonder how long the present state of things can continue, but decaying countries die a very lingering death'.[36] Yet the embers of Tonghak and Independence Club thought still burned in Korea. There were bureaucrats supporting modern enterprises: An Kyongsu, a finance official, helped to establish Korea's first central bank, the Bank of Choson, in 1896, and it was he who pioneered industrial development with the Taehan Textile Mill in 1897. Even though Korea's first railway, joining Inch'on to Seoul from 1901, was built with Japanese finance, there were Korean entrepreneurs with rail plans of their own. The spirit of change was not absent but, whereas the Meiji government had early established close links with business, limiting harmful competition and subsidising major enterprises, Korea (and China) relied for development on politically powerful individuals. All too often, capital-intensive projects withered for lack of funds, while Korean textile producers faced impossible competition with the established mills of Osaka and Shanghai. Thus Korea's foreign trade continued to grow, but not fundamentally to change: of net imports in 1901 of US$6 650 926, cotton goods alone accounted for $2 737 989, while the major export remained food, with gold sales partially offsetting the trade imbalance.

The increasing trade continued to affect Korean demography. By 1907, of the five cities with populations over 20 000, two were the present and ancient capitals (Seoul and P'yongyang) and the other three were international ports (see Table 1.1).

Table 1.1 Major urban populations, 1907					
	Total	Korean	Japanese	Chinese	Western
Seoul	218 225	199 325	16 643	2132	125
Pusan	39 743	23 478	16 040	197	28
Pyongyang	31 576	26 181	4 843	503	49
Inch'on	27 896	14 993	11 467	1373	63
Kaesong	27 701	26 261	1 309	118	13

Source: Son Chongmok, 'Kaehanggi ui tosi ingu kyumo', *Hanguk'sa yon'gu*, no. 39, December 1982, pp. 139–43.

In the rural sector, the Kabo tax reform from payment in kind to payment by cash boosted the commercialisation of agriculture, and rice exports expanded rapidly from 1895. This benefited larger landowners and native merchants, who continued to prosper from trade with Japan, but not the mass of smaller farmers. As a consumer economy evolved in the southern provinces, peasant distress only increased. Kojong, however, provided no central economic guidance and concentrated on feeding his private treasury by the indiscriminate sale of rail, mining and other concessions to foreign interests, or by disbursing government office to the highest bidder. Deprived of protection from the king (now, of course, emperor), some Koreans simply left the country, while others took refuge in Western religion, especially Protestantism. Missionary activity between 1895 and 1905 helped raise the number of fully baptised Protestant converts from 528 to over 12 500, and it was also partly under missionary influence that the first migrants to the United States left for plantation work on Hawaii early in 1903.

External events intruded again with the Boxer Rebellion in China during 1900. Western and Japanese forces entered Beijing, while Russian troops occupied Manchuria. The suddening heightening of geopolitical tension led observers in Seoul to predict that Japan would soon take over Korea, but avoid the costs of annexation and, as Horace Allen presciently noted, 'content herself with securing an agreement whereby she might maintain a sufficient force in the country to preserve order, which would give her virtually the power of a dictator with the happy illusion of independence still maintained'.[37] Yet such a move had first to take account of Russia. With construction of the Trans-Siberian Railway approaching the last of its 6000 miles, Japan still had no continental foothold and Korea remained militarily defenceless. In 1903, Tokyo offered St Petersburg a compromise, effectively renouncing ambitions in Manchuria if Russia would do likewise in Korea. This proposal was unsuccessful and negotiations stumbled into the Russo-Japanese war (February 1904 – September 1905). While internal unrest had brought war to Korea in 1894, a decade later no such excuse was necessary.

As Russian forces held back from the Korean capital, containing hostilities to the north, Japan was free to intimidate Kojong and the Korean government into signing two agreements: the first in February 1904 removed all constraint on Japanese action in Korea; the second, in August 1904, placed advisors with the Korean government informally to control finance and diplomacy. More cautious than in 1894–95 in handling international opinion, Japan deliberately sent an American employee, Durham Stevens, as its diplomatic advisor to Seoul. Early in 1905, a Japanese police advisor also appeared; the Korean army was trimmed to less than 8000 as an economy measure and Kojong's continuing attempts to elicit Russian aid were penalised by Japan taking control of his postal and telegraph services. In this way, Japan was able to exploit wartime exigencies to accrue power over Korea's major institutions, but the control remained informal and thus difficult to implement effectively in the face of passive resistance from Korean officials.

At the outset of the war, Japanese military strategists had emphasised control of the Korean monarch. This, as in 1894, was to defuse the potential for Korean resistance and to legitimise Japanese actions during its occupation of Korean territory. On this occasion, however, Kojong was treated better in public by the Japanese than he was a decade earlier, and he generally acquiesced to Japanese demands. One reason for this was his conviction that Russia, with the largest army in the world, would ultimately triumph, and rumour portrayed him offering novel assistance to this end: as Yun Ch'i-ho noted, 'I am credibly informed that His Majesty is engaged in boiling Japanese maps in a cauldron — a singular means of cursing Japan and her cause'.[38] The accumulation of change in Korean society, however, was producing a new level of civic politics and this was displayed during the war with groups both for and against co-operation with Japan. At the risk of excessive generalisation, opponents might be described as being drawn from the traditional élite and reform Confucians of the Independence Club, while supporters were a mixed bag, including members of the Tonghak, associates of the 1884 coup and some merchants and officials.

The trigger for renewed public politics was a Japanese scheme for Korean land, the literal soil of nationalism. In mid-1904, a Japanese individual named Nagamori Tokichiro sought Korean government permission to develop the country's extensive wastelands. This dovetailed perfectly with Japan's official policy on increasing Korean agriculture as a supplier to Japanese consumers, and opening extra land for Japanese farm migrants to relieve population pressure at home. The terms Nagamori proposed were not wholly disadvantageous to Korea, but the issue was emotive, and alarmist reports in the *Hwangsong Sinmun* had much earlier warned of Japanese designs on Korean land. A wave of Confucian memorials denounced the Nagamori scheme, while officials in Seoul set up the Poanhoe (literally 'Society to Defend Stability') to organise petitions and demonstrations. Newspapers became engaged in the protest, including the *Korea Daily News* (founded by a Briton, Ernest Bethell) and its Korean-language edition, *Taehan Maeil Sinbo*. Although the Poanhoe was forced to dissolve under Japanese and government pressure, it successfully embarrassed Tokyo into shelving the Nagamori plan. The renewal of public activity also gave new life to former Independence Club members who organised the Kongjinhoe to campaign once more for citizens' rights and constitutional government. Renamed the Chajanghoe (Self-strengthening Society) from 1906, it was to spearhead the 'patriotic enlightenment movement', the last of the Yi dynasty's movements for independent Korean reform.

One of the most durable myths of Korean history is that Japan's intention from the start (and some place the start back as far as Hideyoshi) had unswervingly been to annex Korea, and that when this occurred in 1910, it was accomplished largely through the assistance of a handful of Korean traitors: the two arch-villains in this Vichy-like scenario are Prime Minister Yi Wanyong (1907–10) and Song Pyongjun of the Ilchinhoe (Society for United Progress). Part of this overly facile explanation is the assertion that the Ilchinhoe was in the pay of the Japanese from the outset. In fact, the secret Japanese army record *Ilchinhoe Ryakushi* ('Summary history of the Ilchinhoe', held at Gakushuin University, Tokyo) indicates no such payment until 1907, and then only to save the floundering group from utter collapse. To understand the Ilchinhoe's actions, one must follow the Confucian dictum on going back to the roots — in this case, to its establishment in December 1904 from two existing groups, the Chinbohoe and Ilsinhoe.

The Chinbohoe was active among Tonghak believers in Hwanghae and P'yongan. It was directed by Yi Yonggu, a lieutenant to the exiled North District Tonghak leader, Son Pyonghui. In 1900, Son had fled oppression from his own government and, like so many other political refugees, taken refuge in Japan where he, unsuccessfully, sought Japanese government or military aid against the Korean regime. As the Russo-Japanese War commenced, the Chinbohoe saw an opportunity to create a new level of Korean–Japanese co-operation. The Japanese army was desperate to lay railways in Korea for its military transport: primarily this meant completing the Seoul–Pusan Railway, but also laying a new line from Seoul to the strategically vital north-western town of Uiju. Korean coolies, however, sometimes with violence, refused the offer of high wages, because they feared the Japanese would send them to the battlefront. Under Yi Yonggu, however, the Chinbohoe pointedly organised some 3000 men to work without pay on railway construction and in transporting Japan's military supplies. Given its Tonghak roots, the Chinbohoe was not acting out of traitorous intent, but rather to employ Japan's help in reforming Korea, and attempting to do this by supporting the concept of East Asian unity expressed so long ago to Kim Hongjip in Tokyo.

The second group, the Ilsinhoe, was founded at Seoul in mid-1904 with the support of reform officials and merchants. Its leader was Song Pyongjun, formerly a provincial governor in the 1880s who, becoming linked to refugees of the Kapsin coup, had been forced to spend a decade in Japanese exile and had returned to Korea only in 1904 as interpreter with the Japanese army. Members of both the Chinbohoe and Ilsinhoe showed their commitment to modernisation by abandoning the traditional top-knot, the custom which had caused such a backlash in 1895–96. Based in the capital, the Ilsinhoe also attacked government corruption, and openly praised Japan for its public statements and military action in defence of Korean interests. This stand made it deeply unpopular with the authorities and, in view of later events, was to expose its members to repeated threats, but at the time it enjoyed considerable support among the educated: as United States Minister Allen reported: 'This society [Ilsinhoe] has been under suspicion from the first, but it is succeeding among a certain class who are intelligent enough and bold enough to accept the inevitable and try to make peace with the Japanese.'[39] This is not to suggest that either Yi Yonggu or Song Pyongjun was uncritical of Japan. As the two united to form the Ilchinhoe in December 1904, Song wrote to a Japanese colonel, bitterly condemning Japanese officialdom for its support of Korea's corrupt and regressive élite, and pleading for Japanese recognition of the progressive nature of the Korean people as demonstrated by the Chinbohoe and Ilsinhoe. To bring about rapid change, Song voluntarily proposed that Japan oversee Korea's domestic and diplomatic affairs, but he warned against any attempt at colonisation. In preventing this, and no doubt swayed by links with Japanese pan-Asian activists under Prince Konoe Atsumaro, he expressed confidence (ultimately misplaced) in the Japanese public's willingness to intervene against its government in any misdealings with the Korean people.[40]

In the eyes of Japanese diplomats at Seoul, the Ilchinhoe was undeniably a progressive group, and one whose campaign was useful in keeping the Korean authorities in check (not least because the Korean court also suspected Japan was supporting the Ilchinhoe). However, in Tokyo, the imperial government had tied its flag to the Korean monarchy, and Foreign Minister Komura Jutaro ordered his diplomats to avoid contact with the Ilchinhoe. Until the end of the war, therefore, the society waited for events to unfold and concentrated on publishing, the establishment of schools and the development of its own agricultural company to develop wastelands in North P'yongan and Uiju. It also provided funding for at least one bright Korean to study in Japan: this was the future pioneer of Korea's vernacular literature and a leading 'cultural nationalist', Yi Kwangsu.

The belief that Korea's fate depended on improving its ties with Japan was not restricted to the Ilchinhoe. Already, in mid-1904, Horace Allen had urged Korean officials in the 'American group' to join with Tokyo[41] while, at the war's end with Russia's Manchurian concessions shifting to victorious Japan, Reverend Homer Hulbert announced in his *Korea Review* (September 1905):

> So long as there were two powers which Korea could play off against each other just so long would the old regime of conservatism prevail. If there is to be advancement it is plain that Korea must accept the tutelage of some friendly power and that that power should be given a free hand . . . and in spite of serious faults which have necessarily evoked criticism it is patent that Japan is the power to do the work.

Hulbert still accepted Kojong's commission for a last-minute dash to Washington DC, but appeals to President Theodore Roosevelt to defend Korea's independence were futile. Yet Japan remained wary. The eminent Ito Hirobumi, former prime minister and author of Japan's constitution, was despatched in haste to Seoul where, with Japanese troops highly visible around the palace, he forced the Korean government to sign a protectorate treaty on 17 November 1905: this gave Japan control of Korean foreign affairs and placed in Seoul a Japanese resident-general, subsequently Ito himself, to handle the local end of diplomacy. In the Korean cabinet, only Yi Wanyong, back as Education Minister since September 1905, argued to improve the terms, admitting:

> Japan and Korea have already differentiated which is strong and which weak. We have not the strength to resist so we should now, while we are not at odds with each other and time is not pressing in, bring about a satisfactory compromise and have our own demands accepted while accepting those of Japan.[42]

Korea, however, had no international ally and no force at home to use as a bargaining chip. Many Confucians were appalled at the loss of diplomatic authority and Prince Min Yongwhan was just one of those who committed suicide in protest. Only the Ilchinhoe, anticipating the élite's impending demise, was openly satisfied.

Although Japan's authority in Korea had greatly increased, its objectives had now shifted. Following acquisition of southern Manchuria, Japan now viewed Korea primarily as a rail corridor to the north, and its basic requirement of the Koreans was a low-cost trouble-free control. The symbols of Korean independence — the monarchy, the cabinet and local government — were left in place, and though the overweening nature of the protectorate administration was closer to the example of France in Indochina, Ito and his officials continued to evoke parallels with Lord Cromer's informal control of Egypt (significantly, the Emperor Meiji's command lecture for the 1906 New Year was on British policy in Egypt). Echoing Cromer on the Egyptian people, Japanese spokesmen confidently predicted that the benefits of justice and efficiency would reconcile Koreans to the protectorate, but Ito realised that such a turnaround in attitudes required rapid, visible benefits through roads, hospitals, schools and especially agricultural expansion. As always, money was the key. At the start of 1906, a 10 million yen loan was secured in Tokyo for major projects including roads, waterworks and improved medical facilities in Seoul. Ito's hopes, however, were not aided by history, by the exploitative actions of postbellum Japanese carpetbaggers, by the imperious and insulting behaviour of Japanese civilians cuffing and kicking Koreans in the street, nor by Japanese administrative insensitivity such as naming Korean railways the 'up' or 'down' line according to their orientation towards Tokyo.[43]

Beyond the palace, there were three broad political responses by Koreans to Japan's protectorate: the rural-based violent opposition of the *uibyong* or 'righteous armies'; the urban-centred 'patriotic enlightenment movement' of groups such as the Chajanghoe and Sobuk Hakhoe (Northwest Educational Society); and the pro-amalgamation Ilchinhoe with its mixed urban–rural base. The *uibyong*, led by local gentry and centred in the southern regions, numbered less than 2000 until 1907, and their poverty in arms and organisation posed no threat to Japanese control. However, insofar as Korean historians generally consider annexation pre-determined, these early *uibyong* are usually portrayed in heroic colours. In contrast, the patriotic enlightenment movement eschewed violence. The manifesto of the Chajanghoe, established by Chang Chiyon and others under Yun Ch'iho's presidency in April 1906, called on Koreans 'to study and implement educational expansion and industrial development, thus paving the way for national wealth and strength and so establish a base for *future* independence [emphasis added]'.[44] In part, the Chajanghoe shared the Ilchinhoe's respect for Japan's modernisation and its fear of Japanese government policies. This ambivalence underlies the diary entry by Yun in May 1905, upon hearing of Japan's mighty naval victory over the Russian fleet at Tsushima:

> As a Korean, I have no special reason for rejoicing over the uninterrupted successes of Japan. Every victory is a nail in the coffin of Korean independence . . . Yet as a member of the Yellow Race, Korea — or rather I — feel[s] proud of the glorious successes of Japan. She has vindicated the honor of our race. No braggart American, no arrogant Briton, no vain glorious Frenchman, will be, from now on, able to say that the Yellow man is incapable of great things.[45]

This ambivalence has run throughout the history of modern Korea–Japan relations, serving concurrently to provide Koreans with an incentive to catch up with their larger neighbour, but also reminding them of their relative economic and technological (but no longer military) inferiority.

Elite sponsorship of education, of course, had a long tradition in Korea, not least in the establishment in previous centuries of *sowon* by politically disadvantaged *yangban*. The education of the 'patriotic enlightenment', however, was clearly intended to penetrate the various social strata and serve as the engine of a nationalism fuelled by historical awareness. As Chang Chiyon explained in his introduction to a new history of Korea:

> The essence of education is the enlightenment of the people. The departure point of study must be the teaching of national history and the raising of a spirit of national belonging, a spirit of being one people, and a thickening of the blood of patriotism.[46]

Under reformist auspices, a new style of nationalistic history was constructed, and active in its formulation were two young intellectuals who were both to have a far-reaching impact on modern Korean thought: Sin Ch'aeho (1880–1936) and Ch'oe Namson (1890–1957). Influenced by the social Darwinist views of Chinese reformer Liang Qichao, they saw in struggle and expansion the key to international respect, but in their pursuit of an historically expansive, muscular Korea, they had to reach back into the realm of myth and legend before the coming of Chinese influence. Ch'oe was to spend much of his life refining the foundation legends of Korea, while Sin took a more belligerent, combative approach, villifying China for sapping Korea's historical energies and stifling its development with the cold rigidity of Confucian culture; this latter point was expressed also by Japanese nationalists in the nineteenth century. As alternative models, Sin translated or compiled biographies of heroic figures, men such as Yi Sunsin from Korea's resistance to Hideyoshi, and Italy's Cavour. In particular, he emphasised a tradition of conflict between Korea and its neighbours in an attempt to revitalise a square-jawed pride in the Korean past, incidentally establishing a style of confrontational historiography which has endured to the present.

Reformist groups such as Chang Chiyon's Kyongsang Educational Association and Chin Haksin's Association for Women's Education, while promoting the new learning and supporting new journals, nonetheless failed to convert the majority of *yangban* and farmers. It has been suggested that the north-west, historically ignored, commercially advanced and with less social division between people and *yangban*, was more receptive to patriotic enlightenment, but the fact remains that the bulk of Korea's population and the centre of politcs remained in the south.[47] Perhaps the main beneficiaries of Korea's crisis were missionaries: through their energetic prosletysing, and the popular belief that Western religion was one means of defence against Japan, the estimated total of Korean Protestants by 1910 had soared to 200 000. Under Son Pyonghui, a reformed Tonghak called Ch'ondogyo also garnered thousands of adherents, and was to continue to be active even into the 1990s.

The final collapse of Korean independence in 1910 was a result of Japan's inability to duplicate a Cromerist control of the Korean monarchy. Kojong's frequent 'indiscretions' in seeking Russian aid allowed Japan progressively to shackle his financial and physical mobility, but, as in French Indochina, retention of the traditional monarchy was vital to Japan in maintaining social order and preventing an emotional vacuum in which a modern nationalism might flourish. Korean progressives such as Yun Ch'iho were privately contemptuous of Kojong as an individual, but the throne still commanded broad popular loyalty and its only domestic opponent was the Ilchinhoe which, by late 1906, found itself bedraggled in the face of Japanese neglect, without funds for its newspaper, and with its leader, Song Pyongjun, in gaol. At this moment of despair, the Ilchinhoe obtained a new Japanese sponsor, Uchida Ryohei. Uchida was a political activist promoting a Japanese-led alliance of East Asia for defence against Western imperialism. The founder of the Amur Society (Kokuryukai), and with access to senior figures in Japanese politics, he has been portrayed as a major figure in the annexation of Korea. This overstates his importance and the ease with which Japanese decision-makers could be influenced by men on the periphery. However, to maintain the Ilchinhoe as a counter to the anti-Japanese lobby in Korea, Uchida did convince Ito to have Song released, to provide limited subsidies for Ilchinhoe publishing and political activities and, when the group again appeared ready to collapse, to have Song appointed Agriculture Minister in May 1907. Secret funds from the Japanese army were also arranged as a reward for Ilchinhoe help during the Russian war. By this point, however, the Ilchinhoe and Uchida were convinced that no real progress could be made as long as Japan limited itself to informal control and allowed Korean officials to obstruct intended reforms. Thus they began actively working to bring about Kojong's abdication. However, in mid-1907, it was Kojong himself who was to make possible their goal.

Kojong's impulse from the 1880s had always been to seek outside help rather than depend on his own people. In his defence, one might argue that he had a rational view of Korea's inability (though one increased by his own government's repression of the Tonghak and Independence Club as popular forces) to fend off larger neighbours without foreign help. The result of his appeals, however, was only to reduce still further the state's teetering autonomy. In June 1907, the second international peace conference was held in The Hague, and Kojong arranged with Homer Hulbert for a secret three-man delegation in defiance of Japan to plead with the world powers for restoration of Korean independence. Ito had advance warning of the plot and warned Kojong that such a challenge to Japan's treaty authority could not pass without reply. Nonetheless, the mission went ahead, but when news of its dramatic appearance at the conference reached Seoul, there was widespread fear of violent retaliation by Japan. Ito deliberately exploited these fears by maintaining silence on Japanese intentions and leaving the Korean cabinet to pressure Kojong. Yet it should be noted that the Japanese government did not vote to force Kojong's abdication, preferring instead to enhance its sub-surface control and obtain further political concessions. However, there was rising desperation in Seoul and talk of imminent war. Prime Minister Yi Wanyong, and especially Agriculture

Minister Song, bluntly accused Kojong of endangering Korea by his unilateral actions and begged him to abdicate. In view of the crisis, Kojong's own advisors concurred and, after more than three decades which began and ended in international crisis, he made way for the last of the Yi monarchs, Sunjong, in mid-July.

Ito got the desired second Korea–Japan Agreement on 24 July 1907. This gave the Resident-General power over Korea's domestic politics and official appointments, and placed Japanese nationals at vice-ministerial level throughout the Korean administration. However, Ito's hasty disbanding of the Korean army on 1 August 1907 — the risible 'standing joke' — was the error accompanying Kojong's abdication which was ultimately to ensure annexation. Korean soldiers took their skills and organisation to the *uibyong*, instantly raising the military threat to Japan. Japan responded with the callousness for which its forces were much later to be all too well known. British correspondent F.A. McKenzie described one Japanese pacification drive: 'The Japanese soldiers were allowed great licence, wounded were bayonetted, women violated, women and children were shot in scores, and thousands of innocent countryfolk were driven to the mountains.'[48] Commenting on the report, Britain's Consul-General explained: 'The so-called 'atrocities' committed by the Japanese are not much more than is generally to be expected from a victorious army stamping out rebellion in a conquered [sic] territory.' He then added casually: 'The Japanese take no prisoners so far as I can learn, except temporarily for the purpose of obtaining from them information, after which they are shot.'[49] This is confirmed by the figures for *uibyong* dead and wounded between 1907 and 1910 (see Table 1.2).[50]

Table 1.2 Uibyong dead and wounded, 1907–1910					
	1906	1907	1908	1909	1910
Japanese					
Dead	3	29	75	25	4
Wounded	2	63	170	30	6
Uibyong					
Dead	82	3627	11562	2374	125
Wounded	0	1492	1719	435	54
Captured	145	139	1417	329	48

The bloodshed exposed the poverty of Ito's appeals to East Asian co-prosperity. Koreans as a whole had begun the modern era distrustful of Japan, and the clumsiness of Japanese policies since the 1870s had made few converts. Visiting Tokyo in December 1907, Song urged Japanese financiers to invest in Korean villages and use commercial means to undercut the *uibyong*.[51] However, with violence escalating in 1908, Japanese investment and migration were deferred. An offer of amnesty from the Residency-General in September 1907 was largely ignored, while a major Japanese sweep against 'rebels' in Cholla during 1909 encountered few targets and one of the few groups found and shot proved on closer inspection to consist solely of Ilchinhoe members. From 1907, Residency-General policies became increasingly repressive, restricting publication and political assembly, and introducing new regulations from August 1908 on the opening of schools and the content of textbooks. In the aftermath of Kojong's abdication, the Chajanghoe had been forced to disband and, though re-established as the Taehan Hyophoe, it was inhibited in the towns by the new official strictures and in the villages by the widespread unrest. The *North China Herald* of 6 June 1908 reported: 'All trade is in complete abeyance except in the immediate neighbourhood of the railway.' This was exaggerated: Korea's foreign trade in 1908 and 1909 exceeded 50 million yen, but while food and raw materials poured out, little was coming in. By 1909, Japan could boast no success in Korea.

In late 1908, Japanese Prime Minister Katsura Taro returned to power with a program of general housecleaning: the problem of Japanese emigration to California was defused when Katsura promised to restrict the migrant flow — this meant ensuring better access to the Asian continent, especially Manchuria and Korea; at home, policies of retrenchment and debt repayment were instituted to restore economic stability; in Korea, to lower military costs and restore socio-economic stability, the decision was taken in April 1909 on annexation at an appropriate moment — that is, after gaining Russian approval. Ito agreed and, in October that year, travelled to arrange matters with the Russian foreign minister at Harbin where, upon arrival, he was assassinated by a Korean freedom fighter, An Chunggun. An's name has entered the pantheon of Korean heroes but, as annexation had already been decided, the murder served no purpose except to restore a measure of international sympathy to Japan. In Seoul, the Ilchinhoe tried to pre-empt any reprisal for Ito's murder by proposing a voluntary union of Korea and Japan, and the Taehan Hyophoe, recognising the failure of patriotic reforms to date, could only reply that the timing for union was premature.[52] Others were not so passive, and assassins went in search of Yi Yonggu; failing to locate him, they attacked Yi Wanyong instead, stabbing him severely but not fatally. For several months, Korean politics lay in nervous suspension. Japan could not implement its previous decision to annex Korea without Russian approval and, upon news of Ito's death, Tokyo had instantly informed its British ally (who was unaware of the annexation plan) that there would be no imminent change in Korea's situation. However, moves by the United States government late in 1909 towards restoring Chinese control over Manchurian railways had the unforeseen impact of improving Russo-Japanese ties; yet, even if merely for selfish motives, it was only with reluctance that Russia accepted annexation of Korea. Informed in mid-1910, the British minister in Tokyo was furious at what he considered Japanese deceit. As before, however, no power was sufficiently concerned to stand up in defence of Korean interests. In the middle of 1910, General Terauchi Masatake was despatched to Seoul to conclude a treaty of annexation. Yi Wanyong left his sick-bed to negotiate some last-ditch protection for the Korean monarchy and retention of the state name Han'guk. His attempt to preserve the traditional symbols of Korean identity, without which he feared the people would lose the spiritual base for future independence, proved unavailing, and the annexation treaty of 22 August 1910 removed all props of independence, ending the Korean monarchy, renaming Korea as Choson and reducing it to a mere part of the Japanese empire.

At the moment of annexation, Korea was a virtual police state under Japanese control. Political societies, including the Ilchinhoe (still the largest of Korean political groups at 140 000 members), were prohibited, and no opposition to the takeover was allowed. Annexation blackened Japan's reputation in East Asia: the Chinese press warned of similar Japanese designs on Manchuria, and even Japanese intellectuals acknowledged the failure of what for some of them, amidst all the Machiavellianism, had been good intentions. For the Korean people, the brief 35 years of contact with Japan had witnessed a mix of social chaos but expanding horizons; great wealth for some, impoverishment for others; growing violence and, ultimately, despair. For better or worse, however, the traditional state and monarchy were no more and, after a few years of shocked inactivity, a new Korea was slowly to evolve.

Notes

1 Palais, 1975, p. 35. The indomitable British traveller Isabella Bird Bishop visited Kojong later in life and gave her impression in *Korea and Her Neighbours*, NY, 1898, p. 253: '[he is] short and sallow, certainly a plain man, wearing a thin moustache and a tuft on the chin. He is nervous and twitches his hands, but his pose and manner are not without dignity. His face is pleasing and his kindliness of nature is well-known.' It is only fair to state that the Taewon'gun showed a similar concern for the people.
2 Eckert, 1991, ch. 1
3 Lee Yur Bok, 1976, pp. 90–91. By contrast, in 1895 United States exports to Japan were $5 million, and to China $4 million. The first successful American trader was later recalled by a Japanese contemporary: 'He lived in a shabby building in front of the gate of the Chinese government office. While living like a beggar, he sold canned goods and Western liquor which he obtained from Nagasaki.' (Cook, 1981, p. 20)
4 Sugiyama, 1984
5 Ki-baik Lee, 1984, p. 282
6 Yamada Shoji, 'Meiji zenki no Nit-Cho boeki', *Ienaga Saburo kyoju Tokyo Kyoiku Daigaku taikan kinen ronshu kanko iinkai*, ed. Kindai Nihon no kokka to shiso, Tokyo, 1979, p. 64. For details on the Japanese and Chinese commercial presence at Seoul in 1887, see Cho, 1976, p. 33.
7 Sugiyama, 1984, p. 17
8 Huang's memorandum is quoted in Ho Taku-shu, *Meiji shoki Nik-Kan kankei no tenkai*, Tokyo, 1969, p. 90.
9 Watanabe Manabu, *Chosen kindaishi* (Tokyo, 1968, p. 46) describes the Imo incident as 'a riot of the urban poor'.
10 Shin Yong-ha, 1984, p. 20 on origin of modern Korean nationalism; Yong-ho Ch'oe, 1981, pp. 517-18, and Kang Man'gil, 1990, p. 10 on North Korean view.

11 Details of the plan are in Cook, 1972, p. 247; Shin Yong-ha, 1984, pp. 10–17.

12 I.K. Hwang, 1978, pp. 117–18

13 W.W. Rockhill (Seoul) to Secretary of State Bayard, 5 March 1887, in Palmer, 1963, p. 275

14 The history of Ehwa's early years and the experiences of some of its graduates are recounted in Yung-Chung Kim, 1976, pp. 217–31. In 1899, the student population at Ehwa had reached 47, and in the mid-1970s exceeded 8000.

15 Dinsmore to Secretary of State Bayard, 25 June 1888, in Palmer, 1963, p. 211. The rumours also suggested that Korean children were being stolen by foreigners to be converted into medicine and materials for making photographs.

16 Miss L.C. Rothweiler, 'What shall we teach in our girls' schools?', *The Korean Repository*, March 1892, reprinted NY, 1964, vol. 1, pp. 89–93

17 Dinsmore to Secretary of State Bayard, 29 June 1887, in Palmer, 1963, p. 143. See also Young Ick Lew, 1984, p. 101.

18 Quoted in Weems, 1964, p. 23.

19 Details, Han Woo-keun, 'Tonghak nongmin ponggi', Kuksa pyonch'an wiwonhoe, ed. Han'guksa, vol. 17, Seoul 1977, pp. 202–6; Kang Chaeon, 'Kindai shoki no Nihon to Chosen', eds Kim Dalsu et al., *Kyokasho ni kakareta Chosen*, Tokyo, 1979, p. 161

20 Weems, 1965, pp. 39–40.

21 Kang Man'gil, 1990, p. 13, explains that North Korean historians view the Kabo reform group as clarifying the goals of the bourgeois reform movement in its attempt to progress from a feudal to a capitalistic society. See Han Woo-keun, 1970, p. 418, and Pak Chonggun, 'Chosen ni okeru 1894–95 nen no Kim Hongjip (kakikaha) seiken no kosatsu', *Rekishigaku kenkyu*, no. 417, February 1975, p. 42, for a sceptical view.

22 Details of the new ministries and their duties are in Kuksa pyonch'an wiwonhoe, ed. *Kojong sidaesa*, Seoul, 1969, vol. 3, pp. 496–507.

23 Details of the government's school plans and curriculum are in Oh Chonsok (Abe Hiroshi/Watanabe Manabu, trans.), *Kankoku kindai kyoikushi*, Tokyo, 1979, pp. 85–93.

24 Anon., 'The battle of Pyeng Yang as seen by a Korean', *The Korean Repository*, September 1895, pp. 350–53. See also Gale, 1898, p. 200 for an eyewitness report on the Chinese terror at Wonsan.

25 FO881/6605, Korean Foreign Minister to GB Minister O'Conor (Beijing), enclosed in O'Conor to Lord Kimberley, 17 September 1894

26 Quoted in Shin Bok-ryong, 1974, pp. 78–79.

27 FO881/6665, Hillier to O'Conor, 25 October 1894

28 FO881/6665, Hillier to O'Conor, 14 December 1894

29 For an earlier view of the Independence Club, see Henderson, 1968, pp. 65–67. On North and South Korean attitudes, see Kang Man'gil, 1990, p. 13.

30 Chandra, 1988, p. 107

31 Quoted in Chandra, 1988, p. 138.

32 Allen to Secretary of State Hay, 13 October 1898, in Burnett, 1989, p. 52

33 Kuksa pyonch'an wiwonhoe, ed. *Yun Ch'iho Ilgi*, Seoul, 1973, vol. 5, pp. 140–41, entry for 12 March 1898. Yun was elected vice-president of the club on 27 February 1898 and became acting president when Yi Wanyong was appointed to a provincial governorship in March. The events since de Speyer's arrival are also detailed in Synn, 1981, pp. 248–64.

34 Kang Chaeon, *Chosen kindaishi kenkyu*, 2nd edn, Tokyo, 1982, pp. 278–79

35 Allen to Hay, 13 October 1898 in Burnett, 1989, p. 52. The women's memorial is quoted in Nahm, 1988, p. 198.

36 John Jordan papers, FO 350/3, letter to Sir Cyprian Bridge (Weihaiwei), 20 June 1902

37 Burnett, 1989, pp. 62–63, Allen to Secretary of State Hay, 23 August 1900

38 Kuksa pyonch'an wiwownhoe, 1973, vol. 6, pp. 22–23, entry for 26 April 1904
39 Allen to Secretary of State John Hay, 17 October 1904, in Burnett, 1989, p. 137.
40 Gaimusho (ed.), *Nihon gaiko bunsho*, vol. 37-1, pp. 936–41, Song to Colonel Matsuishi Yasuharu, vice-chief of staff, 1st Army, 2 December 1904; also Nishio, 1978, pp. 51–56. For the Ilchinhoe manifesto, see Han Sang-il, 1984, pp. 154–55.
41 W.W. Rockhill Papers, The Houghton Library, Harvard University, Horace Allen letter, 6 May 1904. Grateful thanks to Ms. Jennie Rathbun of The Houghton Library for confirming this reference.
42 Kim Chongmyong (ed.), *Nik-Kan gaiko shiryo shusei*, Tokyo, 1964, vol. 6-1, p. 46
43 Putnam Weale, 'The Corean problem', *North China Herald*, 15 December 1905
44 Kang Chaeon, 1982, p. 442; also Kuksa pyonch'an wiwonhoe, 1973, vol. 6, pp. 227–28, entry for 6 May 1906 on Yun's view of the society
45 Kuksa pyonch'an wiwonhoe, 1973, vol. 6, p. 112, entry for 2 June 1905
46 Kang Chaeon, 1982, p. 465. This was in Chang's introduction to the revised *Tongguk Yoksa* (History of Korea).
47 Kang Chaeon, 1982, pp. 445–47
48 Contained in FO 371/383, undated no. 34377, McKenzie telegram to *Daily Mail* (London), 21 September 1907. McKenzie published his experiences of Korea in two works, *The Tragedy of Korea*, London, 1908, and *Korea's Fight for Freedom*, NY, 1920.
49 Henry Cockburn (Seoul) to Foreign Secretary Grey, FO 371/383 above
50 'Chosen Boto Tobatsushi', listed in Oe Shinobu, *Nichi-Ro senso to Nihon guntai*, Tokyo 1987. Slightly different figures were given the British government by Japan in 1908, but the general trend was much the same, FO 410–53, MacDonald (Tokyo) to Grey, 6 December 1908.
51 Speech to the Toyo Kyokai, 23 December 1907, in Toyo kyokai enkaku, 2 vols, unpublished, Takushoku University Library, vol. 2, pp. 315–28
52 Ichikawa Masaaki (ed.), *Nik-Kan gaiko shiryo*, Tokyo, 1964, vol. 8, p. 318. Regarding the Ilchinhoe amalgamation proposal, some observers acknowleged that it was designed to pre-empt a Japanese annexation. This was the view of Britain's acting Consul-General in Seoul, FO 410/55, Arthur Hyde Lay (Seoul) to Foreign Secretary Grey, 7 December 1909.

2

COLONIAL KOREA 1910–1945

With colonialism, Korea's position in the world virtually resumed its pre-1850s status. Contact with other states was limited and contemporary events or processes, with the notable exception of Christianity, reached Korea through the filter of outside — in this case, Japanese — experience. Korea was the only state in modern East Asia to forfeit its autonomy completely, and the restoration of independence came as an off-shoot of Japan's defeat in 1945, not through domestic struggle. This apparent failure of Korean nationalism is explained by native historians, in contrast with the generally benevolent memory of Japanese rule in Taiwan, by insisting on the unremittingly brutal and exploitative nature of Japanese colonialism. That the Japanese authorities employed repression and widespread arrest is indisputable, but the selective emphasis on official violence to 1919 and the aggressive assimilation polices of the Sino-Japanese War years (1937–45) obscure major shifts in colonial policy and with them the background to social change in Korea.

The colonial period divides roughly with the decades. The first Governors-General, Terauchi Masatake (1910–16) and Hasegawa Yoshimichi (1916–19), were army officers who ruled by intimidation. These years are described in Korea as the dark age, or the era of military rule. After the massive Samil independence uprising of March 1919, Governors-General Admiral Saito Makoto (1919–27, 1929–31), General Yamanashi Hanzo (1927–29) and General Ugaki Kazushige (1927, 1931–36) began to parcel out freedoms to the Korean people in education, print and political organisation, and thereby undercut the militancy of a growing nationalist movement. This conciliatory approach earns the description 'cultural rule' for the period to 1930. With Korean–Japanese tariff barriers being withdrawn on schedule in 1920, the authorities expanded agricultural exports to Japan as a means of developing economic unity, simultaneously increasing Korea's dependency on the Japanese market. The global depression of the late 1920s struck both Korea and Japan, but Japanese army expansion in Manchuria in 1931 and its construction of the client state, Manchukuo, opened new avenues for Korean migration and commercial development. Rising military needs in the 1930s were met by the first heavy industrialisation of Korea. The war years 1937–45 brought militarisation and forced assimilation under a succession of army Governors-General, Minami Jiro (1936–42), Koiso Kuniaki (1942–44) and Abe Nobuyuki (1944–45). Japan's rapid weakening soon after Pearl Harbor enabled Korean officials to extend their authority over local affairs, but also exacerbated oppression and exploitation of Korea's natural and human resources for the war effort. Although Korea was not bombed by the Allies in the Pacific War, it was nonetheless an exhausted people who greeted United States and Soviet forces in 1945.

Of the colonial period as a whole, there are two broad views: that the introduction by Japan of modern production, transport, finance and education, intentionally or not, provided Korea with a modern capitalist system; and alternatively, that the exploitation of Korean resources for Japanese profit, and the control of capital and land by Japanese entrepreneurs, left Korea a semi-feudal dependency. It is generally agreed, however, that in restricting the input of Koreans at the higher levels of administration and preventing the development of democratic participation in affairs, Japan left Korea politically unprepared to deal with sudden independence in 1945. From this, it is argued that Japan indirectly abetted the internal chaos which ensued between 1945 and 1950. What Japan indisputably did provide, however — as with other imperial overlords — was a model of strong social organisation and nationalism. In Japan's case, this was based on education and military service, with the bureaucracy dominant over politicians and working closely with business in what Chalmers Johnson has termed the capitalist-developmental state. This model was to be of considerable value to the future South Korean government.

Between 1910 and 1945, the signal change in Korea was the unprecedented rise in population, which increased by approximately 70 per cent from 14.77 million in 1910 to 25.13 million in 1944. This was the result of declining mortality, both urban and rural, with better social order, public health, campaigns against tuberculosis and smallpox, seaport quarantine to prevent infectious diseases, and with official rewards for larger families. Although the fertility rate declined because of restrictions on child marriage and more women taking employment, improved medical conditions lowered infant mortality and enabled women to produce healthy children later in life. Better health also extended adult life expectancy: between 1925 and 1945, the average life of men rose from 37.9 to 42 years and of women from 37.2 to 44.8 years. The content and distribution of Korea's population was also influenced by colonisation: more men than women either chose or were compelled to seek employment in Manchuria or Japan, while the expansion of heavy industry in north Korea from the 1930s attracted considerable internal migration from the impoverished agrarian south.

As in traditional Korea, Japan and China remained the two primary contacts both in human and economic terms. Foreign residency in Korea was minimal: by 1927, the 51 323 non-Japanese foreign residents included 50 056 Chinese, 743 Americans (most of whom were missionaries) and 228 Britons.[1] Western tourists occasionally made Korea a side-trip from Japan, but travel was a luxury and numbers were few. Economic historian Hochin Choi calculates that there were 30 000 Korean residents of Japan in 1920, but until the massive labour exodus to Japan after about 1931, contact between Japanese and Koreans was largely confined to the Korean peninsula. Even there, the two peoples lived in different philosophical and spatial worlds. Relative to British imperialism in Egypt or India, geographical and cultural proximity resulted in a much larger — and more visible — presence of Japanese in Korea, but they still remained a tiny minority of the population: 1.28 per cent (171 543) in 1910, 2.48 per cent (501 867) in 1930 and 2.91 per cent (707 337) in 1940.[2] Moreover, in excess of 40 per cent of all Japanese residents were located in the two provinces of Kyonggi and south Kyongsang (the sites of Seoul and Pusan). It was only during the war years that Japanese entered the northernmost provinces of Hamgyong and P'yongan in any numbers; in 1942 they constituted 10 per cent and 4.5 per cent respectively of the total population of those two provinces.[3] The age distribution of the two races in Korea was similar: 40 per cent of all Japanese and half of all Koreans were under 19 years of age. Yet adult Japanese were mainly bureaucrats, soldiers of the two army divisions, sailors at the two naval bases or police of the government-general. Products of a modern industrial world, they were attuned to physical mobility with their ships and trains, and to social mobility through universal education. The physical means of mobility they brought to Korea: railway lines, geared to link with Manchuria, expanded from 481 kilometres in 1907 to 3737 kilometres 30 years later, while passenger and freight cars increased four-fold between 1906 and 1926; an autobus service revolving around the railway station was introduced to Seoul and its environs from late 1928; and thrice-weekly air services commenced between Japan, Korea and Manchuria from 1929, with airports at Seoul, P'yongyang and Ulsan (about 80 kilometres from Pusan).

Railways and aeroplanes function according to strict schedules, and the Japanese in Korea lived in urban office time. They also worked according to standards of precision which, much to the gratitude of later scholars, included the tenacious accumulation of vast and detailed records on the societies under their control: this provides a more certain statistical base from which to interpret recent Korean history. In contrast, the Korean people were mainly farmers, indifferent to precise time, unfamiliar with the regime of office and army, and inhabiting a society with little physical or social mobility. This cultural gap was not easily bridged: the ideology of Japanese imperialism was weak, the technological base Western in origin, and Japanese Shintoism too parochial a belief system to generate converts for Japan's 'civilising mission'. In consequence, the authorities, as in Japanese-occupied China later, interfered with the minutiae of life and movement. For the first time in centuries, the Korean farming population was confronted by a highly centralised administration espousing policies on a national scale, but with the force to impose compliance. What the Japanese lacked, however, was understanding of local Korean conditions — even of the language itself. During the colonial era, there was no substantial improvement in Japanese official understanding of the Korean language, despite its basic grammatical similarities. In 1921, the government-general instituted a system of extra pay for officials showing proficiency in the Korean language by examination, but figures in 1937 claimed a cumulative total of only 5000 successful candidates.[4] Inter-marriage was also low: just 2.6 marriages per thousand in 1940. This lack of understanding allowed the Korean people some freedom to conduct their own affairs at the lower level. It also meant that, in times of crisis such as the outbreak of war, the very ignorance of the authorities would bring about a concerted effort to Japanise the Koreans.

The Dark Age, 1910–1919

Karl Marx, writing on nineteenth-century India, acknowledged a positive role for imperialism in its (sometimes unintended) destruction of moribund traditional structures and the freeing of popular energies towards nationalism and social equality. The direction of those energies, however, had to contend with the prevailing ideologies of the time. The military and industrial strength of Western Europe and the United States had created a standard, defined as 'modernity', which involved industrialisation and competition in the global market. For East Asia and others, their relative lateness of industrialisation, coming as it did in a world already divided amongst a few great powers, was inevitably a disadvantage. After 1910, Koreans could envisage no bright future of economic or military parity with the imperialists and a decade was to pass before alternative strategies for nationalist development were to present themselves. Moreover, and not unnaturally, Japan followed in the mould of other imperial powers by seeking local conservative support for its colonial administration. Thus traditional élites and landlords retained considerable status in Korea, while revolutionary movements were suppressed. In addition, imperial powers generally (with the notable exception of Japan in the twilight of empire) avoided developing industry in their colonies, preferring instead to exploit either colonial food reserves or agrarian consumers as a captive market for metropolitan produce: indeed, a corporation law from 1911–20 restricted industries in Korea whether of native or Japanese ownership in order to protect mainland Japanese concerns. This retarded social change and left the colonies dependent on the metropole or ruling power. Korea's relationship with Japan — exporting rice and importing textiles — had been fixed in the 1870s and the colonial government made no attempt to change it until the depression years of the late 1920s.

In its first decade, the government-general concentrated on rebuilding Korea as a modern, efficient field for colonial production. A massive land survey was initiated preparatory to expanding agricultural output; Korea's infrastructure was developed through road, railway and harbour works; while the capital of Seoul was reconstructed with broad thoroughfares, city parks and imposing government buildings as icons of Japanese authority (some of these remained in use in the 1990s). Yet indicative of Japan's underlying weakness was the prohibition from 1910 on Korean political groups and publications. Western missionaries enjoyed some protection due to Japan's fear of international opinion and they were often outspoken in defence of Korean interests; this helped maintain Christianity at the forefront of Korean nationalism, and in part explains the continuing political influence of Protestantism and Catholicism in post-liberation South Korea. In 1911, however, the Japanese authorities fabricated an assassination plot on the life of Governor-General Terauchi and arrested leading Korean Christians as suspects. Several, including Yun Ch'iho, were imprisoned, and intimidation served temporarily to quieten Korean religious nationalists.

As a counterbalance to Christianity, generous official support was given to Confucian learning and Buddhism. Soon after annexation, the government-general established a Society for the Protection of Buddhism (Pulgyo Onghohoe) under the direction of Japanese officials and Korean notables such as Yi Wanyong. From July 1911, the administrative structure of Buddhism was redrawn with the existing 1371 temples being divided into 30 districts under a controlling abbot appointed by the government-general. This gave the authorities effective control over the Buddhist priesthood. However, it had been through the influence of a Japanese Nichiren priest that the prohibition on Buddhist priests or nuns entering Seoul was finally lifted in 1895, and this liberation was followed by a growth in adherents among both urban élite and commoners. Having suffered oppression throughout the Yi dynasty, and being impressed by the energy and high status of Japanese Buddhism, local Buddhist leaders gladly co-operated with the government-general and a new generation of priests went to Japan to study. Between 1912 and 1920, Korean Buddhists used their official support and expanding audience to set up a flurry of journals, publishing scholarly articles on Buddhist matters but also serving to propagate official policies: a leading example of this was the *Choson pulgyo ch'ongbo* (1917–21), edited by Yi Nunghwa, one of the greatest Buddhist scholars of his time.[5]

Influential Confucians, perhaps themselves fearing the inroads of Christianity, also accepted Japanese funding after annexation. Japan's assistance to Confucianism as a shared value system and a prop for the existing social hierarchy was most clearly demonstrated in April 1930 when the government-general established a Confucian Institute (Meirin Gakuin) inside the traditional Songgyun'gwan. This offered students a two-year course in the Confucian classics, as well as Japanese language and civics. The Japanese also introduced Shintoism, the mix of animism and ancestor worship on which Japan's imperial house was founded. A state shrine (Chosen Jingu) was opened in October 1925, prominently located on Seoul's Namsan or Southern Mountain. However, Shintoism did not export well. By 1925, there were 42 shrines and over a hundred 'lesser shrines' (*jinshi*), but controversy centred on whether it was a religion, in which case attendance at shrines was unacceptable to many Korean Christians, or merely an ethical system of ancestor worship as the government-general averred, thus allowing them to treat shrine attendance as a form of civic ritual rather than religious belief.[6] Korean intellectuals writing in the newspaper *Tong-A Ilbo* scorned Shintoism as nothing more than superstition and disruptive to the moral development of Korean children. In 1935, however, as Japanese attitudes hardened, Shinto was to become an object of hatred when all schoolchildren were ordered to make obeisance at shrines. In response, Korean Christians and American missionaries, including Dr George McCune, were staunchly to defend religious freedom and some Koreans, such as the Presbyterian minister of P'yongyang, Chu Kich'ol, were to be martyred for their cause.

Official figures for religious adherence late in the colonial era show the resilience of Christianity, the meagre success of Shintoism and the dramatic rise of Buddhism. In 1938–39, there were 1657 Korean Buddhist temples/preaching places (separate from those run by Japanese sects) with 7244 Korean monks and nuns and 194 800 followers. The Ch'ondogyo church, carrying on Tonghak traditions, registered 82 000 followers. The various Christian churches (including the Japan Episcopal Church) claimed over 470 000 members, 287 000 of these Presbyterian and 114 000 Roman Catholic. Shinto shrines and preaching halls numbered just 53, with 613 priests, and 21 000 Korean followers — many of these were no doubt 'rice bowl' believers, hoping primarily to impress their Japanese overlords.[7]

Japanese troops crossing P'yongtaek Bridge, Ansong River (1920s?)
Source: *Kundae Hanguk*, vol. 1, p. 85

Annexation and oppression had forced into exile Korean nationalist leaders such as Sin Ch'aeho and An Ch'angho, but this led to the formation of an international independence movement, albeit one frequently at odds with itself. Independence groups of varying personnel and ideologies were established in Shanghai, Manchuria, Siberia and the United States. The domestic political movement, however, was left to flounder. Some of those who remained were intimidated by Japanese oppression, while others such as Ch'oe Namson viewed themselves in traditional terms firstly as scholars, not political agitators. However, the lack of improvement under Japanese control, the insistence on Japanese language and textbooks in Korean schools, and the disparity in wages between Korean and Japanese officials fostered resentment which exploded upon the death of Kojong in 1919. This took two forms. On 8 February that year, radical Korean students in Tokyo boldly declared their nation independent, called on the Western powers to honour earlier commitments in support of Korean independence, and warned Japan it would face a bloody war if it did not change its rule. Of far greater impact, however, was the popular demonstration within Korea from 1 March (Sam-il), engineered by Korean religious leaders. It began in the urban centres, but rapidly spread nationwide, ultimately lasting some six weeks and involving perhaps more than a million people. Its opening call for independence, signed by sixteen Christian nationalists, fifteen from the Ch'ondogyo and two Buddhists, was secretly authored by Ch'oe Namson in language which, while quite beautiful, was of a complexity and style beyond the average listener's comprehension. Inspired by President Woodrow Wilson's call for self-determination of the oppressed peoples of the world, Ch'oe stressed pacifism and, to use a term favoured by Kenneth Wells, self-reconstruction, claiming that:

> We have no wish to find special fault with Japan's lack of fairness or her contempt of our civilisation and the principles on which her state rests. We, who have greater cause to reprimand ourselves, need not spend precious time in finding fault with others, neither need we, who require so urgently to build for the future, spend useless hours over what is past and gone. Our urgent need today, is the setting up of this house of ours, and not a discussion of who has broken it down, or what has caused its ruin. Our work is to clear the future of defects in accord with the earnest dictates of conscience. Let us not be filled with bitterness or resentment over past agonies, or past occasions for anger.[8]

Governor-General Hasegawa, however, responded as though confronted by hardened troops instead of the intellectuals, farmers, women and youths who marched in the protests. Japanese soldiers and civilians attacked ordinary Koreans irrespective of age or sex, or indeed irrespective of whether they demonstrated or not. Christian sites were targeted: in at least one village, Cheam-ni, 80 kilometres from Seoul, 35 Christian men and two women were corralled into the local Methodist church and murdered, and then the church itself was razed. In South P'yongan, the Ch'ondogyo villagers of Mangsan were seized by Japanese troops and those who tried to argue were shot. Elsewhere, farmers were terrorised into docility, being lined up for execution and then reprieved to live in fear. Young women were arrested without cause, stripped at police stations before crowds of men and beaten with outrageous brutality. In Hamhung on 4 March, a Canadian missionary described the Japanese fire brigade assaulting a crowd and noted:

> On this same day at least seven Korean men and a number of girls were taken to the police station in a pitiful condition from the wounds received . . . So far as was seen there was no resistance made by the Koreans; they neither lifted a stick nor hurled a stone to defend themselves nor did they utter a word of abuse against the Japanese.[9]

Western missionaries took no part in organising the demonstrations. Yet the Japanese press simply could not believe that the Koreans, so often portrayed as helpless children, were capable of efficient organisation and passionate commitment, and journalists strove to maintain the colonial myths by hinting at American involvement, even claiming United States dollars were funding Soviet-armed Korean guerrillas on the Manchurian border. In fact, Western missionaries had initially welcomed Japan's annexation as a stabilising move, but in 1919 they were unequivocal in publicising Japanese brutality through the Western media. Although the new Governor-General, Admiral Saito, tried to repair the relationship and openly praised the missionary contribution to Korea's enlightenment, the belief that Christian and Japanese aims were fundamentally in conflict was never lost.

Execution of Korean anti-Japanese guerrillas, (cc. 1919)
Source: Mainichi shi sha (ed.) *Icioku nin no Showashi — Chosen* (Showa History of 100 Million People — Korea), Tokyo, 1978, p. 20

The Samil rising is generally viewed as the epochal event in Korean nationalism. Historians in both the north and the south focus less on the intellectual leadership than on the students, workers, women and peasants who agitated in the street, and some southern historians accept P'yongyang criticisms of the movement's bourgeois leaders. For the north, the Samil rising marks the end of the bourgeois nationalist movement, begun earlier by Kim Okkyun and his confederates, and the start of a new worker–peasant-led struggle against imperialism and feudalism. Unsurprisingly, P'yongyang scholars stress the influence of the Bolshevik revolution rather than Wilsonian liberalism in developing Korean political consciousness, and once again there are younger historians in the south who agree. However, while acknowledging the strength and extent of the 1919 protests, and their crucial role in providing material for a tradition of modern nationalism, the fact is that nothing on the same scale was repeated during the the colonial period. Moreover, there were some who considered the Samil rising a failure insofar as Korea remained under Japanese control, and activist youths in the 1920s began promoting violent struggle as the only viable means to liberation.

Controversy exists as to whether Tokyo was already planning reform in Korean policy or whether this was forced upon it by the Samil rising. Rice riots in Japan from August 1918 had brought to the premiership Hara Kei, a party politician and long-time opponent of military domination in Japanese colonies. Although he probably would have altered Japanese rule in Korea, the Samil uprising undoubtedly served to hasten and direct the process. In 1920, Admiral Saito announced a catalogue of major changes. Among these were: regular police to replace the gendarmerie; Japanese teachers and officials to abandon the swords they wore as badges of superiority; and freedom for Koreans to publish vernacular newspapers and hold meetings. In addition, there was to be greater consultation with provincial Koreans on reform; an end to wage discrimination between Korean and Japanese officials; promotion of the Korean language among Japanese officials; government support to develop key industries such as rice production; expansion of sanitation and communications; education to be expanded and brought in line with the system in Japan; new respect for Korean culture, including Korean burial customs; and religious freedom.

The wedding of Korea's Crown Prince Yi and Japan's Princess Nashimoto (Yi Pangja) in April 1920 gave a convenient excuse for releasing several thousand political prisoners, and the new era of 'cultural rule' commenced. There was speculation about Korean political representation, either in the Japanese Diet or in a separate Korean parliament, and relations were improved by recruiting landlords, capitalists and literati sympathetic to Japan into religious and cultural groups. These included the Kungmin Hyophoe (People's Society), established in 1919 by Min Wonsik. Advocating racial harmony between Japanese and Koreans, its ultimate goal was some form of Korean political representation, and in 1925 it delivered a petition to this end to the Japanese Diet, allegedly signed by over 10 000 people. The Japanese Lower House had in 1921 passed a resolution extending the franchise to Korea, and similar moves were to be supported by Governor-General Minami in 1937–38, but on each occasion the Japanese cabinet vetoed the change.

Under Admiral Saito, there was some improvement in Korean official salaries, but the bonus system enjoyed by expatriate Japanese meant a continued disparity in wages. More Koreans were brought into government at various levels, but economically vital regions remained under Japanese direction. Local administration by mid-1931 was as follows: Koreans served as five of the thirteen provincial governors, but as only one of the fourteen prefects; they occupied all but 31 of the 220 district magistracies (a district population being roughly 10 000); but townships were divided into two classes, designated and ordinary (where the designated were commercially or industrially more important) and the 41 heads of designated townships included just eight Koreans — by contrast, of the total 2423 ordinary townships, 2419 were under Korean direction.[10] At the cultural level, there was greater respect for the Korean language and followers of Chu Sigyong in 1921 established what was to become the Han'gul Hakhoe (Han'gul Study Society). Native newspapers such as the *Tong-A Ilbo*, founded in 1920 by educator-industrialist Kim Songsu and others, also expanded the use of *han'gul* and were permitted some freedom to question official policy. Religious toleration improved and Koreans were no longer forced to bury their dead in public cemeteries (so as to use land in a modern, rational manner), but could choose ground according to their local beliefs.

Colonial administration, however, was by definition a mix of freedom and force. Ordinary police replaced the gendarmerie, but their numbers increased rapidly from about 1920, and were supported by an extensive network of plain-clothes officers and informers. In 1925, Japanese recognition of the Soviet Union raised fears that Korea's colonial status and proximity to Siberia made it especially vulnerable to international communism. Japan's catch-all peace preservation law of the same year was immediately applied in Korea, giving the police wide powers of investigation and arrest. In 1926, the army spent heavily on extending wireless facilities across Korea's northern border to strengthen defence, and Japanese intelligence was expert on communist activists attempting to infiltrate from Manchuria or Siberia. However, in the 1920s the vast majority of Koreans were still bound to the land as farmers and it was they who remained the focus of colonial policies.

Agriculture

From 1910 to the late 1920s, agriculture provided employment for about 83 per cent of all Korean households and accounted for 80 per cent of the total value of all Korean production. A third of all farm households were tenants. Shortly after annexation, Japanese landlords owned about 3 per cent of the arable land, but their holdings, which were to remain almost entirely in the southern provinces, were increased by the nationwide land survey conducted by the government-general between 1912 and 1919. As in the takeover of Okinawa and Taiwan, the Japanese authorities realised that their first priority was to systematise landholding and produce a stable base of revenue: the impoverishment of the Yi dynasty offered a clear illustration of what could happen otherwise. No records of land ownership existed and units of measurement varied with locality; hence the survey was publicised as bringing order from chaos, providing clear legal titles to land and equalising the land tax burden. Korean historians, however, are generally sceptical. They see the survey as nothing more than a veil for Japanese appropriation of Korean lands, but this view was challenged by United States scholars in the early 1980s.[11]

Most Korean farmers were illiterate and could not understand the complex rules for registering ownership, nor the methods of rigor such as detailed forms to be completed in all particulars and the absolute deadline for registration. This was a foreign approach, and the near doubling of landlord numbers from 1914–19 (1.8 to 3.4 per cent of total farmers) implies that the survey did benefit landlords above farmers, but also that educated Koreans did not assist smaller farmers in meeting the authorities' demands. However, the regulations on cash payment of the land tax pushed former *yangban* to make their lands more productive and so engage more directly in the cash economy. Thus Japanese land reform did force the pace of modernisation in Korean agriculture.

Japan had long viewed Korea primarily as an agricultural resource. In 1912, the government-general had set up special offices for soil improvement and an Agricultural Technology Bureau for each province to improve animal husbandry, silk, cotton and rice production. The agricultural research station at Suwon, still the centre of agrarian investigation in South Korea, worked to develop solutions for diseases affecting Korean produce of cotton, rice and fruit. However, Japan's own rapid urbanisation, fuelled by the economic war boom of 1914–18 and the violent social unrest of the 1918 rice riots, spurred a major campaign to increase Korean rice exports for the Japanese market. Beginning in 1920, the government-general announced the first of three long-term plans (1920–26, 1927–36, 1937–46) to boost rice production through opening wastelands, expanding the use of natural fertilisers, improving seed quality and introducing advanced farm machinery. Transport facilities were expanded to carry the grains to port, and easier credit was arranged for industries such as rice polishing and rice wine. Between 1919 and 1923 there was also a rapid increase in the number of irrigation associations to lessen the impact of erratic rainfall, but these were mainly controlled by the wealthier landlords and were regarded by some as an imposition on poorer farmers.

The overall aim was to feed Japanese consumers, but the result was to make Korea an archetype dependent colony, fluctuating with trends in a single crop for a single metropolitan market. Unlike their counterparts in Taiwan, where there was considerable diversification into sugar cane, tea, and livestock — or indeed in Japan where supplementary income was derived from sericulture — Korean farmers were almost completely reliant on rice production. This government-assisted over-specialisation kept rural incomes far lower than in Taiwan, with more producers chasing the same market, and while the number of owner-tenants in Taiwan increased in the 1920s, the reverse was true of Korea. The fragility of single-crop production was demonstrated in 1934 when complaints from farmers in Japan, reeling from the great depression, resulted in temporary abandonment of Korean rice expansion with consequent hardship for local farmers.

The government's ambitious scheme to expand cultivated land in the 1920s proved a failure: by 1925 the increased acreage was less than half that anticipated and from 1915–39 the amount of land under cultivation rose only by about 5 per cent. The government-general offered large subsidies for new land development, but profits were safer and easier to obtain on established tenant land. This was particularly so in the congested south where there was bitter competition among prospective tenants. However, high rents meant that any increase in productivity would be taken by the landlord, so farmers lacked the incentive to plant additional crops. Despite this, the yield per hectare did rise by about one-quarter, through improved seed strains and better technology, especially the massive increase in use of chemical fertilisers from 1930. Over the same period, however, rice exports to Japan jumped eight-fold. Much of this originated as rent to absentee Japanese landlords (who by 1930 controlled about 60 per cent of Korean arable land) and was then exported through Japanese hands to the home islands. Exported rice far exceeded the increase in output and rising imports of coarser Manchurian grains failed to stop a qualitative decline in the Korean diet: using 1915 as an index of 100, the level had fallen to 90 by 1939, with an even harsher dip to 82 in the depression years of 1930–34.

Basic figures for rice production, export and consumption by Koreans for the period up to 1926 are shown in Table 2.1.

Table 2.1 Rice production, export and consumption by Koreans, to 1926					
	Production	Index	Exports	Index	Consumption
1912–16	12 302	100	1056	100	0.7188
1917–21	14 101	110	2196	208	0.6860
1922–26	14 501	118	4342	411	0.5871
1927–31	15 798	128	6607	626	—
1932–35	17 002	138	8757	829	*0.444

*Figure for 1930–34

Source: Choi, 1971, p. 216. Figures for production and export are in 1000 *sok*, consumption in *sok* per person in Korea.

Consumption recovered between 1935 and 1939 to 0.641 *sok* per capita, as Korea enjoyed record harvests for 1937 and 1938. However, the catastrophic drought of 1938, which was blamed on insufficient irrigation, led to a 40 per cent crop decline in 1939, and the subsequent war years witnessed only failing confidence among farmers and general economic disruption.[12]

The changed agricultural situation of the 1920s, and the relative political freedom of the Saito years, impelled rural Koreans to organise themselves. The major problem was that of tenant conditions. Without the alternative of industrial employment, the competition for tenant land, as in Japan proper, left many people unable to retain their leases except by enduring exorbitant rents or providing additional services to landlords. Rents were kept at well over half, and often three-quarters, of the tenant's crop, thus further diminishing the prospect of ever saving enough even to become an owner-tenant. Instead, tenant numbers continued to increase annually throughout the 1920s so that by 1928 some 6.7 million people, or 45 per cent of all farm households, were pure tenants with another third as owner-tenants. Tenant familes worked plots of just over a hectare, while owner-tenants averaged just over 2 hectares in total of owned and rented land. However, conditions varied according to region. Tenant contracts in the north were oral and long-term, while in the south, one-year written contracts were the norm. Consequently, of all the 610 landlord–tenant disputes to 1925, about 88 per cent occurred in the southern provinces (especially South Cholla, South Kyongsang and South Ch'ungch'ong), with not a single one recorded in North Hamgyong and only four in South Hamgyong.[13] Most disputes centred on the cancellation of tenant rights rather than demands for lower rents. Disputes were also more common with absentee landlords: where the landlord resided either in the village or nearby market town, traditional paternalism resulted in greater harmony.

Rural groups developed rapidly in the early 1920s, albeit with differing political hues. Song Pyongjun, formerly of the Ilchinhoe, headed the Sojagin Sangjohoc or Tenant Farmers Mutual Aid Society in Seoul. While strongest in the south, it had branches around the country to aid tenant farmers in disputes. Its concerns, however, were generally localised so that the broader organisation was weak and its activity declined after Song's death in 1925.[14] A more radical grouping was the farmer and tenant branches of the Korean Labour Mutual Aid Association; in 1922, the Chinju branch held the first ever county-level tenant conference and attracted over a thousand participants. The association's activities were confined largely to debate and public meetings, but the very fact of tenant organisation threatened established landholders, who were themselves forced to organise for self-defence; in this, some were not content with democratic methods; as the United States Consul-General noted of the Mutual Love Society (Sangaehoe), 'Pak [Chun'gum] and his followers are 'two-fisted' fellows who believe in the strong arm methods and, judged by some of its actions, the party might more properly be called the "Militant Love Society"'.[15]

Emphasising fraternity and mutual co-operation, the early tenant groups included in their activities the relatively well-off independent farmer. As their involvement in group tenant protests increased, however, the independent farmers withdrew and the specifically tenant nature of the groups became clearer.[16] Although the tenant bodies lacked articulation and co-operation amongst themselves, they were increasingly successful in presenting group demands, forcing more landlords to counter with organisations of their own. Disputes became more radical and violent, and this led to police intervention; in 1924, some 344 tenant association leaders were arrested in South Cholla where the movement was strongest. However, political activism among tenant farmers was dominated by young intellectuals returned from study in Japan, and their ambitions lay in journalism at the capital rather than in the mundane task of slowly building rural organisation. Moreover, farmers generally, as in China and Japan, preferred reform to revolution and were slow to welcome communist influence in the labour and tenant movement. They responded coolly to activist students, provoking one college graduate of the 1930s to recall later: 'As time passed, we had to acknowledge the crude fact that farmers and the countryside were not a repository of national spirit and conscience . . . As long as their lives were not threatened and the social order maintained they seemed rather indifferent to the nature of their lordship.'[17]

With conditions in agriculture continuing to deteriorate, the mass of ordinary poor peasants received greater attention from about 1925 when the Ch'ondogyo set up the Korean Peasant Association (Choson Nongminsa). Tenant associations were reorganised as peasant unions and began concentrating on broadening peasant horizons through education, night schools, lecture tours, the creation of consumer unions and campaigns for freedom of speech. These unions expanded rapidly between 1926 and 1928 from 119 to 307. However, farmers continued to be driven into tenancy, and such little progress had been made by Korean farm groups that, in 1928, the government-general established a committee to investigate tenancy and establish regulations to protect tenant rights. An official survey that year revealed just how dire was the plight of most Koreans. The annual income for a farm household, including whatever subsidiary receipts might be gained from sericulture, making sandals, straw bags and ropes, totalled on average a mere US$140. Seventy per cent of owner-cultivators just managed to break even, and over 95 per cent of all tenants, full or partial, ended the year in deficit with debts bearing interest from 12–48 per cent per annum. Half a million people were identified as 'fire-field' squatters, burning forest land in the mountains for bare subsistence, while nearly half of all farm households endured annual 'spring poverty' — eating grass and tree bark to survive after their harvest had been spent on rent and debt repayment.[18]

Both in Japan and Korea, government recognition of the tenant problem came only late as the world depression undercut rural incomes and land values. In 1927, the government in Japan even considered buying land from wealthier landlords for redistribution to local tenants. In Korea, matters had to wait longer. From 1932, Governor-General

Ugaki tried to depoliticise tenant disputes. He ordered all cases to be presented to a county tenancy mediation committee, not on a group basis, but solely by individuals. In April 1934, he instituted legal protection for Korean tenants, with a guaranteed minimum of three-year contracts, and official controls over farm managers to prevent exploitation of tenants. He also set up a rural regeneration scheme from 1932 (with limited success) to cut peasant impoverishment and promote self-reliance. To assist in this campaign, the authorities turned to Korean youth, selecting common school graduates for a year's training as village advisors on household budgeting and farm management.[19] A further aspect of Ugaki's rural program was to promote diversification through cotton and wool production, both items attractive to Japan's military, and sheep were imported from Australia and Canada for pasturage, mainly in South P'yongan and South Hamgyong. Partly as a result of government policies (including pressure on radical organisers, but also due to splits within the movement itself), activist tenant leaders were forced from about 1930 to quit the fertile south and start afresh in the rugged north-east where landlord–tenant relations were generally far better. Despite this, radical organisers of the new Red Peasant Unions (Choksaek Nongmin Chohap) were both commited to and skilled at their task, and managed to develop considerable local support in the Hamgyong region by utilising its distance from Seoul, the proximity to communist influence across the border in Manchuria and Siberia, and the protective cover of the mountainous terrain. The Red Peasant Unions are regarded as the most militant force within the entire peasant movement, rejecting the legalistic tenant associations of the 1920s and, through political publications, theatre, night schools and a semi-militaristic organisation, offering a violent and revolutionary challenge to Japan's authority. For this, they were pursued relentlessly by the police. Their effectiveness, however, was short-lived, as Japanese repression of even moderate groups was increased following the Manchurian incident, and many of their members were arrested from the start of 1932.[20]

Education

Education was arguably the most important arena of colonial activity: to Korean progressives, it was the engine of a modern nationalism; to the colonial authorities, it was a mechanism for discipline, social order and improved economic efficiency. In August 1911, following the example of Taiwan, an educational ordinance established separate school systems for Koreans and Japanese in the peninsula, with Korean common and higher common schools the equivalent respectively of primary and junior high schools in Japan. The common schools gave four years' tuition, while the higher common provided four years to boys and three to girls. In addition, certain professional schools in law, medicine, industry and agriculture, all of which had been established before annexation, offered another three to four years of specialised training.

The 1911 ordinance took Japan's imperial rescript on education from 1890 as its ethical base, the aim of colonial education being the cultivation of loyalty to the Japanese emperor. On a more practical level, as an official publication from the 1930s put it, 'The important point for education in Korea is to acquire a knowledge of the national language [i.e. Japanese], to absorb the spirit of true love for honest toil, to strengthen an inclination for thrift and industry'.[21] In other words, the colonial authorities aimed to foster in their Korean subjects 'character', a quality definable as discipline and service, and a rejection of the individualism current in Chinese and Japanese political youth movements. To this end, and following the practice in Taiwan, the government-general largely refrained from interfering with the traditional village *sodang* which, in 1923, were providing some 280 000 children with a basic understanding of Chinese letters, but more importantly, a grounding in the hierarchical ethics of Confucianism. From 1918, the *sodang* were urged to include Japanese language and mathematics in the curriculum, but it was not until the late 1920s that specifically Japanese ethics were required. The *sodang* provided a degree of intellectual continuity with the past, as well as a more familiar environment than the new schools, and, as late as the Pacific war, over 3000 remained in existence. However, as in Taiwan, Koreans had gradually come to accept that the only route to employment off the land was through Japanese education and, with local revenues funding education, attendance at traditional schools naturally declined.

Western missionaries had pioneered modern education in Korea and by 1910 had established about 800 schools of various grades. These accommodated between 41 000 and 50 000 pupils, nearly twice the total in all Korean government schools combined. Faced with this rival system, the Japanese, under Resident-General Ito, had withheld licences from private schools which ignored new limits on religious instruction, but had also hastened the construction of common schools. Up to 1919, these remained mainly urban but, following the Samil rising and Korean demands for better education, Admiral Saito launched a rapid expansion plan: by 1928 there was a government common school in nearly every township in south Korea and about half the townships in the north. Nominal equality of status was given by an educational ordinance in 1922, placing Korean boys' and girls' ordinary and higher common schools on the same level as Japanese elementary and secondary schools. The curriculum at common schools was extended from four to six years and the age of admission reduced from 8 to 6. Prohibition of religious teaching in private (i.e. mission) schools was also revoked.

In their utilitarian approach to education, earlier in Meiji Japan and colonial Taiwan, and subsequently in Korea, Japanese administrators emphasised primary and practical schooling over advanced studies. The role of schools was to teach language, morals and the modern skills of mathematics and basic science. Thus funds were injected mainly into the common schools, industrial, technical, agricultural and commercial schools. (Practical facilities such as these were expanded even further for wartime needs late in the 1930s.) As colonial rulers, however, the authorities saw teaching of the Japanese language as education's vital role in assimilating the Korean people and the gradual transmission of approved ideals: even after the 1922 educational revision, the Japanese language accounted for the bulk of teaching at all levels of Korean schools.[22]

In terms of cultural identity, history took pride of place next to language, and a leading demand of educated Koreans following the Samil rising was for more teaching of the purely Korean past. However, the first official primary school reader in history, the *Futsu Gakko Kokushi* (two vols, 1923–24), was basically identical to that used in Japan, with just a few Korean materials added to mollify the critics. The text centred on historical biography, mainly of Japanese emperors (as in Japan, children were expected to learn by rote the names of all Japanese emperors) and 'heroes' such as Oda Nobunaga and Motoori Norinaga. Hideyoshi was painted in simple rose-tinted colours: 'He rose from low status, a great man who through wisdom and courage pacified the nation, respected the imperial house, set the people at ease, then, raising an expeditionary force, demonstrated the nation's might overseas.'[23] In a similar vein, figures borrowed from Korean history were largely wise kings and outstanding priests or scholars: the keynote was virtuous rule and, reversing the historiography of confrontation established by Sin Ch'aeho, the text reinforced the myth that Korea was nearly always dependent on some external force, not least Japan from the ancient days of Paekche and Silla.

As in Manchukuo in the 1930s, however, Japanese progressives in Korea discovered freedoms denied to them by the more entrenched bureaucracies at home. This allowed modernist influences to work in colonial policy, and the textbooks developed specifically for use in Korea, especially in the field of natural sciences, are regarded as far superior in stimulating the child's imagination to those used in Japan. For example, while Japanese schoolchildren approached science through a list of culturally symbolic flowers such as the camellia and cherry blossom, their Korean counterparts metaphorically leapt from garden plants to the fields in spring, to the life-cycle of insects.[24] Thus, even while Korean schoolchildren were being trained as loyal and useful subjects, their minds were being opened to a world-view which improved their powers of analysis and which might one day be turned against their colonial masters.

The harsh reality, of course, is that education, even a colonial education, remained denied to most Korean children. In rural areas late in the 1920s, custom and economic hardship resulted in widespread child labour, with children starting farmwork at the age of 10 in the north and 8 in the south: the government's own monopoly cigarette factory gave employment to many children in the capital. Education was not compulsory, as in Japan, though local police were known to pressure families into sending their children to school. Some boys stayed only long enough to gain an understanding of Japanese and mathematics, the two subjects most likely to improve their chances of industrial employment. During the colonial era, ultimately no more than about one-third of Korean children were in school.

Table 2.2 Statistics on student enrolment, 1910–1937				
School	1910	1919	1930	1937
Common	20.1	89.3	450.5	901.2
Higher common*	0.8	3.2	11.1	15.6
Girls' higher schools	0.4	0.7	4.4	7.1
Teacher seminaries	–	–	1.3	3.8
Industrial schools	1.0	2.8	12.1	20.3
Elementary industrial	0.1	1.7	3.2	6.3
Colleges	0.4	0.9	2.5	4.0
University prep. courses	–	–	0.3	0.4
University	–	–	0.6	0.5
Non-standardised schools	71.8	39.2	47.5	142.6**

Notes: *School for Koreans and Japanese
**includes 60 077 students of the short course elementary schools. Figures in 1000 students.
Source: Grajdanzev, 1944, p. 261.

Social attitudes among both Koreans and the Japanese authorities retarded the education of girls, especially in the countryside. As late as 1939, female children receiving primary education constituted only about one-third the number of boys (306 000 girls as opposed to 912 000 boys), and the university at Seoul (established in 1926) simply did not admit women. Despite this, a small number of young women aspired to modern careers: in 1939, some 9535 girls attended high school (as opposed to 19 343 boys), and 1131 were placed at colleges or teachers' seminaries (compared with 5182 boys).[25] Through education, girls developed greater intellectual self-confidence, and through sports shared in that revolutionary awareness of their physical potential only recently gained by Western women. This helped to raise their confidence in political participation and Korean high school girls were noticeably active in protests late in the 1920s. At Sungmyong Girls High School, in May 1927, about 400 pupils united to demand better treatment and more employment of Korean teachers, while girls from nine schools in Seoul, including Ehwa and Sungmyong, joined the mass protests from 1929–30 after an incident involving Japanese abuse of a female student at Kwangju.[26] In strict fairness, one should also note at least one instance of Korean schoolchildren who protested to retain a favourite Japanese teacher.

From 1922, as the legal distinction in Korea between the two races was officially abolished, Korean children were nominally permitted to enter the post-elementary schools hitherto reserved for colonial Japanese. However, ability in spoken Japanese continued to deny access to many Koreans and in 1937 there were only 2050 Koreans in Japanese primary schools and 1040 (580 girls and 460 boys) at Japanese middle and girls' high schools.[27] Korean schools were still regarded as qualitatively inferior and some wealthier Koreans sent their children to be educated in Japan itself. There, the pinnacle of education was the universities. By 1935, either by paying their own way or with assistance from the quasi-government Korean Scholarship Society, there were 2633 Korean students in Japan (234 at the prestigious imperial universities and 897 at private universities), and the figure more than doubled by 1940. Oral testimony suggests those at university found it possible to be accepted by classmates and teachers alike into the élitist student community. This is no doubt correct, as fluency in Japanese was a prerequisite for admission and any Korean gaining entry to a university in Japan was implicitly acknowledging the superiority of Japanese institutions. However, the very élitism of the universities, as at prestigious universities in the West, brought freedoms denied elsewhere, and it was in Tokyo more than in Korea itself that radical ideologies were freely discussed. Thus many Koreans subsequently active in the tenant, labour and nationalist movements developed their political vocabulary among young Japanese in conflict with their own society's prevailing ethics of 'character' and capitalism. In this, Korean students were following in the footsteps of Chinese radicals and nationalists from the 1900s, and modern Japan was continuing its paradoxical role as both liberator and oppressor of East Asia.

Recognising that a home institution of élite learning was needed to provide society's future leaders, Korean mainstream nationalists from 1922 began working for the establishment of a People's University at Seoul. Higher education was the area in which government-general policies were strictest, and existing colleges were mainly those established by Western missionaries a generation earlier. However, the moderate nationalists were emboldened by the new liberalism of the early Saito years and a People's University founding committee was elected in 1923 with Yi Sangjae, former vice-president of the Independence Club, as chairman, and including Cho Mansik, an eminent Christian nationalist from P'yongyang. The *Choson Ilbo* and *Tong-A Ilbo* newspapers spread word of the university proposal and initially there was a wave of popular support. Plans were drafted, envisaging four colleges at the outset: law, literature, economics and science, with those for industry, medicine and agriculture to follow. However, fund-raising was sporadic and public enthusiasm quickly ebbed. In part this was caused by official hindrance, but more especially (as it was meant to be) by the government-general's announcement that from 1926 the doors would open on Keijo (Seoul) Imperial University, an institution with standards comparable to those in Japan. To feed this, a two-year university preparatory school was established in May 1924 with faculties of science and letters: in both faculties, the lion's share of classtime was spent on foreign languages (mainly German in science and English in letters), and this gave pupils some access to the world outside. However, the preparatory school's intake was only about 150 students, of whom approximately one-quarter were Koreans: all teaching staff, with the exception of those for Korean and foreign languages, were Japanese. This predominance of Japanese students and staff was repeated in Keijo Imperial University itself, where many believed an informal quota was being enforced: in 1939, there were 350 Japanese students to 260 Korean and, with the exception of a brief period of Korean staff recruitment around 1930, all teachers were Japanese. However, the testimony of one Korean graduate, subsequently a university departmental head in the Republic of Korea, is that racial discrimination was not apparent among the university's students or staff, and that both academic standards and freedom were higher under Japanese colonialism than Korean republicanism in the 1970s.[28] The university's two departments, one for medicine and one for law and literature (a faculty of science and technology was opened in 1941 for wartime needs), enjoyed high repute, and research publications, albeit framed by a colonialist perspective of Japanese superiority, added greatly to information on Korean society and culture.

It was after graduation that Korean students were really confronted by discrimination: the better jobs were consistently reserved for Japanese and salaries were far lower for Koreans doing the same work. In this way, employment politicised even those who had remained neutral at school. However, education at any level caught only the youth of Korea. As late as 1944, only the provinces of Kyonggi (43.5 per cent) and South P'yongan (34.2 per cent) could boast well over 30 per cent of men aged 20–30 with at least primary schooling.[29] This meant the bulk of the Korean population was relatively untouched by Japanese ideology until the coercive war mobilisation after 1937. A different sort of education, less explicitly ideological and more practical, was to be gained through industrial employment.

Industry and commerce

Between 1911 and 1919, Korean non-agricultural industry lay moored in the traditional areas of mining, garment production and daily necessities such as food preparation and paper-making. Things began to change about 1916: Japanese capitalists, buoyant as the world war took West European competitors from East Asia, pressed for the relaxation of Korea's corporation law; the result was that small household factories of five or more workers increased rapidly and the industrial workforce roughly quadrupled by 1919 to well over 40 000. New businesses brought with them new technology, and skilled Japanese to train and supervise Korean workers. Production values between 1916 and 1918 more than doubled in all major sectors of the economy bar forestry, and while leading industries through the 1920s — food preparation, textiles, alcohol and tobacco — remained tied to agriculture, from this point on agriculture declined as a percentage of overall production value with industry the major beneficiary.

Table 2.3 Percentage of total Korean production by industry, 1920–30 (%)				
	Agriculture	Forestry	Fisheries	Mining	Industry
1920	80.6	1.8	3.7	1.5	12.4
1930	61.6	5.4	7.0	2.1	23.9

Source: Kaneko Fumio, '1920 nendai ni okeru Chosen sangyo seisaku no keisei', ed. Hara Akira, *Kindai Nihon no keizai to seiji*, Tokyo 1986, pp. 179, 197.

In the centrally managed economy of colonial Korea, even more than in Meiji Japan, the government was the propellor of modern industry. One of the largest concerns was the government-general's railway works, employing over 1000 labourers in Seoul to build passenger and freight cars, as well as repair locomotives and cars: depots at Pusan and P'yongyang employed another 450 for minor repairs. The government-general also led the way in capital works which attracted related industries such as the Onoda Cement Factory, established by Mitsui interests near P'yongyang in 1920: this employed between 600 and 700, of whom more than 80 per cent were Koreans.[30] Senior positions in Korean industry, however, were largely monopolised by Japanese until the China and Pacific wars, when army conscription thinned their numbers.

Pusan Customs House, 1920s
Source: *Kundae Hanguk*, vol. 1, p. 203

Korean industry in the 1920s was geographically centred in Kyonggi and South P'yongan. It was largely dominated by textiles and food preparation and, as in China and Japan, depended on low-paid unskilled young women between 15 and 25 years of age. Only late in the decade did a qualitative and geographical shift commence. The catalyst was the Pujon River dam project, developed in south Hamgyong from 1926 by the government-general in alliance with Japanese industrialist, Noguchi Jun. This was part of a broader Noguchi plan: in 1927, he began construction of the Chosen Nitrogenous Fertiliser Company at Hungnam on the south Hamgyong coast. Built on a scale unprecedented even in Japan at the time, the plant employed 4000 and became the centre of a massive electrical-chemical complex. This rapidly expanded the use of fertilisers in Korean agriculture and, joined by concerns such as the Korea Nitrogen Gunpowder Corporation from the mid-1930s, supplied munitions for the expanding Japanese military. In the process, Hungnam was transformed from a small fishing village into a huge industrial basin, and north Korea became the industrial hub of the country. This was to have a fundamental impact on divided Korea after 1945.

The demographic effect of industrialisation, especially on the previously underdeveloped provinces of Kyongsang and Hamgyong, may be seen from Table 2.4.

Table 2.4 Korean provinces as percentage of total population, 1925–1935		
Province	1925	1935
Kyonggi	10.3	10.7
N. Ch'ungch'ong	4.3	4.2
S. Ch'ungch'ong	6.6	6.7
N. Cholla	7.0	7.
S. Cholla	11.1	11.0
N. Kyongsang	11.9	11.2
S. Kyongsang	10.4	9.8
Hwanghae	7.5	7.3
S. P'yongan	6.4	6.4
N. P'yongan	7.3	7.5
Kangwon	6.8	7.0
S. Hamgyong	7.2	7.5
N. Hamgyong	3.2	3.7

Source: Cho Kijun et al., *Ilche ha ui minjok saenghwalsa*, Seoul, 1971, p. 507.

Although colonialism gave the government-general near uncontestable political authority, it had neither the capital nor the philosophical inclination to develop Korea's economy by itself. In the 1920s, both for Japan's wider aims and to support the policies of conciliation and mutual benefit in Korea, it was necessary to seek an injection of funds and permit Japanese capital greater access to the peninsula. Investment was attracted by lowered taxes and wages, cheaper electricity than in Japan, and a friendly government-general. This was especially so under Ugaki. Confronted by the ills of the great depression and the trials of agriculture, his policy was for diversification into cotton, wool, minerals and natural resources, with special emphasis on northern development. From 1931, he assisted Korean migrants from the agrarian south through reduced train fares and guarantees of labour conditions upon arrival in the north. Ugaki created a favourable climate for Japanese investment and was particularly close to Noguchi. As a result of his policies and rising militarism in East Asia, the number of Korean industrial employees rose by the mid-1930s to about 595 000 — more than 50 per cent up on the figure for 1932. Heavy industry, however, favoured male employment and reduced the overall number of women in the labour force. In 1936, the chemical industry accounted for 28.2 per cent of all Korean industrial labour, well ahead of the two other main employers, spinning (22.8 per cent) and food processing (21.9 per cent). Between 1931 and 1936, however, production expanded across the board: forestry and fishery output doubled, textile companies in the Seoul-Inch'on region were booming, and mining leapt from 21.7 million to 110.4 million yen worth of production, increasing a further four-fold within five years of the war with China as Korean gold went to buying war supplies such as oil and scrap iron from the United States.[31]

The shifts in Korean industry were strengthened from 1931 by Japan's military takeover of Manchuria. This provided a greedy market in the Japanese army itself, allowed Korean industry greater access to its northern neighbour, and accelerated cross-border communication links. Najin on Korea's upper north-east coast was developed by the South Manchurian Railway Company in 1935 as a major port and rail link to what had become Manchukuo. Exports in the government-general's monopoly product of opium were also expanded and, even as it promised international bodies to reduce drug addiction in Korea, the government-general was announcing a three-year plan from early 1937 to raise annual production from 57 870 pounds (26 200 kilograms) to 82 670 pounds (37 500 kilograms) — over 71 per cent of all Korean opium was for purchase by the Japanese-controlled Manchukuo government.[32]

Although Manchuria, and especially Kirin province in the south-east, had long been a haven for Korean refugees, economic migrants arrived en masse in the 1920s and 1930s. Figures vary, but the number in Manchuria between 1920 and 1936 rose from approximately 459 000 to over 876 000. The exodus mushroomed under government-assisted migration from 1935, both to solidify Japan's control of Manchuria and relieve rural over-population in southern Korea, and the total climbed to 1.45 million by 1940. This was echoed by a wave of labour migration to Japan: there the figures for 1920–40 show a rise from about 30 000 to 1.26 million. Thus political repression and economic depression combined to empty a significant percentage of the Korean population into the surrounding territories. Up to the late 1920s, most Koreans migrating to Manchuria were farmers, and they were received more kindly by the local people than their compatriots in Japan — there was nothing remotely comparable to the hysterical massacre of Koreans in Tokyo during the great Tokyo–Yokohama earthquake of 1923. However, their situation was increasingly politicised from 1920 by the incursions of Japanese forces attacking Korean guerrilla bases in Manchuria. Nonetheless, the only case of racial violence between Chinese and

Koreans came in the Wanpaoshan incident of mid-1931.[33] Within months of this, however, the Japanese army had seized control of Manchuria and it began a policy of relocating ordinary Korean settlers into strategic hamlets and thereby isolating the guerrilla bands. The merits and demerits of such a policy are, of course, visible in the later experience of the United States in Vietnam. In the Korean case, while the guerrillas were nullified as a threat by 1938, anti-Japanese sentiment actually increased as Korean farmers were uprooted or impeded from developing their crops.

Korea was a typical colony in that virtually all modern industry of any size was in the hands of metropolitan capitalists. Mitsui and Mitsubishi were just two of the monster Japanese concerns dominating the Korean economy. With very few exceptions, native capital was unable to develop large-scale enterprises, instead concentrating on small businesses or usury. Of the nine mines in 1925 capitalised at more than 100 000 yen, only one was Korean-owned, and in 1927, shareholders of the seven private railway companies were listed as 84 per cent mainland Japanese, 14 per cent Japanese in Korea, and just 2 per cent Koreans. The real profits of industrialisation and expansion therefore flowed to Japan and, though the figures for company ownership were sometimes comparable, the level of capital never was. In 1938, there were 740 Korean and 804 Japanese owners of manufacturing companies, and of transport/warehouse companies (the traditional occupation of *kaekchu* and *yogak*), the figures were 258 and 274; yet the ratio of paid-in capital in these Korean and Japanese concerns was approximately 1:7 and 1:10 in Japan's favour.[34] The tendency among Korean entrepreneurs was to seek quick and easy profits, flooding successful areas so that prices collapsed. Those who survived, as in Japan following the boom–bust of the First World War and its aftermath, dominated the economy as a whole (or at least those areas in which they were allowed to prosper). The result was that Korean-controlled commerce, finance and industry were run by a handful of men, and it was they who were to retain influence in the undeveloped economic structure of South Korea after 1945. The major colonial businessmen included Pak Hungsik, owner of the famous Hwasin Department Store in Seoul, Min Taesik, Hanil Bank head from 1920–31, his younger brother Min Kyusik, president of the Tongil (formerly Hanil) and Choheung Banks, and Kim Yonsu, executive director and later president of Kyongsong Spinning, the largest of all native industrial concerns.[35]

The Kyongsong Spinning and Weaving Company (also known as Kyongbang) was founded in 1919 by Pak Yonghyo, veteran of the 1884 coup and still a major influence in Korean politics, and Kim Songsu (1891–1955, elder brother to Kim Yonsu, 1896–1979), a leading educator (he was to establish what is now Korea University) and post-independence statesman from north Cholla. The Kim family fortune, as Carter Eckert has deftly explained, was made through landownership and rice exports following the growth of Korea–Japan trade in the period before annexation. Both Songsu and his younger brother had studied in Japan and developed great respect for its modern achievements. Their experience and understanding also assisted them in forming vital contacts with the Japanese government-general: indeed, only with government-general subsidies did the Kyongbang survive its first difficult years, and the government-controlled Chosen Industrial Bank consistently provided loans on preferential conditions. There were two reasons for this: one was to distract prominent Korean businessmen such as Songsu, who had been instrumental in founding the newspaper *Tong-A Ilbo* in 1920, from involving themselves too deeply in the nationalist movement; on a more positive note, the authorities genuinely believed that economic co-operation was mutually beneficial and that a share of prosperity would reconcile Koreans to Japanese control. Despite this, subsidies alone were not the route to commercial success and, while Kyongbang's paid-in capital increased from 400 000 yen in 1927 to a million yen by 1935, it operated at a loss for the first five years, and profits and expansion remained gradual until the China War. With the onset of war, a number of Korean concerns enjoyed unprecedented revenues from the perfect consumer, the massive and avaricious Japanese military, and between 1937 and 1942, Kyongbang's return on capital invested was to leap from about 5 per cent to well over 30 per cent per annum.

The small group of favoured Korean businessmen developed a network of intermeshing ties to the authorities and Japanese capital. Kim Yonsu, Min Taesik and Pak Hungsik sat on the boards of major Japanese investments such as Keijo Electric, Chosen Petroleum, North Korea Paper and Chemical Manufacture, as well as various railroad companies. They were honoured by government recognition for their support: Kim Yonsu doubled from 1939 as honorary consul to Manchukuo, and in 1944 Pak was to be appointed head of the Chosen Aircraft Manufacture Company, a state-affiliated concern of immense importance to Japan's war effort. These men and their interests moved into Manchukuo alongside the Japanese: for example, near Mukden from 1941, Kim operated the South Manchurian Spinning Company (with Min and Pak as board members), housing 35 000 spinning machines and a hundred weaving machines, while Pak expanded trade with China through his Hwasin company. There was a belief, by no means lost in the late twentieth century (listen to the Toyota company song!), that business itself was a force for modernisation, social equality and advanced civilisation. Using this rationale, Korean entrepreneurs could wrap their collaborative ventures in a coat of nationalism: Kyongbang marketed its heavy-duty cloth as a distinctly native product for native consumption, while maintaining a policy of hiring only Korean workers, and this is often noted by Korean scholars when discussing nationalism in the colonial era. The only concerted movement for a commercial nationalism, however, was Cho Mansik's Korean Products Promotion Society (Choson Mulsan Changnyohoe).

Cho Mansik (1882–1950) was carrying on the Independence Club and 'patriotic enlightenment' tradition of Christian nationalism through moral self-reconstruction.[36] A Presbyterian elder and an organiser of and participant in the Samil rising (for which he had been gaoled), Cho, like Kim Songsu, had studied at Waseda University in Japan. While there, he read about Gandhi's campaign in British India for non-violent protest and nationalism rooted in the activities of native production and consumption. Cho took this same approach for his Korean Products Promotion Society, founded originally at P'yongyang in 1920, and then reformed under the same name with like-minded groups, including Yi Kwangsu's Self-Production Society (Chajakhoe), in December 1922. The movement began with broad social backing: businessman such as Kim Songsu supported Cho, as did moderate intellectuals, while youth and women's groups, Christian, Buddhist and Ch'ondogyo believers were mobilised to carry the message first into provincial cities, then the countryside. That message was quite simple: organise consumer co-operatives for self-protection, buy Korean goods and reject imports, and take an emotional satisfaction in the unifying process of distinctly Korean production and purchase. In practice, buying Korean wares not infrequently meant paying more, and there were unscrupulous businessmen willing to exploit the patriotic label to inflate their selling price. By 1924, moreover, police restrictions, government subsidies to wean Korean businessmen from the movement, and internal factional-ism had dissipated the initial burst of enthusiasm. The society continued to publish its journal, *Industrial World* (San'opkye), to enhance consumer understanding, and to hold successful annual rallies or bazaar presentations of native goods. The great depression late in the 1920s temporarily renewed interest in economic nationalism, but the Manchurian incident brought even harsher Japanese repression of political activities, and the society ceased to be effective by 1937, when all Korean nationalist organisations were abolished.

As for the modern workforce, it was not politicised until the late 1920s and even then most disputes were small in scale, badly organised and aimed primarily at better wages. Industrial jobs were scarce and the over-population of agriculture inhibited labour protest: there were few regulations to protect workers from dismissal, and the level of skill required was low enough that replacements were easily found. Some evidence suggests that larger Japanese concerns, such as the Onoda Cement Factory (where there were only two labour disputes in 22 years), provided better conditions for their workforce than smaller Korean factories in which profits, so much harder to achieve, took precedence over comfort.[37] Consequently, Korean radical agitation was as common in native-owned as in Japanese-owned concerns, with communist groups as much opposed to feudalism or exploitative work practices as they were to imperialism. Wages for Korean labourers generally were about half those of their Japanese counterparts and this was a constant source of resentment, but the key to politicisation was depression: as one village elder put it at the time, 'The economic depression lends wings to Bolshevism'. This is illustrated by the eruption of larger industrial protests between 1927 and 1930, totalling 475 disputes and involving over 45 000 workers.[38] Between 1920 and 1927, a number of centralised labour groups had been established, but factionalism had quickly divided them into provincial sections. One of the largest amalgamations was the Korean Labour and Farmer Alliance, established from over 160 groups in 1924 with a membership in excess of 53 000. Once again, however, internal wrangling caused its dissolution in 1927. The biggest and best organised strike of the colonial era came at Wonsan in 1929, when the Japanese foreman at a British-owned oil company struck a Korean employee, and the remaining workforce, supported by the Wonsan Federation of Labour, went on strike in protest. Over the four months of the dispute, the strikers received popular support from around the country, but nothing of political substance developed in its wake. The Korean labour movement remained weak due to its lack of political unity and persistent official repression. More importantly, Korean industry itself was only just at the formative stage and remained highly fragmented: in 1932, there were 4525 factories, but of these 4277 employed less than 50 workers, and the situation was barely changed before the Pacific War.[39] In these conditions, successful large-scale organisation of industrial labour was obviously remote.

The basis of the government-general's industrial policies was rationality and efficiency. Planning for Korea took place within the broader frame of Japan and Manchuria, or what was in the 1930s to become the yen block. Korea was not expected to be economically independent, nor was this considered desirable. For industrial concerns, however, an educated and available workforce was essential. Around modern factories there arose new communities with schools and improved facilities and, as Wonmo Dong has noted, the government-general increasingly devoted more of its annual budget to the educational and welfare needs of the Korean people.[40] This was not charity, but a commonsense response to the greater technical and physical demands of industry. Industrialisation contributed to the urbanisation of Korea and the evolution of an urban middle class was reflected in the specialist magazines published for youth, women, businessmen and farmers, all introducing new ideas, advertising new products and displaying the elements of a consumer culture. Industrialisation also contributed to the politicisation of the Korean people by attracting workers, and especially young workers, from the villages into factory production or mining. Yet one must remember how recent these changes in Korean society were. Schools took time to build and function, factories even longer. In effect, there was only about a decade between the start of concerted industrialisation and the beginning of war with China. Despite this, there was a variety of nationalist groups battling for the support of Korea's new urban and industrial population.

Competing nationalisms

The dilemma for nationalists under colonialism was that anti-colonial sentiment provided a catalyst for popular mobilisation, but organising that sentiment into an effective, coherent nationalist movement depended on access to modern communications. Such access only became available with the easing of colonial rule, and with it the counter-argument from optimists that better times were on hand without resorting to agitation — as Filipino nationalist leader Manuel Quezon once remarked: 'Damn the Americans, why don't they oppress us more!' Japanese rule in Korea was undoubtedly harsh and political relaxation under Admiral Saito only lasted for a few years between about 1920 and 1926. Even then, moderate groups such as the Products Promotion Society or the campaign for a people's university were undermined by official harassment. The mix of partial freedom and police surveillance ensured the impossibility of a powerful militant nationalism within Korea, but nationalist organisations outside the country were disadvantaged by their very distance from the homeland. The problem of a weak movement at home and estranged but relatively cohesive movements beyond the border was to have an important bearing on post-1945 Korean politics.

The independence movement outside Korea was briefly united in the provisional government, established at Shanghai in April 1919. This involved representatives from all the major political factions: the conservative nationalists under Syngman Rhee, based among emigré communities in the United States; the nationalists-cum-socialists, strong in Manchuria and Siberia, led by the former *uibyong* leader and Christian, Yi Tonghwi; and the moral self-reformers such as An Ch'angho, with their base in the Korean Protestant community. The respective attitudes of these groups were: diplomatic agitation to win support from the Western powers; links with the Soviet Union for armed attack on Japanese concerns; and gradualist campaigns of education and nation-building within Korea. Inevitably, unity was short-lived and threatened from the start by dispute on tactics, control of funds and clashes of personality. Radical nationalists were outraged by Rhee's unilateral proposal to the League of Nations for an interim mandate over Korea (an idea revived by the Western Allies in 1943), and the subsequent resignation of Sin Ch'aeho in May 1921, followed by An, Kim Kyusik and others, left the provisional government with no claim to a command position in the struggle against Japan. The indifference of the Western powers to Korea's case at the Washington conference of 1921–22 further weakened Rhee's influence, and attempts to restore nationalist unity came to naught. Thereafter, Rhee and his followers continued their diplomatic campaign in Washington DC and at the League of Nations in Geneva, but they were largely ignored by the powers until late in the Second World War, and no external nationalist group ever threatened

Japanese domination or offered the Korean people a viable hope for the future.

The principal foreign supporter of Korean liberation was the Soviet Union. Following the success of the Bolsheviks against the Romanov dynasty, Korean groups had met at Khabarovsk in mid-1918 and established the Korean People's Socialist Party under Yi Tonghwi (?–1928). The party needed arms, money and a patron to boost its recruitment. The Soviet Union, for its part, was ideologically committed to assist anti-imperialism, but also in need of allies it could use to distract the capitalist powers from attacks on the nascent Bolshevik government. Through the Comintern, established by Moscow in 1919, the Soviet Union supplied political advisors, economic aid and arms for Korean resistance to Japan. Koreans resident in Siberia allied themselves more closely with the Soviets after the invasion of Siberia in 1918 by Western and Japanese forces, during which Japan used the opportunity to close Korean newspapers and repress militant groups long active in Vladisvostok.

The Soviet Union gave support to Yi Tonghwi because of his fame as a guerrilla leader and status as head of the Socialist Party. However, a rival group of 'Russianised' Koreans based at Irkutsk viewed him as an anti-revolutionary nationalist merely exploiting Soviet aid. Yi retorted by accusing the Irkutsk faction of excessive subservience to the Bolsheviks and, despite his own reliance on Moscow for funds, he clearly made capital out of preserving a nationalist identity: this was a stance later shared by the Chinese Communist Party after 1935, and by Kim Il Sung in post-liberation North Korea. Early in 1921, Yi quit the provisional government at Shanghai, regrouped his followers into the Korean People's Communist Party, and moved his headquarters to Chita, the capital of the Soviet Far Eastern Republic. His main strength in Manchuria, however, was forced to scatter into Siberia by Japanese military incursions. Weakened and disorganised, Yi's followers were then attacked by an army of Irkutsk Koreans and Soviet forces on 27 June 1921 at what is now Svobodnyy. This was the so-called Free City incident, producing in the fratricidal bloodshed hundreds of Koreans killed and many more taken prisoner. At the Congress of the Toilers of the Far East, held in Moscow early in 1922, Soviet delegates attempted to restore unity, but Yi and the Irkutsk group were irreconcilable, and factionalism was to remain characteristic of the entire Korean socialist movement. From the mid-1920s, assistance from Moscow was reduced as the Soviet Union improved diplomatic links with Japan, and the collectivisation of agriculture caused many Koreans to leave Soviet soil, returning instead to Manchuria or Korea. The situation between Koreans and the Soviet Union grew even worse in the 1930s as Stalin became preoccupied with the rise of Nazism and with consolidating his own power base. In the mid-1930s, ethnic Korean regiments in the Red Army were disbanded,

Korean army cadres were persecuted and, in 1937, all Koreans in the Soviet Far East were forcibly relocated to Soviet Central Asia.

The radical movement within Korea was also dominated by Soviet communism. At its forefront were Korean youth, and this in itself indicates a major change from the traditional centrality of age. With the rapid shifts of the late nineteenth century, age became a synonym for the antiquated — a trend clearly echoed in the West with the young 'decadents' and their contempt for society, the rise of a new youth consumerism early in the twentieth century, and in the fascist movements of Italy and Germany, which equated age with weakness and corruption, and youth with beauty, vitality and 'heroism'. In colonial societies, the aged were blamed for loss of sovereignty and old beliefs were abandoned by the young in favour of radical, militant ideologies. In Korea, the Seoul Youth Association (Seoul Ch'ongnyonhoe) became the centre of domestic left-wing activities and formed the headquarters of the Seoul faction of Korean communists. However, throughout the 1920s, this Seoul faction had to battle for control of domestic communism with students returned from Japan (a competition for power between Korean domestic and foreign-educated radicals to be duplicated with communist returnees after 1945).

The Koreans educated in Japan had a sharper perception of political issues, but this only served to polarise ideological differences among their own ranks, ranging from utopian socialists to anarchists, Bolshevists and liberals. The number of extremists was cut after 1923, when the Japanese authorities discovered a Korean anarchist plot to assassinate the Japanese emperor, but the majority of returnees to Korea were communists of various allegiances. Some of these approached the Irkutsk group for support and subsequently established the Tuesday Association (Hwayohoe) in Seoul in 1924; others formed the rival North Star Association (Puksonghoe), heavily active in the rural movement from 1923 and a major force in the All Korea Labour Peasant League. Tenant and labour movements were naturally strongest in the populous regions of Kyongsang and Cholla, but the limited space for political activity exacerbated rivalry amongst the radicals to the extent that, when the Tuesday Association established the Korean Communist Party (KCP) in April 1925 (with support from North Korean communists and legitimised by the Comintern as the sole representative of Korean communism), the Seoul Youth Association simply refused to join. Mass arrests of KCP members in November 1925 and in June 1926 ensured a baptism of fire for the new party and forced it to regroup, but it was competition for control of the domestic movement that caused the All Korea Labour Peasant League to split in 1927 into its constituent halves. Thereafter, the KCP concentrated on the numerically smaller and less developed labour force. However, police surveillance and unresolved disputes within its ranks continued to undermine the KCP's effectiveness.

The adherents of communist ideologies brought a new political approach and a new vocabulary into discussion of Korean politics. However, in trying to emphasise class struggle as the determining factor in social change, they were speaking to a community in which the industrial proletariat and urban bourgeoisie were as yet inchoate groups, and the actual struggle was all too often conducted among the communists themselves.

Youth also took centre stage in the domestic nationalist movement. The mouthpiece of the 'cultural nationalists', as Michael Robinson has termed them, was the newspaper *Tong-A Ilbo*, which first appeared on 1 April 1920. Its editor, Chang Toksu, a follower of Kim Songsu and like him a graduate of Japan's Waseda University, had been a leader of the Korean students in Tokyo, and was the initial guiding force behind both the Korean Youth Federation and the Seoul Youth Association. Journalists on the *Tong-A Ilbo* and *Choson Ilbo* were mostly young men, and it was youth concerns which dominated the press and flourishing journals of the 1920s. The aim of the 'cultural nationalists' was gradually to train Koreans in matters of organisation and co-operation, and through education, economic expansion and moral self-strengthening, create a new Korea. In the meantime, they rejected as futile outright political opposition to Japan. The leading proponent of the 'cultural nationalist' view of reform within colonialism was Yi Kwangsu, a follower of Protestant nationalist An Ch'angho and author of the 1919 Tokyo students' declaration on independence. Yi had quit the Shanghai provisional government along with An, and returned to Korea where he wrote reform articles for the *Tong-A Ilbo* and other journals. One of his most famous essays was *Minjok Kaejoron* (On Reconstructing the Nation), published in the journal *Kaebyok* (Creation) in May 1922. In this, he blamed the Independence Club's failure on its premature involvement in politics, and urged the people to think less of simple forms such as statehood and more about creating the spiritual and cultural entity of a Korean nation. Echoing Sin Ch'aeho and Ch'oe Namson, Yi identified historical subservience to China as the reason behind Korea's moral decay and ruin as a state, and the prerequisite as he saw it for an independent nation-state was a fundamental moral reconstruction led by the educated élite. In other words, nationalism was first and foremost a state of mind. Also echoing imperialists such as Lord Cromer in Egypt, however, Yi warned that a spiritual reconstruction of this magnitude might take a century or more to accomplish.

The gradual approach of the 'cultural nationalists' was dictated by their recognition that nationalism, as with communism, was a foreign import, and that Koreans had first to be educated as nationalists (as Japanese had been) before a viable nation could exist. They viewed nationalism as part of the modernisation process based on the evolution of capitalist society and a strong middle class. It was the middle class and intellectuals who, in terms not dissimilar to traditional Confucianism, were to set the moral example for the rest of society, and this explicit élitism lost the cultural nationalists any chance of a mass following. By emphasising morality over politics, the cultural nationalists tacitly acknowledged the extreme divisiveness of politics in Korea and attempted to replace it with a new national unity based on the essentially apolitical development of education and the domestic economy. Thus the aim was to use nationalism to eradicate differences within Korea rather than as a political tool to expel Japan.[41] The Japanese education of many of the leading cultural nationalists may also have made them loathe to reject entirely the benefits provided by Japanese overlordship in access to new ideas, wider trade and defence security. However, in separating the nation and state, they were seeking evolutionary (and very slow evolution at that), not revolutionary change, and their passivity towards Japanese colonialism smacked too much of collaboration with the enemy. This put them at odds with Koreans on both the right and left of politics and when, in 1924, Yi Kwangsu elaborated on the ideas in *Minjok kaejoron*, re-emphasising the need to work within the colonial structure and progress through capitalist development, the response was condemnation of Yi, a radical boycott of the *Tong-A Ilbo*, and a temporary retreat by the moderate nationalists. For the radicals of left or right, the answer came from Sin Ch'aeho by way of Nietzsche: without destruction there can be no construction. This negativism, however, was anathema to the cultural nationalists (as it had been to Sun Yatsen when confronted with the radical anti-traditionalists in China). They believed there had already been more than enough destruction in Korea and the imperative now was to reconstruct, but their lack of immediate solutions, and their intellectual élitism and moralising restricted their constituency to the educated minority.

The communist and nationalist movements in Korea recognised their separate limitations and in February 1927 formed the coalition Sin'ganhoc. This marriage of opposites was not new: under Comintern direction, the Chinese Communist party and Sun Yat-sen's Nationalists had earlier formed a united front and the same concept was later to recur in Comintern strategy. The Sin'ganhoe's goal of a political and economic awakening of the Korean people, and its twin pillars for reform of school and factory, were little different from those of the cultural nationalists, but where it distinguished itself from the latter was in rejecting compromise with Japanese colonialism and committing itself to independence. Its proposals included an education for particularly Korean needs, with more class time devoted to the Korean language, and additional freedom to study the 'scientific' thought of Marxism–Leninism. At the more political level, it also proposed the abolition of exploitative Japanese organs and practices such as the government-general's encouragement of Korean migration to Manchuria. The Sin'ganhoe's welcome fusion of previously rival elements created a broad support base of labour, peasant, youth and intellectual groups. The reason why the coalition was sanctioned by the government-general may have been that it brought diverse groups together and made them easier to observe. The authorities may also have been expecting the movement to be short-lived, in which case an official ban would be unnecessary. In fact, however, the Sin'ganhoe was to hold together for a surprisingly long four years, despite its internal tensions; at its height, it boasted some 380 branches with more than 75 000 members. It found support from a women's coalition, the Kunuhoe (Helping Friends Society), similarly formed in 1927. Hitherto the women's movement had also been plagued by factionalism, with entrenched divisions between socialist and Christian camps, and those advocating more purely feminist goals, such as the Yosong Tonguhoe (Korean Women's Comrades Society, established in 1922), found themselves counting membership in the tens instead of hundreds. An attempt in 1926 to unite disparate left-wing women's groups under an umbrella organisation had proved ineffective, but the Sin'ganhoe example inspired women across the political spectrum to merge their differences in the Kunuhoe and work in concert with the men's alliance.

The mixed character of Sin'ganhoe membership gave communists and nationalists an entry to spheres of activity previously denied them. The new-found legitimacy was perhaps more significant to the communists, who dominated many local Sin'ganhoe branches and were thus able to increase their grass-roots strength without attracting immediate police repression. Some radical Marxist–Leninists chafed at collaboration with bourgeois nationalists, but at first they remained a minority.

However, it was the Kwangju incident of 1929, and subsequent changes in Comintern policy, that brought the coalition to an end. At Kwangju, the abuse of a female Korean student by Japanese youths was the catalyst for Korea-wide demonstrations, in part directed by the Sin'ganhoe and Kunuhoe. The scale of the protests, though far smaller than those of 1919, nevertheless indicated that Saito's cultural policies had failed to satisfy Korean political aspirations and the police responded by arresting demonstrators en masse. Discontent led radicals in the Kunuhoe to resign late in 1929, and the group dissolved in 1931. The Sin'ganhoe also disbanded in 1931 after a Comintern policy change to avoid subordination to nationalists and instead to seek mass support. Some historians see this disbanding as inevitable, given the polarised views of the membership, and blame the left wing for undermining the group. Others see the dissolution as natural and welcome, with the Sin'ganhoe a transitional movement, a way-station in the process from a bourgeois-led political struggle to one led by the maturing proletariat.[42] However, in the wake of increased repression following the Manchurian incident late in 1931, the continued existence of the Sin'ganhoe could only have been achieved by the complete nullification of its purpose.

It was during the years of the Sin'ganhoe that cinema and radio, the most powerful mediums for creating and disseminating images, became more accessible to Koreans. Cinema houses had appeared in Seoul and other major cities between 1905 and 1915, but most were owned by Japanese and exhibited Japanese films. From about 1919, Koreans had performed kino-dramas, a mix of theatre with film backdrop, with some success, but it was not until 1925 that an independent Korean film company was finally established. However, the attendant cost and difficulties, plus the lack of experience in filmmaking or distribution, often meant the demise of native companies after a single production. Scripts were frequently copied from Japan, with romances being the most popular drawcard. The first avowedly nationalist film, *Arirang*, appeared in 1926. Directed by and starring the 24-year-old Na Un'gyu, the story centres on a Korean youth who has descended into insanity following torture during the Samil rising, and who, returning to the countryside, witnesses an assault on his sister by the farmhand of a pro-Japanese landlord. Infuriated, the youth kills the assailant with a sickle and, at the moment of arrest by the Japanese police, confronts the watching audience to assure them his spirit will rise again after bodily execution.[43] The obvious symbolism of the film was very powerful, and Koreans reacted passionately wherever the film was screened. Singing of the folk song *Arirang*, both then and since in present-day South Korea, has become an emotive display of nationalism. The relatively simple nationalism of *Arirang* was joined in the late 1920s by more complex cinematic attempts under the influence of prevailing radicalism. Directors took up proletarian and peasant themes, but these were often poorly handled and suffered heavily at the hands of Japanese censors. Nonetheless, even into the China War, the Korean cinema managed to develop its skills and produce films with explicit depictions of the lives of ordinary Koreans, such as peasants or river boatmen.

Even more than cinema, radio, with its anonymous entry to any location possessing a receiver, had the power to bridge physical and social distance. For this reason, radio in Japan had been restricted to a government monopoly, but in Korea private radio began with the joint-venture JODK (Seoul) from February 1927. Its directorship was largely Japanese and its main function was to provide reports on the stock market and rice exchange, but the evening and weekend program included both Japanese and Korean music or lectures. However, the 1933 figure of 20 400 subscribers at one yen listening fee per month, plus the expense of the radio set itself, suggests that most listeners were Japanese or wealthy Koreans: the announcers probably reflected the station's racial audience, with two Korean women, two Japanese women and two Japanese men broadcasting.[44]

Communications and literacy remained accessible only to a minority of Koreans. However, the problems of Korean nationalist or communist movements were complicated by the very newness of the foreign ideologies they looked to for guidance. Nationalism was explained in terms of education, language and culture, but was this not a retrospective view? Were nations in fact not defined more cogently, as Sin and others had suggested, by their force and success in expanding over the globe? If this were the case, could a nation develop in a state already occupied and in a world already divided if the imperialist powers did not first destroy themselves? As for communism, it had succeeded in Russia, but what of its failure in Germany, and while Lenin had taken power in the Soviet Union, were not his ideas still subject to trial and error under Stalin? There was no guarantee that socialism would export successfully, and Lenin's theory of the two-stage revolution was a temporary response to essentially unknown conditions in Asia. The Comintern was ignorant of Korea or China, and its directives were often ill-judged. Perhaps this ultimately mattered less to Korean communists than to their Chinese comrades: irrespective of Comintern policy, the government-general was too efficient to let any form of radical ideology plant firm roots. It was only when Japan invaded China, in part to halt the spread of East Asian communism, that Japanese colonialism embarked upon its own destruction and a window for communism opened in Korea.

The war years, 1937–45

The second Sino-Japanese War from July 1937 was to prove a turning point for East Asia. For China, it brought the Communist Party new legitimacy, wider intellectual support and ultimately state control in October 1949. The war exposed Japan's unsuitability to lead a union of East Asia and ended in the ruination of its people. For Korea, it was to bring about despoilation, but also independence, faster than the cultural nationalists or anyone else predicted.

One immediate impact of the war on Korea was a further reduction in the foreign presence. Up to 1937, there were still about 60 000 Chinese residents, but roughly half of these departed at the start of hostilities. Western concerns were represented by mining and by sales of petroleum and petroleum products. Gold was especially lucrative, producing in 1936 about 90 million yen (considerably more than in Japan), of which some 10 per cent came from foreign-owned mines. However, Japanese restrictions on foreign mining had been increasing since 1931: the American-owned Oriental Consolidated Mining Company was forced to sell its exports to a government-general agency and at artificially low prices, while from 1937–38, new strictures were enforced on the import of supplies — by mid-1939 Oriental Consolidated had lost patience and disposed of its Korean mines.[45] As for the Korean oil business, United States firms had dominated the market since the 1890s, and both Standard-Vacuum Oil Company (modern Exxon), pioneer of the early kerosene business, and the Texas Oil Company still kept offices at Seoul in 1937. The British Royal Dutch Shell Company also had Korean interests through its Rising Sun Petroleum Company. However, oil was obviously a vital commodity for the military and, in May 1935, foreign profits were undercut when the government-general established the Chosen Petroleum Company, with refineries at Wonsan sufficient to meet all Korean needs.[46] The new company was designed primarily for defence purposes and it was the beneficiary of rising war consumption as fixed quotas were placed on foreign sales. The reserve stock holding law, whereby oil firms were required to keep six months' supply within Korea at all times, also deterred foreign companies for whom such stockpiling was unjustified by the level of business.

The war produced initial benefits for Korean commerce and industry as hostilities disrupted Japanese labour and shipping, and the gaps to Manchukuo and North China were filled by an increased flow of Korean goods. In December 1937, the first export north of 12.5 million 'My Pet' Korean cigarettes was greeted by the official *Keijo Nippo* newspaper almost as a military strike: "Thus Chosen Tobacco is ready to march upon the field in North China this spring and anticipates delivering a knockout blow to the British and American tobacco trusts.'[47] Rising trade, and exclusion of non-yen block goods, maintained high employment in Korea and by 1938 had turned around its unfavourable trade balance. War-related industries such as chemicals and textiles were hurriedly expanded, while new development of machinery, machine tools and heavy vehicles was rapid in the Ch'ongjin area of the north-east and in the former textile centre of Seoul–Inch'on. The rural labour surplus was quickly exhausted as labour mobilisation from 1939 sent thousands into heavy industry, and more than 50 000 per annum volunteered for work in mines, engineering and factories on mainland Japan between 1939 and 1941: labour conscription was introduced in 1942, and between 1944 and 1945, a total of 500 000 Koreans either went voluntarily or under central directive to Japan.[48]

The move away from light industry towards heavy, war-related industries such as iron and tungsten mining also further reduced the number of women in the workforce. Increased profits hastened the mechanisation of small to medium-sized Korean factories, and forced rationalisation from 1941 ended many of the weaker concerns, bringing the overall Korean economy more closely to resemble that of Japan.

The lean years commenced early. By 1938, mainland Japan itself was rationing rice and petrol and, in Korea, price controls and the shortage of petrol or freight cars quickly slowed the wheels of trade. In August 1938, Governor-General Minami mobilised various bodies, including the intriguingly named Feminine Question Research Society, to lead the way in domestic economies by simplifying clothes, eating less and cooking fewer hot meals. The purchase of articles with military application, including cotton, paper, wool, rubber and metals, was to be reduced, as were smoking and drinking. The government-general also attempted a rapid-fire modernisation of Korean attitudes to time, exhorting the people to 'appreciate, save and utilise time. Strictly observe time to move, time to begin, and time to meet.'[49] There was a renewed effort to expand Korean agriculture as human resources and capital were redirected to the war effort. However, after a bumper crop in rice and cotton for 1937, extensive blight hit crops in 1938, and the level of cultivated land actually decreased between 1937 and 1944 from 1.6 to 1.3 million *chongbo* (1 *chongbo* equals about 0.9 hectare) while output also dropped considerably.[50] In addition, Korean farmers, knowing full well the authorities would requisition livestock and crops at minimal prices, quietly reduced productivity.

As part of its Korean mobilisation, the government-general established a central information committee with branches in each province at the very outset of war. This disseminated propaganda through all available media: newspapers, film, radio, lectures and mass-produced pamphlets in Korean delivered to every few houses. Any sign of dissent was silenced by the police. In 1937–38, Yi Kwangsu and Korean Christians including Yun Ch'iho and Chang Toksu were arrested (though subsequently released) on suspicion of unlawful activities; the following year, the sale of bibles was banned by police in at least one district; other Christians took the warning and some formed 'voluntary' groups to visit Shinto shrines and receive appropriate instruction in Shinto principles. The authorities' real fear, however, was of rural or labour agitators. As a counter-measure, anti-communist bodies were set up throughout the country and all social or occupational groups were placed in centralised organisations under official control. From 1940, the entire population was placed in neighbourhood 'patriotic' associations of ten-family units, with responsibility, as in Japan, for overseeing group visits to Shinto shrines, the raising of the Japanese flag, collection of war donations, distribution of food, maintaining security and making known official instructions.

Through these various sub-units, the authorities were better able to observe and mobilise the Korean public, but the militarisation of Korean society was most evident in those institutions under direct Japanese control, especially the schools. By 1938, teachers dressed in khaki uniforms, while the Japanese-designed school uniforms were military in design: black army style for the boys and sailor-suits for the girls. Morning parades were conducted as at an army barracks; schoolroom maps charted the march of Japanese armies across China; and class songs eulogised Japanese military victories. Schoolchildren were also expected to make their own wooden rifles for the school's 'armory'.

Korea was not mobilised merely to support Japan's war, but to share equally in its prosecution. Governor-General Minami's belief was that only by complete assimilation through a kind of Frankenstein reconstruction of the Korean identity could Japan ever hope to convince others in Asia to accept its leadership in a new regional order. Korea was to be a test case of the difference between Japanese and Western imperialism, the one destructive, the other constructive. While this led Minami to support Korean representation in the Japanese parliament, it also brought about a concerted assault on the Korean language, education, religion — indeed, all the recognised aspects of cultural personality. Educational revision in March 1938 placed Japanese and Korean systems on the same levels of 'elementary', 'middle' and 'girls' high', but also decreed that all education be conducted solely in Japanese and that pupils be forbidden to speak Korean, even out of school. Committees in all schools and government offices were set up to enforce this prohibition and Korean-language papers such as the *Tong-A Ilbo* and *Choson Ilbo* were forced to close.

Colonial restriction on the native language was not unusual to Korea — New Zealand adopted a similar policy in the Cook Islands and the British government had long prohibited the speaking of Welsh. On 10 November 1939, however, Minami introduced a reform which stands out in the history of colonialism: an 'invitation' to the Korean people to adopt Japanese names in place of their own. The underlying banality of this massively ill-judged action is described by Richard Kim in his autobiographical novel, *Lost Names*, in which he observes one aged Korean choosing a new name at the local police station:

> The Korean detective picks up a sheet of paper and shows it to the old man, translating the policeman's words.
>
> The old man shakes his head, looking at the paper, which contains a long list of names. "Anything," he mumbles. "It doesn't matter."
>
> The Korean detective does not translate those words. Instead, he puts his finger on one of the names and says, "How about this one, old man?"
>
> The old man says, "It doesn't matter which. No one's going to call me by that name anyway — or by any other name."[51]

Many Koreans complied with the 'invitation', but it remained a pretence on both sides as official records continued to list individuals by their original Korean names. What is striking about the move, however, is that in Confucianism, a cardinal tenet is respect for one's ancestors, not least through perpetuating the family name. In striking at the very core of the social and ethical make-up of Koreans, Minami's intention was to break their personal historical line and force them to start again from a metaphorical year zero. Of all the Japanese actions in Korea from 1875, perhaps none continues to be more bitterly remembered than this.

And yet, despite the wartime air of intimidation and arrest, there was that persistent ambivalence (apparent in Yun Ch'iho's 1905 comment on Japan's victory over Russia) between hatred of Japan's policies in Korea and respect for Japanese strength. While retaining his nationalist credentials, Ch'oe Namson in the 1930s willingly wrote articles urging China to unite with Japan against Western imperialism, and later exhorting Korean students to fight beside Japan in the 'holy war'.[52] This ambivalence is apparent in a British consular report on Korea for 1937:

> To all appearance, the disciplined enthusiasm of the Japanese people in regard to the undeclared warfare in China had communicated itself to Korea. Troop trains were greeted by schoolchildren and adults of all classes carrying Japanese flags, public prayers for victory at Shinto shrines were attended by large crowds, the press was full of reports of donations by wealthy Koreans to patriotic funds . . . Virtually all these manifestations, however, are either dictated by self-interest or are actively controlled and directed by the police, backed by the Japanese ex-Service Men's Associations throughout the peninsula. If a lantern procession be held in Seoul to celebrate a Japanese

victory, the police designate a quota for each ward to participate in the procession, prescribe street decorations and generally regulate the festivities

Concerning the deeper feelings of the Korean people, the report suggested:

The older people, who have seen their own country and Manchuria swallowed, can hardly be enthusiastic over present developments, but the younger generation, who have attended Japanese schools and have never known independence and are moreover never permitted to hear the other side of any case, accept the Japanese propaganda and follow the line of least resistance. It is the opinion of competent observers that Japan's successful defiance of the League of Nations in Manchuria and of the Western powers in China have stimulated many of the younger Koreans and have implanted in them a thrill of pride in their citizenship in a conquering nation. There is nowhere any unrest or apparent disaffection, but times are good and the people have money in their pockets. A return of the lean years may spoil the picture.[53]

On 22 February 1938, a special government-general ordinance allowed Koreans to become special army volunteers (a similar ordinance for the navy followed in 1943). Over 15 000 Korean youths responded in the first two years, and nearly 800 000 more between 1940 and 1943 (although in total only about 17 500 were actually inducted into the army).[54] The most popular film in wartime Korea was *The War at Sea from Hawaii to Malaya* (*Hawaii Maree oki kaisen*, Tokyo, 1942), a semi-documentary narrative of naval pilot training through all its Spartan rigors. The lead character was a model of dedication, selflessness and technical competence — precisely the kind of youth advocated by the cultural nationalists — and the glory of fighting a war, especially one initially so successful, against Western empires was undoubtedly attractive to many young Koreans. Some no doubt offered themselves by default, being sent to the army for behaviour unacceptable to the Japanese, and thus justifying the general cynicism with which Korean historians dismiss the figures for volunteers. However, there were clearly also young men who, as with Ch'oe Namson, accepted Japan's cause as that of Asians everywhere. As Wonmo Dong's interviews with former Korean army officers indicate, in the Japanese army they generally found themselves better and more equitably treated than in Korea itself.[55]

The opening of the Pacific War from December 1941 altered Korea's administrative relationship with Japan. In 1942, Japan's Home Ministry took over supervision of Korea as an integral part of the empire, and thereafter the appointment of Governors-General was decided by the Japanese Prime Minister with the advice of his Home Minister. Thus the formulation of policies affecting the Korean people became even more remote. The war quickly turned sour for Japan and army conscription was applied in Korea, effective from 1944; about 187 000 men were called up before the war's end, and another 20 000 mobilised for the navy. Between 1941 and 1945, a further 150 000 Koreans were taken for battlefield duties as transport and construction workers, building roads and airfields in the war zone. Young Korean women, some barely more than children, were also rounded up by the army and sent as prostitutes for Japanese troops, while frantic rumours late in the war accused the Japanese of killing teenage Korean girls and extracting their body oil to supplement dwindling supplies.[56] Korean industry and labour was exploited with increasing harshness, and the conditions of Korean workers at home and on the various battlefronts deteriorated rapidly. Many died from disease or accidents, allied bombing or simple murder. As Japan's position collapsed, Koreans working on military production at a factory in north Korea were shot to prevent disclosure at the end of their work.

As of 1944, only one Korean had been appointed to Japan's parliamentary upper house and only one Korean resident of Tokyo elected to the lower House of Representatives. Under imperial injunction, the Japanese Diet late in 1944 finally passed a bill to extend Japan's constitution and election laws to Korea and Taiwan from 1946. This was to give Koreans over 25 years of age and paying 15 yen in direct taxes the right to elect a total of 23 representatives. In 1933, the civil administrator of the government-general had written: 'the day is not far distant when Koreans will occupy seats in the cabinet, and when the governor general himself will be a Korean'.[57] Coming at the end of the war, it was too late.

From mid-1944, Korea was being prepared to repel invasion from the Soviet Union in the north and from the United States in the south. Troops and fortifications were concentrated on the south coast and especially on the island of Cheju-do. Thousands of Koreans were pressed into service as defenders. Ultimately, however, the use of nuclear weapons at Hiroshima (in which the victims included many Korean labourers) and Nagasaki, and the declaration of war on Japan by the Soviet Union, saved Korea from further havoc and brought the dogs of war to heel.

Under Japanese colonialism, Korea was physically modernised, but the Korean people were never actively involved in the process. Instead they were pushed and shoved according to Japanese designs and they worked largely for Japanese profit. They were exposed to city life, modern schools and work in factories, but they rarely sensed a positive connection with the changes around them, and the majority of Koreans observed modernity as if through a store window. In terms of imperial history, there is nothing unusual in this, although the relative lateness of Japanese imperialism resulted in a greater application of 'scientific' principles and ambitious socio-economic planning than in earlier and more remote Western imperial outposts. Thus Korean society as a whole felt the experience of colonialism more directly than others, and in a shorter period, for it is well to remember that the Japanese empire was a very brief phenomenon. Social dislocations were most rapid after the start of the second Sino-Japanese War. Between 1935 and 1940, Korea's urban population doubled from 7 to 14 per cent, and whereas in 1925 there had been an urban-agricultural ratio of 1:22, that had contracted by 1944 to 1:6. The dizzying growth of large cities between 1930 and 1940 is illustrated by Table 2.5.

Table 2.5 Urban growth of major cities, 1930–1940			
	1930	1935	1940
Seoul	394 240	444 098	935 464
Pusan	146 098	182 503	249 734
P'yongyang	140 703	182 121	285 965
Taegu	93 319	107 414	178 923
Inch'on	68 137	82 997	171 165
Kaesong	49 520	55 537	72 062
Wonsan	42 760	60 169	79 320
Hamhung	43 851	56 571	75 320
Chinnamp'o	38 296	50 512	68 656
Mokp'o	34 689	60 734	64 256
Kwangju	33 023	54 607	64 500

Source: Yunshik Chang, 1977, p. 70

Perhaps most remarkable was the genesis of Ch'ongjin, linked to the new port development of Najin in north-east Korea. A key military–industrial centre during the war, it grew from a small city of 20 000 in 1925 to 55 000 in 1935, but just five years later boasted a population of 197 918. Yet it was not merely the internal make-up of society that had been so violently affected. Millions of Koreans were now in China, Manchuria, Japan, the Soviet Union or the South Pacific. Some chose to return home; others decided to wait and see what would happen and who would now run the country. Imperialism had acted partly as Marx described in changing society and reducing the authority of traditional élites, but the imperial powers, unlike some dying sun, had not obliterated themselves entirely, and the new imperialism of the Cold War was to prevent Korean classes from resolving their differences in isolation. In that sense, the collapse of Japanese dominion was not an end entire in itself, and the respite from foreign intrusion was to be brief indeed.

Notes

1 *Japan Year Book 1930*, p. 475
2 Cho Kijun et al., *Ilche ha ui minjok saenghwalsa,* Seoul, 1971, p. 498
3 Kajimura Hideki, 'Shokuminchi Chosen de no Nihonjin', ed. Kimbara Samon, *Chiho bunka no Nihonshi vol. 9: chiho demokurashii to senso,* Tokyo, 1978, p. 340
4 Government-general of Tyosen, 1937, pp. 88–89
5 Sorensen, 1990
6 Han Sokhwi, *Nihon no Chosen shihai to shukyo seisaku,* Tokyo, 1988, pp. 160–62
7 *Japan Year Book 1940–41*, p. 879
8 Quoted from the official translation presented to President Woodrow Wilson by the Korean National Association, 7 April 1919, in Records of the State Dept. relating to the internal affairs of Korea, 1910–29, document 895.01/2.
9 Quotation and reports from United States Consul General Leo Bergholz to Secretary of State, 17 and 23 April 1919, 22 May 1919, Records of the State Dept. relating to the internal affairs of Korea 1910–29, items 895.00/622, 895.00/625, 895.00/639

10 US State Dept records, John K. Davis, United States Consul (Seoul), 'Extension in the sytem of local self-government in Chosen and its significance', report dated 30 July 1931
11 Pak Kyongsik, *Nihon teikokushugi no Chosen shihai*, 2 vols, Tokyo, 1973, vol. 1, pp. 63-66. The opposing view of United States researchers is noted in Myers and Yamada, 1984, pp. 429–30.
12 E.B. Schumpeter (ed.), *The industrialization of Japan and Manchukuo, 1930-1940*, NY, 1940, pp. 280, 288
13 Yoo Se Hee, 1974, p. 64
14 Ranford S. Miller, United States Consul-General, Seoul, to United States State Dept, 29 May 1925, itcm 895.00/705.
15 ibid.
16 Discussion of the tenant movement is derived largely from Yoo Se Hee, 1974.
17 Young Hoon Kang, 1977, p. 288. Also Yoo Se Hee, pp. 114–16.
18 United States State Dept. records, Ransford S. Miller (United States Consul-General, Scoul) to State Dept., 31 August 1929, 'The farmers and farm lands of Chosen (Korea) in 1928', document 895.61/5; Grajdanzev 1944, p. 119
19 Early results of the rural regeneration campaign are noted in government-general of Tyosen, 1937, pp. 213–16.
20 Yoo Se Hee, 1974 provides a detailed analysis of the Red Peasant Unions.
21 Quoted in Grajdanzev, 1944, p. 269
22 Cho Kijun et al., 1971, p. 585
23 Hatada Takashi, 'Chosenjin jido ni tai suru Chosen sotokufu no rekishi kyoiku', ed. Hatada Takashi, *Nihon wa Chosen de nani o oshieta no ka*, Tokyo, 1987, p. 32
24 Yamanaka Seigo, 'Kyokasho kenkyu no kadai to hoko', in Hatada, 1987, pp. 20–21
25 Grajdanzev, 1944, p. 266
26 Cho Kijun et al., 1971, pp. 588–90
27 Government-general of Tyosen, 1937, p. 80
28 Vacante, 1987, pp. 208–19
29 Chang, 1971, p. 178
30 Park Soon Won, 1985
31 Ki-baik Lee, 1984, p. 352
32 Reports from O. Gaylord Marsh, United States Consul (Scoul) to Secretary of State, 4 and 25 February 1937, United States State Dept. records, 895.114
33 A Korean farmer developing a lengthy irrigation channel interfered with the water rights of Chinese farmers and boatmen, resulting in local riots. In retaliation, Chinese resident in Korea were attacked, with 37 killed at P'yongyang and some 10 000 fleeing to Manchuria in just one week.
34 Hochin Choi, 1971, p. 236
35 For details of these men and their activities, see McNamara, 1990 and Eckert 1991.
36 This section relies on Kenneth Wells, 1985.
37 Park Soon Won, 1985, p. 108
38 Pak Kyongsik, 1973, vol. 1, p. 315
39 Pak Kyongsik, 1973, vol. 1, p. 293. Of the 2093 Korean-owned factories in 1930, 97 per cent, or 2031, employed less than 50 workers.
40 Wonmo Dong, 1973, p. 177
41 Robinson, 1988 interprets the cultural nationalists program; see especially pp. 74–77; Yi Kwangsu's 'Minjok kaejoron' is discussed on pp. 64-73.
42 Kang Man'gil, 1987, pp. 4–5 discusses the various interpretations.
43 The early Korean cinema and a summary of *Arirang* are from Lee Young-il, 1988.
44 United States Consul-General (Seoul), 7 March 1927, US State Dept records, item 895.74/8

45 United States State Dept., O. Gaylord Marsh, Consul (Seoul), 19 May 1937, item 895.60/2; United States State Dept., item 895.63
46 Details from United States State Dept records, W.R. Langdon, Consul (Seoul) to Edwin Neville, Charge d'Affaires (Tokyo), 29 October 1935, item 895.6363/5; U. Alexis Johnson, vice-consul (Seoul), 'Present position and future prospects of American oil firms operating in Chosen', 26 January 1938, item 895.6363/13
47 Contained in United States State Dept records, U. Alexis Johnson, vice-consul (Seoul) to Secretary of State, 27 December 1937
48 Chong-sik Lee, 1985, pp. 16–17
49 Quoted from Chosen Shoko Shimbun, 13 August 1938, in O. Gaylord Marsh (Seoul) to Secretary of State, 25 August 1938, US State Dept records, item 895.5017/1
50 Ik Whon Kwan, 1965, p. 100
51 Richard E. Kim, 1970, p. 104
52 Takeuchi, 1988, pp. 232–33, 254
53 FO 371/22190, British Consulate-General, Seoul, *Annual report on Korea for 1937*, dated 24 December 1937
54 Kimijima Kazuhiko, 'Chosen ni okeru senso doin taisei no tenkai katei', eds Fujiwara Akira/Nozawa Yutaka, *Nihon fashizumu to higashi Ajia*, Tokyo 1977, p. 96
55 Dong, 1973, p. 160
56 Lee See-Jae, 1987, p. 9
57 Quoted in Brudnoy, 1970, p. 186.

The Korean War was a civil war, yet unlike most civil wars in history it ended not in victory for one side or the other, but in stalemate, with the combatants retreating exhausted from the battle. About 3 million people were dead, 10 million were divided from members of their families by the ceasefire line, and the whole nation was uprooted and destitute. The country was laid waste to such an extent that it would take a generation to recover economically, and much longer to recover psychologically and emotionally from the horror of internecine violence. Furthermore, unlike most civil wars, this one was complicated by foreign intervention on such a scale that it is sometimes seen as a surrogate world war. Understanding the interplay of domestic and foreign forces is the key to understanding the Korean War.[1]

This understanding has been rendered acutely difficult by the fact that the war was embedded in social and international problems which it failed to resolve: that of the unification of Korea itself, and the form of political and economic order appropriate to it, on the one hand, and that of the tensions and confrontation between East and West that was known as the Cold War on the other.

The Korean War is normally dated from the morning of 25 June 1950. After events in and around the 38th parallel which are disputed, the (northern) Korean People's Army (KPA) crossed in force, capturing the southern capital, Seoul, a few days later, and triggering a United States-led intervention by a sixteen-nation force under the United Nations flag and sponsorship. Three months later, the United Nations force's drive back across the 38th parallel and towards the Chinese frontier prompted the intervention of a large force of 'Chinese People's Volunteers'. The two sides fought on until an eventual truce was signed on 27 July 1953.

Beyond the bald facts of this account, much else is disputed. Although the major, and initial, forces involved were indisputably Korean, and although the conflict stemmed from the failure to reach a settlement between the competing northern and southern claims to legitimate representation of the national interest, the view that the war began with external aggression was long held by major proponents on both sides: the aggression was said to have been planned and initiated by Stalin on the one hand, or by Truman (and MacArthur) on the other, as part of regional or global strategies of super-power hegemony. The Cold War polarisation of the world into hostile camps helped to create and sustain this view on both sides.

However, the shift towards a 'Korea-centred' view of the conflict gathered momentum during the 1970s, with a growing consensus among historians that the prime responsibility for initiating the war rested with Kim Il Sung, to whom the Soviet Union and China played subordinate roles as supporters and possibly stimulants, but not controllers. Early in the 1980s there occurred a further major shift in interpretation, intensifying this aspect of the 'civil' quality of the Korean War by looking at the processes at work in Korean society from 1945 as a revolution, and the war as part of a revolutionary nationalist struggle. In this perspective, the primary historical focus shifts to the relationship of all parties to the central and evolving dynamic of Korean nationalism, and the explosion of June 1950 is seen as a stage — albeit a dramatically new and violent one — in that evolution, with outside parties being assessed in terms of their role in facilitating or obstructing the achievement of the goals of Korean revolutionary nationalism. The depth of the social ferment and the violence of the struggle were evident long before June 1950; at least 100 000 people died in various bitter struggles in the south, and an unknown number had fled from the revolutionary changes taking place in the north, before the actual 'war' began.[2]

Liberation and the drawing of the line

The collapse of 35 years of Japanese imperial control in Korea created an immediate vacuum at the centre, and the convergence of Soviet and American armies (and the political forces they represented) around Korea meant that nascent Cold War rivalries were quickly felt. Indeed, the impact of the Cold War on domestic politics was felt earlier, and in more dramatic ways, in Korea than anywhere in Europe.

Soviet forces crossed the border into Korea on 9 August 1945. By the time of the Japanese surrender on 15 August, they had already captured much of northern Korea and were pushing southwards against diminishing Japanese resistance, while the nearest United States forces were hundreds of kilometres away, on Okinawa. Once their shared wartime purpose was achieved with the collapse of Japan, rivalry between the two allies was inevitable over the degree of relative power and influence each would hold over the collapsing Japanese empire. The notion of coexistence between capitalism and communism was still a generation away.

Thinking about Korea had not figured high in the planning of either Washington or Moscow before the surrender. At the Cairo Conference of November 1943, an eventual post-war trustee status under the great powers was agreed, although with little discussion. At Yalta in February 1945, a term of between ten and 30 years was put on this period of trusteeship. In other words, the shared assumption on both sides was that it was neither possible nor appropriate, at least in the short term, for Korea to become a sovereign and independent state. In this belittling of the Korean capacity for self-rule, both Soviet and American thinking unconsciously adopted a Japanese imperialist perspective.

In Washington, the early Soviet advances in Korea (in accordance with the Potsdam Agreement) aroused concern, particularly in light of the hubris generated by the 'successful' nuclear attacks on Japan. On 10 August, one day after the Soviet declaration of war on Japan, two young colonels were commissioned by the War Department to find an appropriate line along which to divide Korea into separate Soviet and American zones of occupation. One of them, Dean Rusk, who was later to become Secretary of State, has given his account of their searching the map for an appropriate line, finding only the 38th parallel, a line of no previous political or cultural significance but which would place the capital, Seoul, and most of the population, under American influence.[3] Stalin accepted the American initiative and immediately ordered the withdrawal of his forces to the line. Unlike Europe, therefore — where the aggressor state, Germany, was divided — in Asia it was the victim of Japanese imperialism, Korea, which suffered that punishment.

The United States, South Korea and anti-communism

With the announcement of the Japanese surrender, Seoul was swept by a mood of joyful anticipation and hasty organisation for independence; the thought that the outcome could be anything other than independence was far from people's minds. A spontaneous network of popular local organisations, known as 'People's Committees', emerged as the core of the new national order to take over from Japan.[4] Despite the disparate political tendencies emerging in a community where free political expression had for so long been repressed, a readiness to compromise around certain agreed core policies was clear, with the central consensus being on the need to root out the supporters and beneficiaries of the old (pro-Japanese) order, and to create a more just and equitable society. These two aspirations had the potential for a radical national and social revolutionary transformation of the society of the kind that classically had given birth to new democratic nation states.

Where the United States occupation of Japan proceeded on the basis of a set of priorities which had been decided after detailed planning — and the priority of demolishing military and fascist structures and establishing a new and democratic order was unequivocal — in Korea neither a plan, nor experts, nor even speakers of Korean existed. Instead, the main policy objectives were negative and pre-emptive: to deny the territory to the Soviet Union and to consolidate a co-operative regime that would reflect United States strategic interests in the region. The idea of independence played no part in such thinking. Thus the tone of General MacArthur's 'General Order Number One', issued on 7 September, was foreboding. Pending the arrival of United States forces from Okinawa, Koreans were to obey the Japanese authorities under threat of severe penalties.[5] In the exchanges between the Americans on Okinawa and the Japanese before the American arrival, the Japanese characterisation of the local nationalist movement as virtually communist was quickly accepted by the Americans.[6]

When the Americans did land in Korea, on 8 September, they refused to deal with or recognise the Provisional Committee for Korean Independence (PCKI) or its leaders (such as Yo Un Hyong), or to hear any talk of the establishment of a Korean Republic such as had been declared on 6 September. In place of any of these local Korean leaders was the arch-conservative and anti-communist Syngman Rhee.[7] The network of local People's Committees, as well as the incipient political framework of the Korean Republic, was seen from the start as a communist-front movement. There is no denying that communists were part of the nascent movement — and it would be surprising otherwise given their prominent role in organising what resistance there had been to the Japanese. However, scholars who have examined the social and political composition of the committees and of the Republic recognise the broad base of the former and agree with Dae Sook Suh's assessment of the latter that there was 'a serious effort to form a government acceptable to the Communists as well as to the Nationalists'.[8] United States policy, however, turned to the task of wiping them out and instead building a regime which would share American priorities.

By December 1945 the United States military commander, General Hodge, recognised that 'pro-American' had become an epithet akin to 'pro-Jap [sic] national traitor, and Jap collaborator',[9] and the popular organisations which were being 'consciously and systematically' rooted out were understood to be representative of the popular will.[10] In February 1946, United States intelligence reported that leftist elements would be bound to win in any fair election.[11] According to an American military government survey in the same month, 49 per cent of the people thought they had been better off under the Japanese colonial adminis- tration than they were under the Americans.[12]

In place of the organisations they were weeding out, the Americans chose to work through the conservative, landlord and business élite and the Korean Democratic Party (KDP) which evolved out of it. The institutions and forces of the 'old order' built up by Japan were not only retained, but were given an enhanced role in the 'new order' created by the Americans. The system of control embedded in the Japanese 'peace preservation' laws and the Japanese-trained police force which had learned to implement them, the prosecutors and judicial authorities who had served Japan and built careers on rooting out anti-Japanese tendencies among their countrymen, and the Japanese-trained military who had served in various Japanese armies gained rapid promotion as their former Japanese superiors were removed, but the essential quality of their work remained unchanged. The state structures which were gradually built around them fused the ideological anti-communism of the Americans, the rural conservatism of the local élites, and the revamped security and police apparatus bequeathed from the old Japanese colonial state.[13] Rhee, with his close American connections and commitment to the new 'roll-back' phase of anti-communism on the one hand, and his autocratic and conservative Korean élite background on the other, was well placed to head the emerging structure.

Other Korean politicians also returned from abroad in late 1945, including the members of the so-called Korean Provisional Government which had maintained a precarious existence in China for 25 years. Its leading figures, men such as Kim Ku and Kim Kyu-sik, although politically conservative, were nationalists who found offensive the strength of collaborators in the United States-sponsored structures which were evolving, while they also did not share the ideological passions of Rhee and the Americans.

In December 1945, there was a final allied attempt to work out an agreement on the future of Korea: the Moscow Conference of Foreign Ministers. Its prescription was for a joint commission to supervise economic interchange between the two sectors and consult with Korean leaders with a view to establishing a provisional all-Korean government in a five-year trusteeship arrangement to be supervised by the four powers pending full Korean unity and independence. This American initiative was accepted with the utmost reluctance by the Russians and by political groups in the north, and was fiercely attacked by rightist elements in the south with United States encouragement.[14] Negotiations within the Moscow formula gradually broke down, first in 1946 when the Russians disallowed consultations with any group opposing the terms of the agreement, and conclusively in 1947, by which time political events in Korea had developed such a momentum that the kind of inter-zone co-operation envisaged was all but inconceivable. Truman's top advisers told him in September 1946 that: 'The language of military power is the only language which disciples of power politics understand . . . Compromise and concessions.are considered by the Soviets to be evidence of weakness.'[15] In place of any compromise with the communists of Moscow (or P'yongyang or Seoul), the thrust of occupation policy remained firmly the creation of an anti-communist bastion in Korea, whether in part or the whole of the country.

Polarisation sharpened in south Korea, as those associated with the People's Republic, especially communists, were frozen out of the structures nurtured by the occupying forces. In the summer of 1946, leading communists were arrested or driven underground. Violent clashes grew as the popular aspiration for liberation was denied. A series of rebellions in the autumn of 1946 was described by the correspondent of the *Chicago Sun*, Mark Gayn, as 'a full-scale revolution', and he estimated that they involved 'hundreds of thousands, if not millions of people'.[16] The unco-ordinated peasant and local attempts to resist the assaults on the People's Committees, and actually to seize local and provincial power, were no match for the (largely) Japanese-trained security forces, but 1000 people were killed, including 200 policemen, before they could be quelled.[17] In July 1947, the man who had been at the heart of the People's Committees and the Korean People's Republic in 1945, and who had struggled since then to build a broad, united nationalist front and reach accommodation with the north, Yo Unhyong, was assassinated.

The tragedy of this phase of the occupation of south Korea was that the 'democracy' for which the allies had fought the war was defined for Korea in the global, geo-political terms of anti-communism, which in practice meant a repudiation of the expectations of national liberation and radical social change that had stirred Korean hopes in 1945, and the crushing of the spontaneous organs of Korean self-expression, the People's Committees, and their attempt to achieve democracy from below. Paradoxically, therefore, while the occupation of the former enemy, Japan, was experienced as liberating, and even the Communist Party of Japan co-operated with it, the occupation of Korea was experienced as one of division followed by American-sponsored repression.

The Soviet Union, north Korea and revolution

Any consideration of the evolution of north Korea from 1945 faces two initial problems: the assumption that anything created as a result (or consequence) of Soviet military operations at the end of the Second World War, or subsequently, must have been a Stalinist puppet creation, without intrinsic legitimacy; and the assumption that the political and social order which may be observed in north Korea today, headed by the man who emerged to prominence during the Soviet occupation, Kim Il Sung, must be the same as that which was constructed during the occupation. Both assumptions contain some truth, but they also over-simplify, and they distract attention from the unique and evolving character of north Korea.

The most striking contrast between the occupation of the two zones was that, initially at least, it was the Soviet Union which recognised a much greater degree of autonomy, and was more sensitive to the aspirations for national and social liberation in its zone than were the Americans in theirs. This is not to imply that Soviet policy was dictated by any particular virtue, but to recognise the convergence between Soviet national interest and the revolutionary dynamism of Korean society in the aftermath of liberation. Stalin's relative lack of interest in Korea may also have helped.

On 26 August, once established in his P'yongyang office, the Soviet commander, General Chistiakov, ringingly affirmed the end of Korean liberation and independence, which was strictly in accordance with his instructions from Stalin that 'anti-Japanese groups and democratic parties and their activity should be aided', but announced that it was no part of Soviet policy to introduce the Soviet system to Korea.[18] The People's Committees and the Korean People's Republic, rebuffed from the start in the south, enjoyed 'real power' during the initial phases of the Soviet occupation.[19] Initially, and until it became clear that the People's Republic and the federation of People's Committees upon which it rested were not to be recognised in the south, the northern committees looked to Seoul for direction and leadership. Only in February 1946, when national co-ordination had become clearly impossible, was a Provisional People's Committee for North Korea established. Thereafter it functioned as a provisional government and proceeded to implement a series of radical, but broadly popular, social and economic reforms. These included the purge of Japanese collaborators, land reform, emancipation of women and the transfer to public ownership of all former Japanese assets.

At the head of this new structure emerged Kim Il Sung, who remained the dominant figure in North Korea for the next half-century. The full details of his emergence to power may only be clarified when archival material from North Korea becomes available, but this much is clear: Kim was a prominent guerrilla leader from the anti-Japanese struggle of the 1930s whose exploits made him seem a legendary figure and who, the American CIA reported, 'was conceded by all circles to have vast popular prestige'.[20] His anti-Japanese credentials were impeccable, and the reform program implemented from early 1946, including land reform, labour reform and women's rights, was in accord with the internal dynamic of Korean society, though there is some reason to think it followed a direction from Moscow.

The social base of the regime was made up of poor peasants and veterans of years in the anti-Japanese struggle, in striking contrast with the regime that was being put in place in the south.[21] As the liberal American scholar, George McCune, wrote:

> The mass of the Korean people in the north reacted favorably toward the Russian regime especially when it was accompanied by many of the revolutionary benefits of a socialist society.[22]

It is also true, however, that Kim would not have gained power in the first place had he not been approved by the Soviet leaders. He was chosen in 1945 as head of the 'Korean Task Force' sent to P'yongyang by the Soviet Red Army, apparently on the basis of a consensus among Soviet, Chinese and Korean communists.[23] Once in P'yongyang, which he reached on 22 September 1945, he made a more positive impression on the occupying Soviet commanders than anyone else (although readiness to do the Soviet will must have been a major factor in earning this favour).

His first rival for power in North Korea was Cho Mansik, a popular P'yongyang Christian nationalist. Cho was detained by the occupying authorities for opposition to the Moscow Agreement on trusteeship (December 1945) and was apparently executed shortly after the beginning of the Korean war in June 1950.[24] In February 1946 Kim became head of the provisional administration, and from the establishment of the Democratic People's Republic in 1948 he was clear leader, initially as premier.

His anti-Japanese credentials were impeccable, but his service prior to liberation in 1945 had been either with Chinese units (to 1940) or Soviet units (as captain in the Soviet 88th Special Brigade outside Khabarovsk between 1940 and 1945). As a prominent figure in the guerrilla forces of North-East China, he was 'trusted and respected' by both his superior officers and the men who served under him, while at the same time being hated and feared by the Japanese, especially after his successful raid on the North Korean town of Pochonbo in June 1937 and his annihilation of the Japanese 'Maeda Unit' which had been sent to destroy him in February 1940. He featured in the Japanese wanted lists as the 'tiger' (*tora*), while other guerrilla leaders were known as 'bear', 'lion', 'bull', 'horse' or 'cat'.[25] In July 1946 he was personally selected by Stalin in preference to his rival, Pak Hon-Yong.[26] To Stalin, he must have seemed both more likely to serve Soviet interests than anyone else and (probably) more competent, dynamic and young.

The truth about Kim Il Sung is particularly difficult to discern between the official North Korean line that he is a god-like figure of infinite genius and the South Korean propaganda which completely denies his anti-Japanese guerrilla record. What seems most likely is that, as Dae-Sook Suh puts it, he was neither fraud nor saviour, but one who, like many of his compatriots, had fought against Japan, had ability and drive, and was favoured by circumstances and luck.[27] During 1946, however, the diametrically opposing paths followed by the northern and southern zones of occupation gradually weakened the prospects of unification. The merging of a revolutionary and a counter-revolutionary regime could only be achieved by the surrender of one or other side, or by war.

The failure of the United Nations

In the summer of 1947, negotiations under the trusteeship formula worked out in Moscow broke down. The final attempt to break the deadlock between the two powers was made in a proposal by United States Acting Secretary of State Robert Lovett at the end of August. Lovett advanced a seven-point plan which called for separate elections in the two zones and a provisional national legislature and government to be established in accordance with relative population, followed by discussions with the 'Moscow powers' on aid, and under United Nations supervision.[28] Superficially attractive, the proposal concealed an uncompromisingly hard United States position. It implicitly denied any legitimacy to the elections that had been held in the north in 1946 and, given the population disparity between the two zones, it amounted to a formula for assimilation. Furthermore, the proposal to extend the arena for decisions from the bilateral of the two occupying powers to the quadrilateral of the four allied powers and then the multilateral of the United Nations, in which United States influence progressively strengthened as that of the Soviet Union declined, was effectively one to deny the latter influence over the eventual settlement. While the American proposal was unacceptable to the Russians, theirs was equally so to the Americans, since their call for withdrawal of all foreign troops as of the beginning of 1948 would certainly have led to the resumption of the processes of revolutionary change arrested in the south since 1945.

So, on a unilateral American initiative, the problem was transferred to the United Nations in September 1947. No compromise was to be brooked in seeking 'to secure the widest possible mobilisation of public opinion behind United States policy',[29] even if, as United States commander General Hodge put it prophetically, the outcome in South Korea might be 'a reactionary Fascist government, with which it might become difficult, if not impossible, to deal'.[30] A United Nations Temporary Commission for Korea (UNTCOK) was set up by a resolution of 14 November to see to the holding of elections for a National Assembly not later than 31 March 1948.[31] Thus commenced the involvement of the United Nations which was to lead, in due course, to a step it has never taken anywhere before or since — the direct prosecution of a war.

From the circumstances of UNTCOK's creation it was clear that co-operation would be unlikely from the Soviet Union, and indeed requests to enter the northern sector were rebuffed. Despite the commission's 'all but unanimous' opposition, according to the chairman, K. P. Menon, the principle of separate elections was endorsed on 26 February by the United Nations' Interim Committee. Even as the committee was meeting in New York, the communist coup took place in Czechoslovakia, and some members at least were persuaded that if the communists had won in Czechoslovakia they must be prevented from 'winning' in Korea.[32] The strongest opposition in the United Nations Committee, whose members had been personally chosen by John Foster Dulles, came from the Australian and Canadian delegates.[33] The situation in Korea as observed on 11 November 1947 by Patrick Shaw, then head of the Australian diplomatic mission in Tokyo, was that:

> Real Power is apparently in the hands of the ruthless police force which works at the direction of the G-2 Section of the American G.H.Q. and Syngman Rhee and Kim Koo [sic]. Korean prisons are now fuller of political prisoners than under Japanese rule. The torture and murder of the political enemies of the extreme Right is apparently an accepted and commonplace thing.[34]

The instruction of the UN Interim Committee to go ahead with separate elections did not allay these misgivings and sustained United States pressure was necessary to achieve the desired result. Australia and

Canada still voted (11 March) against the decision to conduct elections
two months later in such parts of the country as were accessible, provided
there existed 'a reasonable degree of free atmosphere'.[35] Furthermore,
in the event it turned out that the Indian delegate had indeed been
'open to persuasion', since the Indian vote for the resolution was cast
only because of the Indian delegate's passionate attachment to a Korean
woman poet.[36] The Indian vote, determined in this tragi-farcical manner,
was crucial in determining the 4:2:2 outcome in favour.

For their temerity in opposing the United Nations plans, the
Australian and Canadian delegates were denounced by General Hodge
for 'general appeasement of Soviet Russia' and for 'not understanding
the bitter cold war against communism'.[37] Their position remained
stubborn, however, since it seemed clear to them that such elections
would not advance the cause of Korean unification, and that they would
be boycotted by 'all but the extreme right'.[38]

Even as events moved towards separate elections and a deepening of
division, the most prominent members of the south Korean leadership,
excepting only Syngman Rhee, wrote to Kim Il Sung to propose a north–
south political conference. This was supported by the Australian and
Canadian delegates.[39] A north–south conference was held in April, with
240 southern delegates, including the most prominent liberal and
rightist nationalist leaders.[40] However, the joint declaration, calling for
immediate withdrawal of all foreign troops, rejection of 'dictatorship and
monopoly capitalism' and the formation of a united government, was
overtaken by events.

The elections were held on 10 May, boycotted by the left and the
nationalist right, and after a campaign of officially sponsored violence
and intimidation which saw 589 people killed. The Australian government pronounced itself 'far from satisfied' with the election.[41] None of
the UNTCOK members thought of the elections as creating a national
parliament, but after seven weeks' debate and continuing United States
pressure,[42] and only in the absence of the Syrian and Australian
delegates,[43] agreement was reached to declare the elections 'a valid
expression of the free will of the electorate in those parts of Korea which
were accessible to the Commission'.[44] Despite all the reservations, the
elected representatives were constituted a national assembly, a
constitution was drawn up and Rhee was installed as president of the
'Republic of Korea'. On 12 August the United States government
recognised the new body as a National Assembly and the government as
that which had been envisaged in the 1947 United Nations resolution.[45]
On 12 December the United Nations General Assembly declared the
new body 'the only legal government in Korea', although it did not
pronounce on its claims to jurisdiction over the whole of the country.[46]

The Republic of Korea was thus born under inauspicious circumstances, marked by violence, the overriding of principled objections and
the exercise of consistent and determined United States pressure on the
United Nations and its commission. In the fiercest display of opposition

to the conduct of separate elections, the people of the island of Cheju, off the south coast, rose in rebellion: between 10 and 25 per cent of the population was massacred, scores of villages were burned, and the panoply of anti-guerrilla measures later developed to the full in Vietnam — herding of the population into strategic hamlets or fortified villages, destruction of the crops, scorched earth, slaughter of villagers — was put into operation.[47] Only after the uprising had been mercilessly put down could the elections be held on Cheju, one year later than the rest of the country. The United Nations Commission was impressed by the peace and order, and pronounced that the elections proper had been 'marked by quietness'.

The north followed Seoul by holding its own elections (on 25 August) and establishing rival institutions, a Supreme People's Assembly, which also claimed legitimacy as a national parliament, and a government headed by Kim Il Sung as Prime Minister. The United Nations' intervention, far from accomplishing the unification and independence of Korea, served to entrench the division and set the scene for civil war.

Beginning the war

Korea now had two governments, communist and anti-communist, each determined to extend its writ over the whole country. In the south, a reorganised United Nations Commission (UNCOK) was supposed to lend its good offices to promote reunification, to be available for 'observation and consultation' as free and representative institutions developed, and in due course to observe the withdrawal of foreign troops.[48] In fact, however, its capacity to exert leverage over the ROK government in the south was slight, and its influence with the DPRK government in the north was non-existent.

UNCOK delegates in Seoul were frustrated by their inability to influence events, and disturbed by the repressive nature of the regime. The Indian and Australian delegates in particular were concerned over arrests of National Assemblymen, intimidation of the press, and 'the fact that public meetings frequently could not take place'.[49] In the countryside, guerrilla warfare continued, and in the areas in which guerrilla activity had been crushed, order was maintained 'only through Police State machinery of espionage, censorship, propaganda and repression'.[50] In June 1948, the rightist leader, Kim Ku (who had visited P'yongyang in April and had been denounced by Syngman Rhee as a 'traitor'), was assassinated. The murders of Yo in 1947 and Kim in 1948 removed the two outstanding south Korean non-communist nationalist leaders, one of the left and one of the right, who had been passionately opposed to any split of the nation.

By July 1949, according to the Head of the Australian Mission in Tokyo, progress in the development of representative government was 'unlikely while the Government remains an arbitrary dictatorship of the President and a few members of the Cabinet, enforced by ruthless police action'.[51] The CIA thought Rhee 'senile', if also 'indomitably strong-willed and obstinate', while in the British embassy he was regarded as 'a dangerous fascist, or lunatic'.[52] Large-scale military campaigns for the suppression of resistance within South Korea continued through early 1950, to the extent that the *New York Times* wrote in March of the country being 'darkened by a cloud of terror that is probably unparalleled in the world'.[53] As instability continued, Rhee grew strident in his calls for a march north to unify the country and his forces stepped up raids across the border. In October 1949 he boasted that it would take him just three days to capture P'yongyang.[54] Australia's Department of External Affairs in Canberra noted: 'The [Seoul] Government's only proposed solution to the problem of unification is bullets and bayonets.'[55]

Neither side was free from responsibility for the border incidents. The head of the American Military Advisory Group, General Roberts, blamed the South Korean side for those of the summer of 1949,[56] and Admiral Yi Yongun (Lee Yongwon) admitted that naval units which he commanded were responsible for initiating attacks in August on the northern port of Monggump'o.[57] From September, however, the flow of Soviet military supplies into North Korea began to shift the balance, and on at least three occasions in September and October 1949 northern forces crossed the border and showed clear superiority in clashes against their southern counterparts.[58] Thereafter, until the war began in June of the following year, sporadic violence continued on the border.

As Soviet and American troops were withdrawn (in December 1948 and June 1949), and full governing powers were assumed by regimes locked in frontal opposition to each other, the danger of military escalation of the north–south tension led UNCOK in March 1950 to request the Secretary-General to provide field observers along the 38th parallel. Early in the morning of 25 June 1950, however, war began and northern forces quickly poured across the border. Within three days the southern capital, Seoul, had fallen and Rhee's government was in flight.

Both sides allege that they were attacked that morning, but whatever the truth about the initiation of hostilities, three things are clear. First, the failures of the postwar settlement and the United Nations intervention to come to grips with the force of Korean nationalism made violent attempt at resolution likely — and in fact, both sides anticipated and planned for war. Second, of the two regimes which confronted each other, one preserved intact the central features of the Japanese-created colonial state and the organs on which that state had rested, while the other was created out of forces which had struggled for decades against Japan and gave form to deeply felt demands for radical social and economic reform. Third, the outcome of the civil war phase of the conflict was swift, but massive external intervention prolonged and intensified it. The assumption in much of the literature that war responsibility should attach exclusively to whichever side moved first that morning ignores the considerable responsibility for the interventions between 1945 and 1950 which served to make the eventual conflict virtually inevitable, and fails to account for the enormously destructive character of that intervention once the war began.

However, the circumstances surrounding the beginning of the conflict in June 1950 are important. The initial despatch from United States Ambassador John Muccio in Seoul said that, 'according to [South] Korean Army reports which are partly confirmed by Korean Military Advisory Group field adviser reports', north Korean forces had invaded the south at several points that morning.[59] Independent confirmation of the report was sought from the United Nations Commission, but all it could do was to corroborate that it had been told the same thing.[60] With only one-sided information before it, the Security Council of the United Nations was hastily convened, and described the events as 'an armed attack' by North Korean forces, calling on those forces to withdraw, and on United Nations member states to co-operate in securing that goal.

However, the United Nations Secretary-General, Trygve Lie, strongly suggested that United Nations sources had confirmed the south Korean reports. Furthermore, by Lie's own account, we know that he intervened to persuade several members of the Security Council (India and Egypt, and possibly Norway) to vote for the United States resolution,[61] and from a 'Top Secret, Emergency' cable despatched to its government on that night by the Australian United Nations mission it appears that the French and Egyptian delegates had actually been persuaded to change their vote because of information from the United Nations Secretariat to the effect that 'ten of the twenty captured tanks were not only of Russian origin but were actually manned by Russian troops'.[62] There is no record of any such information being transmitted by UNCOK. It must therefore have come from South Korean or American sources but, since no Russian prisoners were produced, either at this or at any other stage of the war, the report was obviously a fabrication. Nevertheless, its effect on the delegates to the emergency session of the Security Council may well be imagined. The vote was carried by nine votes to zero, with one abstention (Yugoslavia) and in the absence of the Soviet Union.

On 27 June, the Security Council met again to consider a second resolution, the crucial vote under which the United Nations then actually went to war. This time there was one piece of apparently incontrovertible and impartial evidence — a report by the two Australian officers who constituted the UNCOK Field Observer team. Major F.S.B. Peach and Squadron-Leader R.J. Rankin had made a series of visits to points on the 38th parallel between 9 and 23 June, returning to Seoul on the 23rd and writing their report the following day, the eve of the war.[63] They noted that the south Korean forces were lightly armed and defensively deployed, and that, apart from some reports of increased military activity on the Ongjin Peninsula to the west, there was no indication of any unusual level of military activity in the north either. In the context of collapsing southern defences, this was enough to persuade UNCOK, meeting in Seoul at 10:00 hours on 26 June, that the northern regime was carrying out a 'well-planned, concerted, and full-scale invasion of south Korea' — in effect, that since the southern side could not have launched an invasion, the northern side must have. It was the UNCOK interpretation, not the Field Observers' text, which reached the United Nations Security Council for its second debate. The actual Peach–Jamieson text, because of various difficulties in communications, was not placed before the Security Council until 30 June.[64]

United States forces were in fact committed before the United Nations resolution,[65] and after it the international commitment gradually built into a sixteen-nation force — Australia, Belgium, Canada, Columbia, Ethiopia, France, Greece, Luxemburg, the Netherlands, New Zealand, the Philippines, the Republic of South Africa, Thailand, Turkey, the United Kingdom and the United States — but only gradually stiffened resistance against the (northern) Korean People's Army (KPA) into a line that by late July began to hold firm in the south-eastern corner of the country. The government retreated to Pusan, but its ability to hold even a final defensive line along the Naktong River remained doubtful.

The United Nations action was based on the hypothesis that the invasion of south Korea was unprovoked, deliberate and planned. Under the circumstances, it was a reasonable inference from the available evidence, but there were other hypotheses, including the north Korean case that it had responded to an attack from the south, and in any case the jurisdiction of the United Nations was highly problematic, given that this was a dispute between two rival claimants to national sovereignty (i.e. a civil war), to which therefore the peace enforcement powers of the Security Council should not have applied.

The fact that south Korean defences crumbled is frequently taken as evidence that the north had mobilised vastly superior resources for a premeditated assault. Yet United States intelligence before the war believed that the balance, if any, favoured the southern side,[66] and the reluctance to supply items such as tanks and aircraft was precisely because of the fear that Rhee would carry out his promise to 'march north'. Neither army was at the time particularly large; even including police and constabulary, the figure still comes to about 152 000 for the south and 139 000 for the north, the south having a clear superiority in regular forces and being more concentrated in the border area than the north.[67] Had the war begun a few months later, in September, the northern forces would have had an additional five divisions, but in June they were still only in effect half-mobilised.[68] MacArthur's headquarters estimated that the initial attacking army numbered about 38 000, and that there had been about 50 000 southern troops facing them in the region between Seoul and the 38th parallel.[69] The invading forces also lacked any equipment for crossing the Han River, the first major obstacle they would encounter in any drive southwards,[70] and they faced the worst possible weather conditions for the use of their tanks (flooded paddy fields) and planes (low cloud and an imminent typhoon). Even their tanks might have been rendered ineffective had the south deployed the anti-tank mines that had been supplied in abundance.[71]

The attack was said to have come as a complete surprise. This is hard to believe, however. United States and south Korean intelligence noted increased military activity in the north and on 10 May the Defence Minister issued a warning of impending hostilities.[72] Since the last Sunday in June had been the time chosen by the south in 1949 to launch a major cross-border attack, the apparent relaxation of southern defences on the same day in 1950, to the extent of issuing leave passes to many officers, is not easily understood. In Washington, too, senior officials were notably absent from their posts — away fishing or relaxing — despite the fact that a major international crisis, in the form of a Chinese communist invasion of Taiwan or a United States-supported coup against Chiang Kaishek, had been predicted for this weekend. The restraining hand of General Roberts, head of the Military Assistance Group in Korea, had also been removed.[73]

The extent to which the Soviet Union was involved in the outbreak of hostilities is disputed. It was certainly widely assumed at the time that Kim Il Sung was Stalin's proxy, but little evidence was available about the relationship between the two until the publication early in the 1970s of the memoirs of Nikita Krushchev.

Krushchev refers to a visit to Moscow by Kim Il Sung at the end of 1949, at which Kim persuaded an initially reluctant Stalin to sanction an attack on the south. Since the only officially recorded visit by Kim to Moscow was in March 1949, when a treaty to establish economic and cultural (but not military) relations between the newly established DPRK and the Soviet Union was signed, it was thought that Krushchev must have been mistaken in attributing to the end of 1949 a meeting which had taken place much earlier and of which he could not have had any direct knowledge. Furthermore, any agreement to support a war must have been in the vaguest of terms if that war did not begin until fifteen months later.[74] However, in 1990 the fact of a second (secret) Kim visit to Moscow, in February 1950, was made public by the head of the Soviet Institute of Military History.[75] During a secret three-day visit to Moscow, Kim's 'Korean People's Army Preemptive Strike Plan' was apparently approved by Stalin,[76] and in a secret telegraphic exchange between Kim and Stalin, also in February, Kim apparently requested, and Stalin approved, equipment for the existing Korean People's Army's seven infantry divisions, plus another three divisions, 'so long as success is completely guaranteed'.[77]

According to Krushchev, Kim proposed to take military action to unify his country and insisted that the southern leadership would split the moment an attack was launched. Stalin, 'as a communist', could not oppose him, and Kim was told to make detailed preparations and return again to report to Moscow. Kim completed his preparations and returned, a third time, to tell Stalin that he was certain of victory. The initiative, Krushchev makes clear, was Kim Il Sung's, but Stalin did not try to stop him. Krushchev further claimed that Mao Zedong was consulted and gave positive support to Kim's plan, arguing that United

States intervention would be unlikely. On this third Moscow visit, however, and on the consultations with Mao, the (taped) Krushchev material was extremely vague,[78] although there is some Chinese confirmation of a Kim visit to Beijing in April, while en route from what might have been such a third visit to Moscow.[79] Substantial deliveries of Soviet weapons and equipment, enough to supply three newly established divisions and including tanks, arrived in April 1950 by sea and road from Vladivostok.[80]

These pointers to Stalin's complicity, even in a purely supporting role, are difficult to reconcile with the fact that Soviet military advisers in north Korea had been reduced to 120 (compared with about 500 Americans in the south) by the time of the outbreak of war,[81] and that, when the war broke out in June, the Soviet Union was absent from its seat on the Security Council, persisting in a long boycott over its position that the China seat should be transferred from Taiwan to Beijing; it was thus unable to block United States mobilisation of the world body.[82] One hypothesis is that both moves were deliberate actions taken by Stalin in order to appear to be distancing himself from North Korea, thereby diverting suspicion away from the Soviet Union and, by not attempting to plead the P'yongyang case in the United Nations, reducing the risk of escalation to world war. Stalin in this view was not incompetent, but cautious and subtle.[83] Furthermore, although most military advisers were withdrawn, there remained a substantial number of 'Soviet Koreans', or Koreans who had come to North Korea from the Soviet Union after 1945, apparently continuing to speak Russian among themselves while holding high positions in the party, government and army. Chong-Sik Lee says of them that they were controlled by Stalin, as 'Soviet citizens before they were Koreans'.[84] There were estimated to be about 500 of them in important positions.[85]

The evidence of Soviet military aid to North Korea is at least consistent with such a hypothesis. The (north) Korean People's Army was substantially reinforced in the months leading up to the war, to the point where it had 1600 artillery pieces and 258 T34 tanks.[86] That meant (according to a 1985 report by the Soviet historian G.K. Plotnikov) an overall superiority of eight times the tanks, four times the aeroplanes, 1.4 times the number of troops and 1.5 times the firearms.[87] It should be noted, however, that Plotnikov was probably wrong about the numbers of troops, and the aerial superiority he mentions was not of great significance since the northern planes — antiquated, propeller-driven craft — were totally destroyed in a matter of days once the war actually began.[88]

While the military buildup in the north was clear, it still did not make obvious sense for it to have launched the attack. A resounding defeat in the elections of 30 May 1950 had plunged the Rhee regime into such serious crisis that a propaganda campaign to overthrow it might have been effective, while avoiding the risk of United States military intervention that the Dulles speech made clear would be great in the event of war. North Korea must have gambled that the outbreak of war would precipitate a political collapse in the south and quick victory before international intervention could be organised. It clearly was not ready for the kind of prolonged warfare which ensued, but it may have believed a marginal military superiority would be sufficient given the political vulnerability of the south.

As for Mao, whether or not he was 'positive' about Kim's plans, he certainly co-operated in important ways with helping advance them to maturity. The ferment of revolution and war into which the region was cast by Japanese imperialism and the struggle for liberation greatly reduced the significance of national distinctions. The struggle for national liberation, through revolution and civil war, was seen by many in China and Korea as one and indivisible. The figure of 100 000 Koreans fighting in the Chinese People's Liberation Army in the 1940s is probably accurate,[89] and from 1945 North Korea had played an important role as secure base and support area in the vital battles against the Kuomintang.[90] With the achievement of victory in the Chinese civil war and the proclamation of the People's Republic in October 1949, those forces became redundant, and at the same time flushed with a sense of victory and a conviction that the liberation of Korea would follow. It is not at all surprising, therefore, that Kim Il Sung should have requested, and Mao authorised, the return to Korea of these troops *with their weapons*. The numbers were considerable, around 42 000 in September 1949 and another 14 000 early in 1950, with whole units simply changing their names upon incorporation into the KPA.[91] These men were battle-hardened veterans, who saw themselves as moving to a new field in the same liberation struggle.

As tension deepened after the establishment of rival states in 1948, both sides drew up contingency plans for a military resolution to the problem of national unification. Rhee spoke openly of his, but was slow to grasp the military realities and too reliant on his American sponsors; Kim was reticent, more vigorous in pursuing military preparations, and much more able to persuade his powerful friends to see things his way.

As these preparations fell into place, it is not surprising that Kim Il Sung was said to have expressed excitement on hearing of the speech on 12 January 1950 by United States Secretary of State Dean Acheson which defined a free world defence perimeter which did not include Korea.[92] The speech was misleading. It was not intended to signify any intention to abandon South Korea, but rather to stress its ability to defend itself, or the responsibility of the United Nations to support it.[93] United States thinking during early 1950 was undergoing important shifts, which were to make Kim Il Sung's venture much more hazardous than he anticipated. The 'double shocks' of communist victory in the Chinese civil war and successful explosion of the first Soviet nuclear weapons had shaken Washington. A memorandum submitted to President Truman on 12 April 1950, known simply as National Security Council 68 (NSC 68), outlined a Manichean view of struggle against a 'fanatic' Kremlin design for world hegemony, and called for increasing taxes and doubling or tripling the defence budget, while laying the groundwork for a strategic shift from containment policies to a 'roll-back' of communism.[94]

John Foster Dulles' visit to Seoul in June 1950 suggested a renewed United States commitment to supporting Rhee. In the National Assembly in Seoul on 19 June, Dulles spoke in unequivocal terms of support:

> The American people give you their support, both moral and material, consistent with your own self-respect and your primary dependence on your own efforts . . . You are not alone.[95]

In Tokyo, subsequently, Dulles spoke with General MacArthur about positive action by the United States to preserve the peace in the Far East.[96]

A showdown seemed to be approaching, whether in Korea, Taiwan[97] or elsewhere, but the evidence suggests that it was Kim Il Sung who moved first to try to resolve the otherwise intractable problem. Although documents purporting to be northern orders to launch the attack had long since been published by South Korean sources, it was impossible to dismiss the suspicion of forgery.[98] When similar, but apparently more damning, documents were found among the mass of material captured by United Nations forces in P'yongyang late in 1950, but held unread in the United States for many years, however, it began to seem that P'yongyang had indeed planned and initiated the attack (although rather hurriedly). These documents, apparently authentic, make it clear that written orders for the attack were delivered to KPA units on 17 June and preparations were completed by 23 June, with the attack being launched on the night of 24 June.[99] There is no reference in these materials to maintaining readiness against any possible attack from the south. It may even be that the original text of those orders was in Russian, as South Korea has long claimed, since a former KPA officer, Ju Yonbok, testified that he had personally translated the orders handed to him by (Soviet) Colonel Tolkin relating to the engineer detachments, and that he had then seen the originals burned.[100]

The war actually began on the Ongjin Peninsula, at the western extremity of the 38th parallel, on 25 June. This is, as Cumings points out, a strange place for the north to choose to launch an invasion. It was held by the best forces in the south's army, and it led nowhere, being a geographical cul de sac. From the southern point of view, on the other hand, it was the obvious attacking route, since just across the border northwards lay rail and other communications giving easy access to P'yongyang. The last Sunday in June 1949 had been the occasion for the south to launch its most intense assault of that year. Not only that, but there is strong evidence to suggest that similar military action was planned for the precise day on which the war began in 1950. The former Rear Admiral in the South Korean Navy, Yi Yongun, has stated that in 1950 he was in charge of a small naval detachment which launched

attacks across the border against 'Haeju districts' in order to divert
attention from a general invasion of the north planned to commence at
5 a.m. on 25 June.[101] Some evidence from intelligence material tends to
confirm what Admiral Yi says, although it does not establish any plan of
general invasion.[102]

What all this seems to point to is the astonishing hypothesis that both
sides chose to launch a war on *precisely the same day*, or at least (and the
difference is significant) to launch cross-border military activity of some
kind. Once the fighting started, the failure of the south to offer more
than token resistance, and the rapid abandonment of points where it
had clear superiority of force, thus opening the route to Seoul, is also
quite puzzling.[103]

Cumings suggests a hypothesis to account for all this: that the south
(and its United States backers) may have deliberately provoked the north
in the Ongjin area with a view to inducing attack, securing United States
(and United Nations) intervention, and saving the tottering Rhee
regime, while also initiating a new aggressive ('roll-back') phase in
United States policy towards Asia and the communist world. With the
benefit of hindsight, it is as plausible as the hypothesis adopted by the
United Nations in 1950.

Fighting the war

SEOUL SUMMER

By the end of August 1950, the war was stalemated along the lines of
greatest northern advance, the so-called 'Pusan Perimeter', but the
length of northern supply lines, their vulnerability to United States air
attack and the gradual build-up of men and equipment on the United
States/United Nations side made further advance extremely difficult.
Their forces had lost 58 000 casualties, and the remaining 70 000 were
substantially outnumbered and outgunned.[104] When General MacArthur
launched his 'Inchon Landings' operation on 15 September, effectively
cutting the northern forces in half by landing his huge armada behind
their lines, the north Korean army appeared to collapse almost as
suddenly as it had exploded across the border less than three months
earlier.

The (northern) Korean People's Army occupation of Seoul and much
of south Korea lasted only about two months, but the process of
'liberation' of part of a country by forces representing a sharply
contrasting set of values was inevitably traumatic. However, the
occupation does not appear to have been particularly brutal or vindictive.
General William Dean, commander of the United States forces at the
battle of Taejon, who spent several weeks cut off from his command
before being captured, remarked later that: 'To me, the civilian attitude
seemed to vary between enthusiasm and passive acceptance.'[105] A United
States Air Force study of the occupation of Seoul noted that it was a time

of 'music, theatre, parades, huge spectacles', during which the invaders 'in general were not ruthless'. A simple program was propounded, of 'a united and free Korea, land redistribution and nationalisation of industry, equal status for women, a broad program of social betterment, lower prices and an assured living for workers, and more efficient and honest government', and there was little doubt that many of the people approved the program presented.[106] The restoration of People's Committees and the implementation of land reform were undoubtedly popular.[107] Youth were forcibly impressed into the northern forces,[108] and executions occurred, especially as collapse became imminent, but they seem in the main to have been sporadic, and the responsibility of local units rather than main force KPA.[109] While the 'masses' did not rise up with spontaneous enthusiasm to welcome the KPA,[110] nevertheless the overall picture adds up to something less than 'bestiality', the term chosen by the authors of the Air Force report to characterise it.

At the end of July, the south Korean government had been described by the special assistant to the United Nations Secretary-General, Colonel Alfred Katzin, as 'a useless mob', and 'all authority' was held by the Army and American Ambassador.[111] These impressions may have been superficial, however, since Rhee was able to write to MacArthur on 12 August describing the withdrawal as 'tactical', 'in the hope that American reinforcements would arive soon enough to launch an offensive before losing too much ground.'[112] If so, the plan certainly worked. By the end of September, Rhee was back in Seoul. The fortunes of war suddenly turned dramatically in his favour, and the crumbling of north Korean resistance before the massive assault launched at Inchon fed his hopes of dominating a united Korea.

YALU AUTUMN

The United Nations forces might have rested content with dispatching the KPA back across the 38th parallel, but instead quickly resolved to pursue it across the old frontier and destroy it. Initiatives towards holding United Nations-supervised elections were rejected, and instead a resolution calling for 'all appropriate steps' to be taken to establish a unified, independent, democratic Korea was adopted on 7 October in the General Assembly.[113] In place of the United Nations Commission on Korea, a United Nations Commission for the Unification and Rehabilitation of Korea (UNCURK) was set up. The move across the old north–south border and towards the Chinese and Soviet frontiers not only threatened the extinction of the Kim Il Sung regime, but also carried a risk of widening the conflict from regional to world war. Both Chinese and Soviet forces became directly involved in this next phase of the war. A Chinese force of 250 000 men actually crossed the Yalu River frontier on the night of 19 October.[114] When repeated warnings against continuing the United Nations advance were ignored, they launched a massive counter-offensive against the United Nations forces on

25 November, bringing another sudden and dramatic reversal in the fortunes of the war and forcing a retreat that for a time seemed likely to turn into a rout. By 5 December, P'yongyang had been recaptured, and the decision was taken once again to ignore the old north–south frontier and strive for total victory against the United Nations forces rather than negotiate a settlement. On 25 December, the combined force of the KPA and the Chinese People's Volunteers (CPV) crossed the 38th parallel and on 4 January recaptured Seoul.

New evidence emerged in the 1980s to clarify the thinking behind China's decision to enter the fray in Korea. It is clear that China's leaders had no foreknowledge that the war was about to begin — the process of demobilisation of 1.4 million men of the People's Liberation Army had begun only five days before the Korean War started, and China had neither a diplomatic mission in P'yongyang nor any substantial body of troops in the vicinity at that time. However, the probability of involvement was foreseen from the start, and the need to prevent United States forces from advancing to the Yalu River frontiers of China, and therefore to prevent the destruction of Kim Il Sung's regime, was recognised. Though deeply reluctant to commit Chinese forces outside the country when all efforts needed to be concentrated on national reconstruction after the devastation of long civil war, the advantages of facing the United States in Korea rather than either of the other likely places, the Taiwan Straits or Vietnam, were appreciated by Mao and others.[115]

Even when it seemed that Kim Il Sung's advances down the Korean peninsula in June and July were irresistible, and long before Inchon, the Chinese leaders began preparations. The 13th Army Corps (a force made up of four armies) was ordered from the Central-Southern Military Region to the Yalu on 7 July, where it was renamed the North-Eastern Frontier Defence Army. This was the main element in the force which later became the CPV. An ambassador and a military observer mission were also sent. On 18 August, Mao ordered that preparations for dispatch of the force to Korea be completed by the end of September. He (and others in the leadership) clearly foresaw the dangers in the long extension of the KPA lines and their vulnerability to a United Nations counter-attack by sea from somewhere behind their lines — precisely what happened at Inchon. Mao apparently pleaded with Kim Il Sung and Stalin for caution, but to no avail.

After Inchon, and an urgent appeal from Kim Il Sung on 1 October, an enlarged Politburo meeting of the Chinese leadership decided, despite strong reservations, that intervention was necessary. On 2 October, Mao cabled Stalin to request air support (since China still had no air force) and material help with supplies. Stalin at first agreed to both, but the fear of provoking the United States to direct, and possibly nuclear, conflict made him change his mind (on 10 October) to the extent of withdrawing the promise of air support. Despite an urgent personal plea from Zhou Enlai who immediately flew to see him, Stalin persisted in this refusal. In Beijing, after 60 sleepless hours'[116] brooding on the costs that were bound to follow, including the possible nuclear devastation of China's cities, Mao made up his mind on 13 October. On the night of 19 October, 250 000 Chinese soldiers, described as 'volunteers', crossed the Yalu River into Korea. Kim Il Sung was delighted.[117]

Furthermore, although China had decided to send in its forces even without the benefit of air support, Stalin again changed his mind on this question. He is said to have been so moved by the Chinese decision that he wept.[118] Not until 1989 was it made clear officially in the Soviet Union that a Soviet Air Force unit had fought in Korea, and the significance of the fact that for two and a half years a secret full-scale war had been fought between America and Russia in Korean, Chinese and Russian skies, involving thousands of aircraft and lives, was only slowly appreciated.[119] Departing from Moscow by train in mid-November, this unit and its 200 MIG fighters, commanded by Lt General Georgy Lobov, operated in the northern parts of North Korea, dressed in Chinese uniforms, with Chinese markings on their planes and only flying missions over territory controlled by north Korean–Chinese forces. They also helped train the new Chinese Air Force which expanded rapidly from 400 MIG's in June 1951 to 2000 by July 1953. Although their losses, especially initially, were heavy, they claim to have shot down over 1300 United States planes, damaging hundreds more for losses of 345 of their own.[120] Lobov himself is said to have shot down fourteen United States planes.[121] Chinese pilots suffered much heavier casualties, well over 2000.[122]

What had begun as a civil conflict between north and south was massively expanded by the intervention, first, of the United States, then of the other nations that made up the United Nations Command, then of a top-secret Japanese naval unit, under the command of [later] Rear-Admiral Okubo which undertook in October 1950 to clear north Korean harbours of mines and facilitate the United Nations' northwards push,[123] and then of China and the Soviet Union in November. As the tide of battle turned against the United Nations forces, a further escalation was seriously considered, this time a qualitative one — the use of nuclear weapons.

The bomb

The American mood turned from optimism in mid-November to gloom and desperation after the Chinese assault. Evacuation, and the establishment of a 'new Korea' by relocating 328 000 South Koreans to the remote islands of Savaii and Upolu in the Western Samoa group (administered by New Zealand under a United Nations mandate), was one option considered.[124] The other was escalation.

On 30 November, President Truman announced that the use of nuclear weapons was under active consideration, adding that he saw no need for United Nations authorisation. This caused such consternation among America's allies that British Prime Minister Clement Attlee flew to Washington to urge restraint. In fact, Truman was considering not only the use of the bomb, but also air attacks on China and a blockade of the Chinese coast, and his Joint Chiefs of Staff were also contemplating assisting the Kuomintang in an effort to recapture the mainland. MacArthur, on 9 December, asked for 26 atomic bombs and the right to use them at his discretion, listing cities such as Peking, Dairen, Port Arthur, Vladivostok and Khabarovsk as possible targets. He also developed a plan to end the war in ten days by dropping atomic bombs across the 'neck' of Manchuria (i.e. north of the Yalu River frontier), introducing half a million Kuomintang troops from Taiwan, and then spreading from the Sea of Japan to the Yellow Sea 'a belt of radioactive cobalt . . . [which] has an active life of between sixty and 120 years'.

Contrary to his assurances to Prime Minister Attlee, Truman did order bombs to be sent, unassembled, to aircraft carriers off the Korean coast, and also authorised 'dummy' nuclear runs over North Korea.[125] Ultimately, however, it was the combination of doubt about whether nuclear weapons could be used *effectively*, given the gradual deepening of the Chinese–Korean defensive bunkers and tunnels — ultimately a 1250 kilometre labyrinth'[126] — and the difficulty of finding appropriate targets (large military and industrial installations) without launching all-out war on China; whether they could be used *safely*, given the closeness of the opposing forces; and whether they could be used *without overwhelmingly adverse international reaction*, either in the form of enemy counter-attack (perhaps against Japan's cities), or allied condemnation of the United States for escalation of the war and use of 'terror' weapons, rather than any moral scruples that prevented the bomb being used in Korea.[127]

Furthermore, the application of massive 'conventional' firepower, including napalm, eventually arrested the Chinese–Korean advance and made it possible in late January 1951 to launch a counter-offensive. Nuclear weapons were seriously considered from time to time thereafter during the war, however — and long after the dismissal of General MacArthur on 11 April 1951. General Ridgway sought authorisation in May 1951,[128] and there was another period of extreme danger at the end of 1951. Between March and May 1953, President Eisenhower was also greatly attracted by the nuclear option, which he noted was 'cheaper dollar-wise' than conventional methods.[129] Ultimately allied pressure, combined with a pragmatic concern over the possibility of Soviet retaliation and a breakthrough in the peace talks, saved Korea (and possibly the world) from nuclear conflagration

Germ warfare

The question of whether bacteriological ('germ') warfare was also employed in Korea is still unclear, but the purely pragmatic nature of the thinking on the nuclear issue — and also the issue of chemical warfare, which is known to have been seriously considered, with huge stockpiles of Sarin nerve gas being readied for use in Korea[130]— suggests that ethical considerations were of little import and that the Chinese–North Korean allegations, still not conclusively disproved, deserve attention. As of the early 1990s, this remained perhaps the largest single question still to be clarified from the Korean War.

The allegation of use of bacteriological warfare by United Nations forces was first made by the Chinese–north Korean side in May 1951, after smallpox and typhoid had broken out in areas abandoned by United States troops as they began their retreat from north Korea in the winter of 1950–51. In February 1952, the further claim was made that low-flying United States planes had dropped bacterial bombs designed to disseminate plague, typhoid, anthrax and other diseases. Confessions of captured United States airmen were broadcast in support of the allegations, and details of locations, casualties, types of bacteria and mechanisms of conveyance were published.

The allegations were quickly developed into a campaign by Soviet and Chinese propaganda organs, and were as vehemently denied by the United States. The confessions were attributed to 'brain-washing'. An 'International Scientific Commission for the Investigation of the Facts Concerning Bacterial Warfare in Korea and China' was organised under the auspices of the World Peace Council, with experts from Brazil, Britain, France, Italy, Sweden and the Soviet Union; it conducted investigations in Korea and China between June and August 1952. The commission's 700-page report, published in English in Peking in 1952, concluded that such weapons had indeed been used. Though attacked as a 'fellow-travelling' organisation, the credentials of this group were impressive, with perhaps the most outstanding being the Cambridge embryologist (and later eminent historian of Chinese science) Joseph Needham.

In the Cold War atmosphere of the 1950s, two points in particular were attacked: the feasibility of the military use of bacteriological weapons and the credibility of the confessions of the United States airmen. On the former, the report linked the allegations from Korea with evidence of Japanese use of bacteriological weapons against China before and during the Second World War, noting the apparent similarity between the diseases and the methods of delivery. In the 1950s, the principal evidence of these matters was the Soviet War Crimes trials, which had been held at Khabarovsk in 1949 and had tried and found guilty a number of Japanese officers of a unit known as 'Unit 731' or the 'Ishii Unit'.

This Japanese unit had employed at its headquarters in Harbin in Northeast China up to 3000 researchers to work on the development and military use of organisms to spread a wide variety of diseases, and had experimented on and killed many Chinese, Russian and other prisoners. The Soviet revelations about it, however, were treated in the 1950s as 'vicious and unfounded propaganda'. Only in the 1970s did it become clear that they had been true in every particular, since many of those involved began to speak openly about their work, and documents released in the United States under Freedom of Information legislation showed that the United States government had known of the facts and had deliberately lied to cover up its knowledge, while protecting the principals of the Japanese unit and taking over all its documents and materials.[131] The view that it was impossible to harness bacteriological material for warfare, influential at the time in expert opinions by other scientists, was incorrect. Likewise, the analogy between the pathogens and the means of delivery employed by the Japanese and those alleged to have been employed by the Americans, and the possible direct linkage between the two, called for close investigation rather than angry rebuttal. Furthermore, apart from the United States connection with Japanese work in this area, we now know that the United States itself had long been interested in bacteriological warfare possibilities and had considered using such means to destroy Japanese food crops during the last stages of the war in 1945.

Furthermore, independently of the Japanese link, it has been established that the United States had a clear capacity to wage bacteriological warfare at the time when the Korean allegations were launched. Its usefulness had been debated in military circles and journals, and in the very month (December 1950) in which the former head of United States Naval Intelligence, Rear Admiral Elis M. Zachharias, had told a Congressional Committee that 'Germ warfare combined with a devastation of crops and cattle could soon reduce the Russians and their satellites to impotence', smallpox broke out in those provinces of north Korea from which the United States forces had just withdrawn, with a typhus outbreak following shortly afterwards.[132] The tactic of 'seeding' territory about to be abandoned with pathogens was one developed and practised by the Japanese in China in 1941–42. Furthermore, in 1976 William Colby, Director of the CIA, admitted that the Army Bacteriological Warfare Laboratories at Fort Detrick in Maryland had been commissioned early in 1952 to develop both bacteriological agents and delivery systems, while extensive experimentation had been carried out in various places in the United States, including the New York subway system and the Pentagon water supply system. In other words, there is plenty of circumstantial evidence to make credible the Chinese–north Korean charges.

The reliance of the International Commission on evidence in the form of confessions by captured United States pilots is much more controversial. Statements by people in captivity can never have the same value as those by people who are free, and in fact most, but not all, of the captured American pilots who 'confessed' while in captivity recanted their confessions later. However, the gap between the extremely specific nature of the material of the confessions and the very general terms of the recanting leaves some room for doubt. The circumstances under which the latter statements were drafted, while facing the threat of possible prosecution for treason, were scarcely more conducive to objectivity and detachment than those under which the original claims were made.

It is true, of course, that the diseases of which north Korea and China complained were basically contained, by dint of a massive public health campaign. However, one disease, epidemic haemorrhagic fever (EHF), which had been previously unknown in Korea, broke out there in April 1951 and has continued to this day to be a serious health problem, having spread in the meantime also to parts of China and to Japan. This is a disease with an offensive potential which is known to have been the subject of considerable research by the Japanese germ warfare establishment in the 1930s and 1940s, and it is probable that both detailed research information and specimens passed into American hands between the autumn of 1945 and the spring of 1947.[133] The hypothesis that this disease may have been deliberately introduced into Korea, in a move which backfired and then led to pollution of the entire region, remains plausible. So too does the general question of whether there was a larger, covert United States operation, perhaps partly experimental and partly designed to sow panic and confusion rather than actually to annihilate the enemy.

'CONVENTIONAL' WAR

So-called 'conventional' weapons were themselves enough to exact a terrible toll. Napalm was employed on a massive scale, 7.8 million gallons (35.4 million litres) of it in only the first three months of the war.[134] In London, Winston Churchill protested without avail to his advisers about 'splashing it [napalm] about all over the civilian population',[135] and some pilots expressed shock at having 'killed civilians, friendly civilians, and bombed their homes; fired whole villages with their occupants . . .'[136] General Curtis LeMay, hero of the saturation bombing of Japan in 1945, boasted that 'over a period of three years or so . . . we burned down every [sic] town in North Korea and South Korea too'. [137] Attacks on the fabric of civil society also included a June 1952 raid by 500 bombers which destroyed a complex of hydroelectric power stations on the Yalu River, the huge assaults of July and August 1952 on the city of P'yongyang (697 tonnes of bombs and 10 000 litres of napalm) which produced a civilian death toll of 6000, and finally, in May 1953, the bombing of the irrigation dams on which the agricultural infrastructure of the country depended. The latter raid was designed to starve the enemy into submission.[138]

Whoever started the war, it was the forces of the United Nations which devastated the country, and an overwhelming proportion of casualties were civilian. The northern side, whatever its moral qualities or the justice or otherwise of its cause, simply did not have the capacity to mete out indiscriminate death to the civilian population by bombing, strafing, napalming, blasting dams or destroying food crops.

ATROCITIES

Despite this striking fact, it is remarkable that the reverse should have been commonly assumed about Korea. Though it should be clear that the acts listed above qualify as atrocities, they are not commonly considered so. Instead, the torture and murder of civilians, prisoners or combatants is generally considered an atrocity only when the act is carried out in direct, person-to-person, 'low-tech' fashion, not when delivered by 'hi-tech', remote control from a bomber or as the result of a bureaucrat's decision.

This is a very delicate subject. Civil war excites bitter passions which are notoriously difficult to contain in structured and disciplined military activity. In the Korean War in particular, the fact that Seoul was repeatedly 'liberated' by both sides meant that those seen by the 'liberating' force at any time as having collaborated with the preceding occupation were liable to be rooted out and punished, often by torture and execution. When Seoul was recaptured from the KPA after Inchon, many people were executed, perhaps as many as 29 000; [139] by the time Seoul was recaptured a second time by United Nations forces in March 1951, its population was down to 200 000 (from 1.5 million), its water supply had collapsed and illness was rife.[140] The fate of P'yongyang and many other cities and villages was similar. There is no agreed figure for the number of those killed during the South Korean 'liberation' of P'yongyang and much of North Korea in 1950, but internal United States intelligence and governmental reports indicate that what happened was 'a nauseating reign of terror,'[141] and one Japanese estimate is that 150 000 people were executed or kidnapped during the 'liberation'.[142] A consideration of these very unpleasant issues suggests that, while the Geneva Conventions were little honoured in Korea, there was a political difference in the character of the war both sides were fighting, and consequently in the tactics appropriate or necessary.

At the outbreak of war in 1950, one of the first acts of the Rhee regime was to order the execution of political prisoners, whose deaths were in due course attributed to atrocities by the incoming northern forces. In Seoul, there was only time to execute 'about a hundred communists' (according to an Australian diplomatic source), but in Pusan an estimated 50 000 were killed,[143] and Gregory Henderson, then a United States Embassy official in Seoul, estimated that throughout the country, 'probably over 100 000' people were killed without any trial or legal warrant at this time.[144] The northern occupation of Seoul, by contrast, began with the opening of the gaol and the release of all who had survived (because there had not been enough time to shoot them). Some of those released clearly had vengeance on their minds, but the studies of the northern occupation (as noted above) indicate only sporadic incidents of brutality.

Undoubtedly, the chaotic conditions of the summer of 1950 that followed the invasion bred the worst atrocities. There is no doubt that prisoners were on occasion murdered by their north Korean captors,[145] although the major American study of the matter concludes that:

> There is no evidence that such acts of barbarism against UN soldiers were ever countenanced by NKPA commanders — in fact, orders were issued by the Advanced General Headquarters of the North Korean Army to prevent the unnecessary slaughter of prisoners of war.[146]

However, the official United States Army report issued at the end of the war gave a total figure of civilian victims of atrocities of 7334 (which it will be noted is a small fraction of those executed by Rhee in the first moments of the war alone). Of that 7334, the deaths of unnumbered civilians, variously estimated from 5000 to 7500 (sic), were attributed to a single incident, known as the 'Taejon Massacre'. This incident, described as 'worthy of being recorded in the annals of history along with the Rape of Nanking, the Warsaw Ghetto, and other similar mass exterminations', was the centrepiece in the United States case of brutality against north Korea, and since the majority of civilian victims of the entire war seem to stem from it, it must be treated very seriously. The United States Army report, including some shocking pictures, was given massive publicity around the world in October 1953.[147]

The first thing to be noted about this report is that it was seriously inaccurate in some obvious respects. The Australian government was astonished to find a figure of twenty Australian atrocity victims listed. Its investigations showed that all were confirmed battle deaths, and the twenty comprised seventeen Australians, one new Zealander, one American and one other unidentified person. Interrogation of Australian POWs after release revealed 'NO (sic) evidence of torture or atrocities to Aust POW'.[148]

As for Taejon, a massacre undoubtedly occurred, but what precisely happened, when and who was responsible remain to be settled. The first published references to the massacre appeared in an article in the English (communist) paper, the *Daily Worker*, dated 9 August 1950.[149] Its correspondent, Alan Winnington, accompanying the (Northern) Korean People's Army on their march southwards, reported having inspected mass graves at a village called 'Rangwul' near Taejon, which is about 160 kilometres south of Seoul.[150] He concluded from inspection of the graves, photographic evidence and discussions with villagers in the vicinity, that approximately 7000 prisoners from the gaols of Taejon and nearby had been summarily executed at that spot between 6 and 21 July (when the area was captured by the KPA), and buried in mass graves dug by locally press-ganged peasants. His report was reproduced in a pamphlet, *I Saw the Truth in Korea*, which so distressed the British Cabinet that serious consideration was given to trying him for treason (sic).[151] Except in the sense of the outrage they provoked in London, Winnington's allegations, repeated in his posthumously published autobiography, were never treated seriously, were never investigated, and were not mentioned in the subsequent United States Army report.

As it happened, the two Australian officers who earlier had constituted the UNCOK Field Observer team, Major Peach and Wing Commander Rankin, were in the Taejon area at the precise time that Winnington concluded the massacre must have taken place, acting as liaison officers between the United Nations and south Korean forces.

On 9 July (according to Peach's 1950 dispatch), he and Rankin were on the 'road from Taejon to Konju . . . along the Kum River, a few miles short of Konju'. Trucks loaded with prisoners were going south before the northern advance.[152] As Peach later recalled the incident: 'Before my very eyes I saw at least two or three killed, their heads broken like eggs with the butts of rifles.'[153]

Later, in Konju, he was told that prisoners from the Konju gaol were being shot.[154] Peach reported details to the South Korean Home Minister but believed that nothing was done. A contemporary photograph in the London *Picture Post* shows a truckload of such prisoners on the banks of the Kum River abour halfway between Seoul and Pusan 'on their way to execution'.[155] They were described as 'South Korean suspected traitors'. Four days later, on 13 July, the northern forces crossed the Kum River, and on 20 July captured Taejon. When Winnington reached Taejon, the city was still burning. The sequence of events strongly suggests that Winnington, Peach and Rankin were all witnesses to different stages of the same terrible event.

There was one further witness, whose testimony strengthens the suspicion. Philip Deane, in 1950 correspondent for the London *Observer*, was told this story while in a prison camp in north Korea after his capture of a massacre in Taejon just before the town fell to the communists. His informant was a French priest, Father Cadars, and Cadars' veracity seemed beyond dispute. Deane wrote as follows:

> [Fr Cadars] told me that just before the Americans retreated from the town, South Korean police had brought into a forest clearing near his church 1700 men, loaded layer upon layer into trucks. These prisoners were ordered out and ordered to dig long trenches. Father Cadars watched. Some American officers, Cadars said were also watching. When a certain amount of digging was complete, South Korean policemen shot half the prisoners in the back of the neck. The other half were then ordered to bury the dead.[156]

After Father Cadars' protest was dismissed, the remainder were likewise killed. He was told they were 'Communist guerrillas who rebelled in the Taejon gaol'.

Unless, by some terrible fate, there were two massacres in the Taejon vicinity — the one described by Winnington and Cadars which occurred in July and was perpetrated by the Rhee forces, and the one which is described by the United States Army as having occurred in late September and having been comitted by the KPA — it is hard to avoid the suspicion that the events witnessed by all these men were aspects of the same unfolding massacre. In 1992, however, more than 40 years after the events occurred, a full account was published for the first time in a South Korean monthly journal.[157] What Winnington wrote was confirmed (except for some discrepancy in the numbers involved) by eyewitnesses and men who had actually taken part in the massacre. The only matter which remained unclear was whether Americans had been directly involved or not.

We now know, therefore, that the atrocity which the United States Army describes as the worst of the war, ranking with the Rape of Nanking and Belsen, was committed by forces acting in the name of the United Nations.[158]

Ending the war

The hubris of victory led the United Nations side into strategic error and severe military reverse when it crossed the 38th parallel and tried to wipe out the Kim Il Sung regime in October 1950. Likewise, it led Mao and the joint Chinese–north Korean forces into mistake and caused an immense prolongation of the war when they crossed the same line southwards early in 1951. With the United Nations committed, there was clearly no way to wipe out the Rhee regime; the best to be hoped for was a negotiated settlement on advantageous terms. That might have been possible had the advance been stopped before Seoul, at a moment of triumph. Instead, the victorious forces drove on, Mao and Kim Il Sung repeating the mistake of Truman and MacArthur.

The United Nations counter-offensive soon forced the northern forces to give up Seoul again, and the war gradually entered a phase of virtual stalemate and positional warfare, with huge armies more or less evenly balanced on the ground, see-sawing back and forth across a relatively narrow band of territory in the general vicinity of where the war had begun. Behind the lines, there was no such balance, since the United Nations side had virtually total control of the air and the sea, using it to pound north Korea mercilessly — the siege of Wonsan by aerial and naval bombardment lasted for 861 days.[159] In July 1951, however, talks towards a settlement opened in the town of Kaesong. The north Korean delegate, Li Sang-Jo, who as of 1990 was living in the Soviet Union, has remarked that his side expected the talks to last a few days; the war, having begun at the parallel, would also end there.[160] Actually the war was to last another two years.

The first problem was where to draw the new line — on the 38th parallel again, or on the 'actual line of contact on the battlefield', which was difficult to define since much territory was contested. Initially the understanding was that the line would be the former, but the United States refused, 'as a matter of major principle', to accept that, and began a new push northwards.[161] Then the problem became one of defining the 'battle line', with the United States attempting to persuade the other side to cede teritory actually in its control in return for a United States–United Nations agreement to refrain from exploiting its air and naval supremacy. This attempt to 'persuade' was reinforced by a bombing raid on the supposedly 'neutral' city of Kaesong, which narrowly missed the

Chinese–north Korean negotiating team.[162] While an international propaganda campaign was launched to blacken the Chinese–north Korean side as the perpetrators of atrocities and as fanatical and unreasonable negotiators, the efforts of a couple of Western journalists covering the peace talks — Alan Winnington of the British *Daily Worker* and Wilfred Burchett of the French *Ce Soir* — in exposing the actual negotiating positions of the parties were extremely embarrassing.[163]

The talks resumed on 25 October 1951, at the new site of Panmunjom, after intense nuclear intimidation and sustained bombardment of North Korea and some of the fiercest land battles of the entire war, on 'Heartbreak Ridge' or Height 1211. But this time, with the line more or less agreed, a new bone of contention emerged, the issue of prisoners-of-war and their repatriation. The Communist side proposed the implementation of the 1949 Geneva Convention (Article 128), which called for immediate and total repatriation of all prisoners upon cessation of hostilities, but the United States countered with a new principle, 'voluntary repatriation' — ostensibly (and at least in part) on the humanitarian ground of provision of freedom of choice, but also out of determination to inflict severe propaganda defeat on the other side by demonstrating that, given a choice, many prisoners would refuse repatriation to 'tyranny'.

The general principle of 'voluntary repatriation' is clearly just and correct, as demonstrated by the cruel fate of those Soviet citizens compulsorily returned to Stalin after 1945, but a 'major' United States objective was 'to inflict upon the Communists a propaganda defeat.' As the chief United States–United Nations negotiator at Panmunjom, Admiral C. Turner Joy, later wrote:

> It was thought that if any substantial portion of the ex-Communist soldiers refused to return to Communism, a huge setback to Communist subversive activities would ensue. I regret to say this does not seem to have been a valid point.[164]

Whatever the validity of the point, much of the war was fought because of it. The United Nations side suffered 140 000 casualties, including 9000 American dead, and in all about 500 000 civilian Koreans died as the war dragged on.[165] Within the camps, the determination to gain a propaganda victory on the United States side, and the determination likewise on the Chinese–north Korean side to resist, led to the imposition of a reign of terror and brutality, during which, on the admission of General Ridgway's Head Office, more POWs were admitted to have died in United Nations camps than in north Korean camps where conditions were said to be so bad.[166] Most of the camp control was given to south Korean or Chinese (Nationalist) guards, and those prisoners who expressed a wish to return home were tattooed with anti-communist slogans and 'either beaten black and blue or killed (sic)', according to Admiral Turner Joy.[167] Major rebellions occurred, which were put down with tanks and flame-throwers, and 334 prisoners were killed by their guards.[168]

Ultimately 21 839 prisoners were not returned to north Korea or China,[169] but the outcome was far from being a propaganda triumph, as even one in five of those Korean prisoners whose homes were in the south chose to go north.[170] There had been little of the atmosphere necessary to make any free choice, and the December 1953 report of the Neutral Nations Repatriation Committee concluded that 'any prisoner who desired repatriation had to do so clandestinely and in fear of his life'.[171] The experience of captivity under such conditions so over-whelmed some of the prisoners that they refused to have anything to do with either south or north Korea afterwards, preferring instead to go into exile in India, and later Brazil.[172]

The counterpart of the reign of terror that 'voluntary repatriation' brought to the United Nations prisoner camps in the south was an intense propaganda campaign to establish that camps in the north were worse. In November 1951, the Judge-Advocate of the United States 8th Army, Colonel James Hanley, claimed that over 5500 prisoners had been massacred since the war began. That figure was much later reduced to 365 (sic) United States POWs whose deaths as a result of 'atrocities' could be confirmed.[173] Allegations of 'brain-washing' of prisoners, particularly of United States pilots who 'confessed' to taking part in bacteriological warfare bombing raids, were also widely circulated. In general, however — and setting aside well-known cases of murder and various ill-treatments of prisoners during the chaotic conditions of 1950–51 — official studies of this problem concluded, as did the Australian Army, that 'interrogation of Austn (sic) P.O.W. revealed no evidence of torture or atrocities to Austn P.O.W.'[174] No less an authority than Britain's (former) chief of the Defence Staff, Lord Carver, agreed that 'The UN prisoners in Chinese hands . . . were certainly much better off in every way than any held by the Americans' (italics added).[175] Despite this, the intense American propaganda effort to establish the opposite was largely successful.

A further factor which delayed a peace settlement was the stubborn refusal of the Syngman Rhee regime to countenance an end to war on any terms other than victory, and the use of terror and intimidation by the Rhee regime — at the heart of the 'free world's struggle for democracy' — to maintain Rhee himself in power. On 23 May 1952, Rhee declared martial law in Pusan and its adjacent areas (where the government was then functioning) and two days later began arresting political opponents. James Plimsoll, Australian delegate on UNCURK, described it as 'virtually . . . a coup d'etat', which involved the 'wiping out of public life (and perhaps killing) those persons on whom we depended to build a new democratic Korea.'[176] As conspiracy trials ground on in the courts and intimidatory mobs surrounded the National Assembly to ensure passage of the constitutional reforms necesary for Rhee to retain power, the United States authorities agonised over plans for their own coup, to overthrow him.[177]

Eventually the 'voluntary' principle was accepted, prisoners were exchanged, and a ceasefire was signed on 27 July 1953, after just over three years and one month of fighting, restoring a border which gave the south territory at the centre and eastern end of the 38th parallel, and the north territory at the western end. The ceasefire, signed by China and north Korea on the one side and the United States (but not south Korea) on the other, had still not, as of the early 1990s, been converted into any permanent peace settlement. Shock and devastation in both Koreas was profound. If there was no victor, there were countless victims — relatively more in north Korea in terms of population than there were in the Soviet Union at the end of the Second World War.

By 1953, the peninsula was devastated. The generation that survived, scarred for life by the experience, was still seeking to heal the physical and psychological wounds of war 40 years later, and to resolve the problem that gave rise to the war in the first place: national division. However, the violence of war had torn people from their village and traditional roots, mobilising them into armies and political movements, and confronted them with 'modernity', albeit it in its most brutal form. War therefore cleared the way for profound social, economic and political transformation, and released enormous energies in both halves of the country in the years that followed.

Notes

1 The following account draws from Gavan McCormack's 1983 book on this subject, *Cold War Hot War: An Australian Perspective on the Korean War*, Sydney, 1983, but updates and in some respects substantially revises that account.
2 See especially Cumings, 1981. One 'conservative' estimate of the numbers fleeing from north to south between 1945 and 1947 is 800 000: Scalapino and Lee, 1972, p. 349n.
3 Cumings, 1981, pp. 120–21
4 ibid., especially Chapter 8
5 United States Department of State, *Foreign Relations of the United States*, 1945, vol 6, pp. 1043–44 (hereafter: FRUS)
6 Cumings, 1981, pp. 127ff
7 On the circumstances surrounding the 18 October return of Rhee, see Cumings, 1981, pp. 188–91
8 Dae-Sook Suh, 1967, pp. 298–99
9 Cumings, 1981, p. 209
10 ibid., p. 350
11 Joyce and Gabriel Kolko, *The Limits of Power*, New York, 1972, p. 291
12 ibid., p. 290
13 Cumings, 1981, pp. 91–100. See also Cumings, 1990, pp. 185–93
14 ibid., pp. 216ff
15 'American relations with the Soviet Union', Report submitted to the president on 24 September 1946, quoted in Yonosuke Nagai, 'The Roots of Cold War Doctrine', in Nagai and Iriye, 1977, p. 22
16 Gayn, 1981, p. 263
17 For a detailed account, see Cumings, 1981, Chapters 10 and 11.

18 Wada Haruki, 'Soren no chosen seisaku, sen kyuhaku yon-ju go nen hachi-gatsu — ju-gatsu', *Shakaikagaku Kenkyu*, vol. 33, no. 4, November 1981, pp. 91–147, at pp. 124 and 128; and for an English (if slightly different) text of the Chistiakov proclamation, see Wilfred Burchett, *This Monstrous War*, Melbourne, 1952, pp. 27–28.

19 Cumings, 1981, p. 393. See also Yi Kyongmin, 'Kita Chosen ni okeru 8.15', part 1, Sapporo University, *Keizai to keiei*, no 1, June 1991, pp. 41–63.

20 Quoted in Cumings 1981, p. 402

21 Halliday and Cumings, 1988, p. 57

22 George McCune, *Korea Today*, Cambridge, Mass., 1950, p. 181

23 See Wada Haruki, *Kin Nissei to Manshu konichi senso* (Kim Il Sung and the Manchurian Anti-Japanese War), Heibonsha, 1992, pp. 330ff.

24 Robert A. Scalapino and Chong-Sik Lee, *Communism in Korea*, Part 1, *The Movement*, Berkeley, LA and London, 1972, pp. 339–40

25 ibid., pp. 140, 185ff, 273ff, 306

26 'Stalin ga Kin Nissei o mensetsu tesuto' (Stalin's interview test for Kim Il Sung), *This is Yomiuri*, February 1992, pp. 84-87. This is a Japanese translation of the Korean text originally appearing in *Chungang ilbo* of inerviews with both General Lebedev and Colonel Mekler.

27 Quoted in Aeba Takanori and NHK shusaihan, *Chosen senso*, Tokyo, NHK, 1990, p. 73 (hereafter cited as NHK)

28 McCune, pp. 291–92

29 From an April 1947 State Department document quoted in Cumings, 1990, p. 66

30 Hodge on 21 November 1947, quoted in Cumings, 1990, p. 68

31 The United Nations adoption of jurisdiction in the Korean question may have been illegal on three grounds: it amounted to unilateral revocation of the Moscow Agreement; it was in breach of Article 107 of the charter which excluded postwar settlement issues from United Nations jurisdiction; and it was in breach of Article 32 which prescribed consultation with parties concerned in disputes (no Korean voice was heard). See Chung Kyung-Mo, 'Arata no "fukakujitsu no jidai" o mukaete', unpublished manuscript, July 1991.

32 Leon Gordenker, *The United Nations and the Peaceful Unification of Korea. The Politics of Field Operations, 1947-1950*, The Hague, 1969, p. 71

33 For details on the role of the various United Nations committees, see McCormack, 1983, or in the revised Japanese text of 1990: *Shinryaku no butaiura — Chosen senso no shinjitsu*, Tokyo.

34 Australian Mission in Japan, Departmental despatch no 29, 11 November 1947, AA (Australian Archives) 19/301/1208

35 Stueck, 1981, p. 97

36 K.P.S. Menon, *Many Worlds: An Autobiography*, London, 1965, p. 259

37 Department of State (Washington), *Foreign Relations of the United States*, 1948, vol. 6, Washington, 1974, p. 1126

38 Statement by S.H. Jackson, Australian representative on UNTC0K, 12 March 1948, *First Part of the Report of the United Nations Temporary Commission on Korea*, vol. 1, General Assembly, Official records, 3rd Session, supplement no. 9, A/575, Lake Success, New York, 1948, p. 38

39 Stueck, 1981, p. 97; and see Jacobs (Political Adviser) to Secretary of State, 22 April 1948, FRUS, cit., p. 1180

40 McCune, p. 263

41 Ralph Harry (of Department of External Affairs), quoted in Secretary of State to Jacobs, 4 June 1948, FRUS, cit., p. 1215

42 Stueck, 1981, p. 103

43 The Australian delegate was instructed to absent himself from the country, since 'the government as now constituted in Seoul cannot be regarded as the government envisaged in the resolution of the General Assembly of 14th November 1947': Telegrams of 3 and 4 August 1948, Canberra to Tokyo, AA 3123/7/3/1.

44 Leland M. Goodrich, *Korea: A Study of U.S. Policy in the United Nations*, New York, 1956, p. 113

45 McCune, p. 303

46 Gordenker, 1969, p. 143

47 On Cheju, see John Merrill, 'The Cheju-do Rebellion', *Journal of Korean Studies*, vol. 2, 1980, pp. 139–97; Kim Sop-bon, *Chejudo — chi no rekishi* (Chejudo — History of Blood), Tokyo, 1978; and Cumings, 1990, pp. 250–59. For a brief account, see also Halliday and Cumings, pp. 36–38. The Governor of Cheju estimated that about 60 000 people had been killed and 40 000 had fled to Japan as a consequence of the suppression: Cumings, 1990, p. 258.

48 Gordenker, 1969, p. 270

49 ibid., p. 161

50 Mr Shaw, despatch from Tokyo, 12 July 1949: AA 19/301/1208

51 ibid.

52 Quoted in Cumings, 1990, p. 227

53 Walter Sullivan, *New York Times*, 6 and 15 March 1050 (quoted in Cumings, 1990, p. 289)

54 Rees, 1964, p. 16

55 Patrick Shaw (in Tokyo), cable no 105, 22 March 1949, and Department of External Affairs to Washington (Australian Embassy), cable no 186, 24 March 1949: AA 3123/4/9, Part 1

56 Merrill, 1982, and for detailed analysis of the intelligence and other information, see Cumings, 1990, pp. 388–98.

57 Quoted in John Gittings, 'The War Before Vietnam', in McCormack and Selden, 1978, p. 63

58 See John Merrill, quoted in NHK, p. 45.

59 McCormack, 1983, p. 73

60 ibid.

61 Trygve Lie, *In the Cause of Peace: Seven Years with the United Nations*, New York, 1954, p. 329

62 AA, MP 1217, 1963

63 For detailed discussion, see McCormack, 1983, pp. 75–84

64 ibid.

65 On the basis of decisions made exclusively by Dean Acheson, as Cumings, 1990, pp. 626–27 shows.

66 General Roberts, head of Korean Military Assistance Group (KMAG), quoted in Kolko, 1972, p. 570

67 Cumings, 1990, pp. 452–53

68 ibid., p. 453

69 Halliday and Cumings, 1988, p. 73

70 Kim Chum-Kon, 1973, pp. 324–25

71 Cumings, 1990, pp. 452–53

72 McCormack, 1983, p. 81

73 Cumings, 1990, passim

74 For a detailed, and sceptical, treatment of the Krushchev material on Korea, see John Merrill, 'Krushchev Remembers', *Journal of Korean Studies*, vol. 3, 1981, pp. 481–91

75 Kobayashi Keiji, 'Chosen senso no shikakenin ha dare ka', *Aera*, 1990, vol. 9, p. 22. My attention was drawn to this source by the discussion in Wada

Haruki, 'Chosen senso ni tsuite kangaeru — atarashii shiryo ni yoru kento', *Shiso*, no. 795, September 1990, pp. 6–29. Wada's discussion of the Krushchev evidence, and of Korean–Soviet–Chinese relations generally, is stimulating and persuasive.

76   *The Korea Times*, 30 August 1992
77   Odagawa Masaru, 'Nanshin e no shien yosei' (Support for the move south), *Asahi shinbun*, 4 April 1992
78   See analysis by Merrill.
79   See Wada, 1992, p. 14.
80   Aeba Takanori and NHK shusaihan, *Chosen senso* (The Korean War), Tokyo, NHK, 1990, pp. 94–95.
81   Halliday and Cumings, 1988, p. 60
82   The decision not to return to the Security Council was (according to Gromyko) taken personally by Stalin, and was resented and seen as a serious mistake by senior officials including Gromyko (Andrei Gromyko's 1989 memoirs, quoted by Wada, 1992, p. 17). Michael Kapitsa, formerly vice-Minister for Foreign Affairs makes the same point in NHK, p. 92.
83   For a different interpretation, see Cumings, 1990, pp. 636–37.
84   Quoted in NHK, p. 72
85   Wada, 1992, p. 16
86   According to the 1977 Soviet *Military Encyclopedia*, vol. 4, 'The Korean War', cited in Wada, 1992, p. 15
87   Wada, 1992, p. 15 (citing Soviet sources)
88   Cumings, 1990, p. 446
89   Halliday and Cumings, 1988, p. 62
90   See Wada, 1992, pp. 18–22 for a resumé of recent material in Chinese and Korean on this important and little-understood relationship.
91   ibid.
92   Merrill, quoted in NHK, p. 46
93   McCormack, 1983, p. 68. For a full and detailed study of this speech and its context in United States strategic thinking, see Cumings, 1990, pp. 408–38 (i.e. the whole of his Chapter 13, which is entitled 'The Speech').
94   'United States Objectives and Programs for National Security', 14 April 1950; *Containment: Documents on American Policy and Strategy, 1945–1950*, eds Thomas Etzold and John Lewis Gaddis, New York, 1978, pp. 385–87; see also discussion in Cumings, 1990, pp. 177–81.
95   Quoted in Goodrich, 1956, p. 85
96   McCormack, 1983, p. 70
97   For an analysis of the importance of the Taiwan issue as of late June 1950, see Cumings, 1990, passim.
98   For a recent discussion of this material, see Cumings, 1990, pp. 588–93.
99   Wada, 1992, pp. 9–11, gives details of the documents, which are analysed in an article by the Korean scholar Bang Sunju in the Hannim University journal *Asea Munhwa*, in 1986
100   Chu Yongbok, 'I Translated Attack Orders Composed in Russian', in *The Truth about the Korean War*, ed. Kim Chulbaum, Seoul, 1991, pp. 115–30
101   McCormack, 1983, p. 87. And for recent accounts of the fighting in that area by leading south Korean participants, see NHK, pp. 55–56.
102   Cumings, 1990, pp. 577–80 (and more generally, pp. 569–80)
103   ibid., p. 585
104   Kolko, 1972, p. 589
105   William F. Dean, *General Dean's Story*, London, 1954, p. 68
106   Riley and Schramm, 1951, pp. 35, 65–67, 118
107   Cumings, 1990, pp. 668–73
108   See, for example, Kim Chum-kon, *The Korean War*, Seoul, 1973, p. 389–90.
109   Cumings, 1990, pp. 668–73

110 There were , however, reports from American sources of such spontaneous risings in certain cities, such as Taegu and Kwangju. See Suzuki Masayuki, 'Kita chosen shiryo kara mita chosen senso', *Gunji shigaku*, no. 103, December 1990, pp. 57–66, at p. 64; see also Cumings, 1990, p. 688.

111 Quoted in telegram no 18, Mr Hodgson, 25 July 1950, AA 2123/1

112 Quoted in Kolko, 1972, p. 591

113 Goodrich, pp. 129–30, and text of United Nations resolution at pp. 223–25

114 Hao Yufan and Zhai Zhihai, 'China's Decision to Enter the Korean War: History Revisited', *The China Quarterly*, no. 121, March 1990, pp. 94-115, at p. 111

115 For Mao's explication, see ibid., p. 106.

116 ibid., p. 111

117 Details drawn from various recent accounts, including Hao and Zhai (op cit.), Wada, 1992, NHK, 113.

118 Wada, 1992, p. 28 (quoting a Chinese source)

119 Jon Halliday, 'Secret War of the Top Guns', *The Observer*, 5 July 1992, pp. 53–54.

120 Figures given by Lobov, NHK, p. 107; see also Halliday, p. 54

121 Halliday and Cumings, 1988, p. 132

122 Halliday, 1992, p. 54

123 Okubo Takeo, *Uminari no hibi*, Tokyo, 1978, and author's interviews with Admiral Okubo, Tokyo, 1981

124 Joseph C. Goulden, *Korea: the Untold Story of the War*, NY, 1982, p. 409

125 On 'Operation Hudson Harbor', see Cumings, 1990, p. 752.

126 NHK, p. 191

127 For a concise discussion of the nuclear issue, see ibid., pp. 121–28, Cumings, 1990, pp. 748ff, or NHK, pp. 184–94. For a detailed study, see Foot, 1985.

128 NHK, p. 190

129 *Mainichi shinbun*, 8 June 1984; *Korea Herald*, 8 June 1984

130 Halliday and Cumings, 1988, pp. 128–29; John Gittings, 'The War Before Vietnam', in *Korea North and South: The Contemporary Crisis*, eds Gavan McCormack and John Gittings, New York, 1978, p. 71

131 For a fuller discussion of these matters, see McCormack, 1983, pp. 147–58 and sources cited there.

132 ibid., p. 155

133 The authority on this question is Tsuneishi Keiichi of Kanagawa University in Japan. Tsuneishi is author of several works in Japanese concerning EHF, and was interviewed by this author in Tokyo in 1987.

134 McCormack, 1983, p. 124

135 *The Australian*, 3 January 1983

136 Walter Karig, Malcolm Cagle and Frank A. Manson, *Battle Report: The War in Korea*, New York, 1952, pp. 111–12

137 Quoted in Cumings, 1990, p. 756; and for examples of KMAG's requests for the obliteration of towns and villages, see ibid., p. 706

138 McCormack, 1983, pp. 124–27

139 Cumings, 1990, p. 702

140 NHK, p. 201

141 Cumings, 1990, p. 719

142 Quoted in ibid., p. 721

143 McCormack, 1983, p. 128–29

144 Gregory Henderson, *The Politics of the Vortex*, Cambridge, Mass., 1968, p. 167

145 See, for example, the UN Observer report discussed in McCormack, 1983, pp. 141–42.

146 T.R. Fehrenbach, *This Kind of War*, London, 1963, pp. 200–201

147 Interim Historical Report, War Crimes Division, Judge Advocate section, Korean Communications Zone, AP0 234, Cumulative to 30 June 1953. Copy in Australian Archives (AA), Victorian Division, MP 729/8, Department of the Army, Classified Correspondence Files, 1945–1957, File 66/431/25. Extracts appeared, with photographs, in newspapers throughout the world around 30 October 1953. See, for example, *Daily Telegraph* (Sydney) of that date.

148 AA (Victoria), MP 729/8, File 66/431/25

149 'US Belsen in Korea: Americans Drove Women to Pits of Death', *Daily Worker*, 9 August 1950

150 The village, though pronounced as Winnington wrote it, should actually be written as 'Nangwul'.

151 Jon Halliday, 'Anti-Communism and the Korean War (1950-1953)' in *Socialist Register*, eds Ralph Miliband, John Saville and Marcel Liebman, London, 1984, pp. 130–63, at p. 146

152 Extract from the Peach report contained in Dispatch by A.B. Jamieson, 2 August 1950, in Australian Mission in Tokyo to Canberra, 10 August 1950, AA 3123/5, part 4

153 Interview, Sydney, 14 August 1982

154 Rankin confirmed this account in a 12 August 1982 interview with this author by referring to his 1950 diary.

155 'War in Korea', by journalist Stephen Simmons and cameraman Haywood Magee, *Picture Post*, vol. 48, no. 5, 29 July 1950, p. 17. The caption to the photograph described the incident as one 'which has been investigated by a United Nations observer'.

156 Philip Deane, *Captive in Korea*, London, 1953, p. 83. The 1953 United States Army report locates the headquarters of the north Korean forces it alleged were responsible for the September massacre 'in the Catholic mission' in Taejon.

157 No Ka-Won, 'Taejon hyong-mu-so sa-chon san-baek myong hak-sal sa-kon' (The massacre of 4300 men from the Taejon prison), *Mal*, February 1992, pp. 122–31. I am grateful to Chung Kyung-Mo for bringing this material to my attention, and to Kim Hong-Ja for translating it into Japanese.

158 Cumings, 1990, p. 700 refers also to American internal evidence' which corroborated Winnington, though giving the figure of 2000–4000 rather than 7000 victims.

159 Halliday and Cumings, 1988, p. 157

160 Quoted in NHK, p. 205

161 Evan Luard, *A History of the United Nations*, vol. 1, *The Years of Western Dominance, 1945–1955*, London, 1982, p. 263

162 For an eyewitness account, Wilfred Burchett, *This Monstrous War*, Melbourne, 1952, pp. 182ff, or *Again Korea*, New York, 1968, pp. 38ff.

163 See Gavan McCormack, 'Korea: Wilfred Burchett's Thirty Years' War' in, *Burchett Reporting the Other Side of the World*, ed. Ben Kiernan, London, 1986, p. 166 and passim.

164 Quoted in Gittings, 1978, p. 68

165 McCormack, 1983, p. 123

166 ibid.

167 Quoted in Halliday and Cumings, 1988, p. 178

168 McCormack, 1986, p. 175

169 See table in ibid., p. 178.

170 Cumings, 1990, p. 812, n. 28

171 Quoted in McCormack, 1986, p. 179

172 Takahashi Yukiharu, *Rumin no daichi*, Tokyo, 1984

173 McCormack, 1986, p. 168

174 Department of External Affairs (Canberra) to Australian Mission (New York), 3 November 1953, AA (Canberra), Al 838/T 184, 3123/5/7/2 pt I

175 Quoted in Halliday and Cumings, 1988, p. 181
176 Plimsoll to Department of External Affairs, Canberra, 27 May 1952, and to General Mark Clark, 2 June 1952, in AA, CRS A 1838, T 154, 3123/3 part 3
177 Halliday and Cumings, 1988, pp. 187, 197

4

THE REPUBLIC OF KOREA

The history of the Republic of Korea (ROK) has been dominated by three related factors. The first and most far-reaching was the division, and subsequent civil war — the first time the state of Korea had been divided in a thousand years. Up to the start of the 1990s, no peace treaty had been signed to end the civil war, and thus south Korea's evolution was that of a garrison-state. This produced benefits in efficient state-making and social mobilisation, but it also shaped culture, influenced history and was used to justify political repression.

The division of Korea deprived the south of industrial resources and compounded its dependence on the external world during the early stages of modernisation. It also inflicted a tremendous psychological scar at the very moment that a sense of modern nationalism was expanding across regions and social classes. The division, and the conviction that it resulted from foreign intervention, not fraternal conflict, has been the bass note running throughout south Korean public discourse.

The second distinguishing factor is the unprecedented socio-political role of the military. A powerful army emerged from the international-ised conflict of 1950–53, but it was the subsequent failure of south Korean leaders to set aside factionalism and address domestic problems that brought about military control of government in the 1960s. The military's success in spreading basic skills and enforcing socio-economic cohesion through conscription and managerial efficiency in government has been an undeniable reason for south Korea's later affluence. However, while Japan's early modernisation is often attributed to its samurai heritage, Korea had no such tradition on which to draw, and this has increased the intensity of intellectual, and especially student, opposition to successive army-based regimes.

Finally, in the 1960s south Korea chose a policy of export-led develop-ment, and this commited it to expand its contacts beyond its traditional horizons and enter more fully than at any previous time into the Western capitalist system. It was forced to alter its values at home, and at a minimum to foster a cosmopolitan class of businessmen, diplomats and intellectuals. Ordinary Koreans as tourists were only to surface in any numbers late in the century. South Korea's quandary, unlike the anti-capitalist north, was to buttress its policies with modern nationalism while relying on the international economy, yet without appearing either too 'nationalist' to the outside nor too 'Westernised' to its own people. This dilemma also confronted China and Japan into the 1990s, but the presence of the north, ever ready to attack southern toadyism, made Seoul's foreign contacts considerably more tortured than those of Beijing or Tokyo.

In contrast with Japan (if less so with China), insecurity left the politics of both Koreas dominated by personality. Replacing the monarchy, presidents in Seoul and P'yongyang often acted above the law or simply manipulated the legal system to their own advantage. In the north, Kim Il Sung also assumed the semi-religious powers of a pre-modern king, but in south Korea, the strength of politically active religious groups (in 1988, in a population of about 22 million, there were 6.5 million Protestants, 1.9 million Catholics, and 8 million Mahayana Buddhists) served to inhibit the emotional allure of a father-president. While modern presidents usually lack the moral authority of kings, the state machinery of police, communications and social organisation through education and conscription allows them (in the absence of enforced legal restraint) to exercise power with far greater effect. For this reason, the history of south Korea, more than the remote court history of the Yi period, is a dialogue (albeit frequently degenerating into a monologue) between the president and citizenry.

The first republic, 1948–60: Metropolitan politics and the control state

The Republic of Korea was formally established on 15 August 1948, the third anniversary of Japan's surrender and Korea's liberation. It had a crippled economy, blackmarketeering and banditry flourished, Seoul was a wasteland and the people relied for food and other supplies on international — primarily American — aid. Urban congestion increased with the massive influx of returnees from Manchuria and Japan, and refugees from the north settling mainly around Seoul. An American visitor in 1949 described the capital:

A city with housing, transportation, schools, and utility facilities for 500 000, it now has a population swollen to over a million and a half. Several thousand people sleep in the Seoul streets, thousands more live in caves and other temporary shelters, and existing homes are crowded with two and three times as many people as they should shelter . . . Long lines of waiting people are customary; so are shortages and high prices. But so are patience and cooperation, and the willingness to do without and to share.[1]

Whatever goodwill remained was dissipated after 1950 as war brought renewed chaos. Indeed, the early years of the republic witnessed more devastation and social and cultural dislocation than the entire Japanese colonial period.

One of the tests for south Korea's entry to the Western system was a functioning constitutional democracy. This was inevitably a long and difficult process of trial and error, and over four decades there were to be constant amendments to the form of presidential election and the level of presidential powers. The first — and to some observers the fairest — constitution was promulgated on 17 July 1948. Indicating the relative lack of concern of the United States (whose officials had independently drafted the 1946 Japanese constitution), the framing of the document was undertaken almost wholly by Koreans alone. The nascent republic bore some similarities to Japan in the 1880s, emerging into a violent world, militarily and economically weak, with neither national education nor conscription for unity. One may see the influence of Japan's 1889 statist constitution on south Korea, with its strong central president and broad but poorly defined commitment to democracy. Mass primary education was guaranteed, and a conscription law followed in August 1949, but the underlying assumption was that the south Korean people, like the Japanese of the 1890s, were unprepared to exercise full democracy and should be guided in a traditional paternalist fashion by the educated élite. Ultimately, as William Faulkner said of American negro emancipation, freedom could not be legislated, it would have to be taken.

The circumstances of 1948 limited south Korea's choice of political style and leadership. The United States wanted capitalist democracy and opposed leftist influence. Those who had lived under Japanese rule were easy targets as collaborators — this left the field open to expatriate nationalists. Most prominent amongst these were Kim Ku, friendly with the Nationalist Chinese but whose base was in north Korea (in 1948, following the presidential election, he was to be assassinated by one of his own followers); Kim Kyusik, a graduate student in the United States, friendly with left-wing believers, gentle in character, and the preferred choice as president of United States officials, missionaries and press; and most famous of all, Syngman Rhee, with nationalist credentials going back to the 1890s Independence Club and his imprisonment by the Yi dynasty. Rhee is often misrepresented as the hand-picked president and intimate ally of the United States, but his relationship with General Hodge, United States military commander in south Korea to 1948, was irretrievably bad. Frustration with Hodge and United States policy was bluntly expressed in 1947 by a member of Rhee's tiny Washington lobby:

> If these two foreign delegations [United States and Soviet] in Korea were deliberately considering the Korean people to be their worst enemies, they could have devised no more diabolical plans to destroy Korean morale, to steal Korean economic resources, to annihilate Korean nationality, to promote civil hatred and fratricidal war . . . American officials insinuate that the Korean question is not important in and of itself. It must be considered in the 'larger' scope of world-wide relations with Russia. Is not this simply

another way of saying that the welfare and interests of the United States are
not the same as the welfare of the Korean people? . . . This is no less a critical
juncture in Korea's life than were the fateful years of 1905–1910. Then the
decisions were forced upon us by foreigners and our country was betrayed.
This time the Koreans must decide for themselves.[2]

The phrasing was impolitic, but the sentiment that Korea was once
more being exploited by outside powers was then and later shared by
many Koreans.

At some other time, Kim Kyusik may well have triumphed in the 1948
presidential election. Rhee had been overseas for nearly 40 years, had
no local base, and was estranged by age from Korea's youth. Yet the
republic was born amid confrontation and baptised by war: Rhee was a
commanding figure, certain of himself and obstinate in defence of
Korean interests as he saw them, even when this brought him in conflict
with United States desires. Like many others, the Korean people had no
inkling in 1948 of what lay ahead for the world. An extremely clever
politician, Rhee's views were nonetheless quite simple, and the people
not only elected him first in 1948, but continued to re-elect him for the
next twelve years.

The early limits of Rhee's influence were exposed by his need to
appoint cabinet members from the major interest groups. Louise Kim, a
long-time Rhee supporter and leading women's educator, received the
portfolio of commerce and industry, but Yi Pomsok (perhaps better
known as Lee Bum Suk), head of the openly fascist-style Korean Youth
Corps (860 000 members), was appointed vice-president, and a former
communist, Cho Pong'am, became agriculture minister. As Rhee
secured his position, he shed these uncertain allies, separating Yi from
the Youth Corps and having Cho executed as a north Korean sympathiser
in 1959. Until 1950, however, he was under frequent attack: a local
autonomy law was passed over his objection in 1949 (though remaining
on the shelf until 1952), land reform was implemented in 1950 over
presidential veto, and opponents did notably well in the National
Assembly election of May 1950. Ironically, Kim Il Sung's attack in June
1950 undoubtedly aided Rhee, allowing him the excuse of wartime
exigencies to revise the constitution and eliminate opposition.

After 1953, Rhee's constant public theme was reunification of the
peninsula and liberation of fellow Koreans from communism. This
enabled him to sustain the psychology of wartime crisis, perpetuate
massive armed forces and expand the means of central state control. The
army, police and officialdom swelled, so that by 1953 the bureaucracy
for south Korea alone was three times larger than the entire Japanese
colonial administration. Rhee used the state apparatus to balance
contending forces and preserve his individual authority. As at the end of
the Yi dynasty, high office was shuffled relentlessly and appointees milked
government positions before the months or even weeks of their tenure
came to an end: Gregory Henderson, a United States diplomat in Seoul
and a Korean scholar, writes that there were only two of Rhee's total of

129 ministers to 1960 who did not make money in this fashion: 'one through ferocious personal honesty, the other through not having been at his desk long enough'.[3] Thus the first republic was dominated by politicking and patronage.

Rhee had something of a Confucian disdain for economics and various development plans were left to gather dust. United States aid, much of it in commodity goods, was accepted to satisfy a growing consumerism, but one side-effect was to retard native production and reinforce the patron–client nature of United States–south Korean relations. The largesse of commodity aid also highlighted disparities between the well-off, ostentatiously displaying their foreign wares, and the impoverished majority. Rhee directed Korean capital not to industry, but to the armed forces, and secondarily to import substitution of non-durable consumer goods such as food and beverages, tobacco, clothing and footwear. With this malign neglect, south Korean exports in the late 1950s averaged only about US$22 million. Officials kept a tight hand on domestic credit and supplies of foreign exchange, and businessmen often had to resort to bribery to obtain capital. A favoured few enjoyed government protection and the bases of some of the huge *chaebol* conglomerates were laid at this time. The economy as a whole, however, was poorly co-ordinated and carelessly developed.

With the growth of schools, communications and techniques of popular mobilisation, Rhee's élitist high culture nationalism could, as elsewhere in Asia, be undermined by populist rivals. To counter this, he exploited the catch-all *National Security Law* of December 1948, not only to suppress communism but also to intimidate or imprison opponents. The National Assembly, judges and prosecutors, the military, press and education were all ruthlessly purged: between September 1948 and May 1949, seven leading newspapers and one news agency were ordered to close, and about 90 000 Koreans (including the future president, Park Chung Hee) were arrested. In 1954, Rhee remoulded the still-wet constitutional clay to permit himself more than two presidential terms, and he was re-elected in 1956 with no apparent barrier save mortality to his remaining there forever. Certainly the opposition party was not, as it never has been, independently capable of challenging a sitting president — the Democratic Party, established in 1955, was based in the same class of landowners, capitalists and bureaucrats as Rhee's Liberals (established in 1951), and instead of seeking a popular base, it concentrated on constitutional reform to obtain power. Only a new but diffused (and therefore difficult to suppress) political force could unseat Rhee: that role would fall to Korean students, but it was not until the start of a new decade in 1960 that they were to find their political voice.

While the domestic situation ossified under centripetal politics, the Cold War forced Seoul to restructure its longest-standing historical ties — those with China, which were severed with the Communist victory of 1949, and those with newly demilitarised Japan. China remained as a potential strategic threat, but its direct contact with south Korea was only renewed in the late 1970s, and then, in an historical seachange, as a junior economic partner to Seoul. Japan was south Korea's natural ally, through its complementary economic and political system, but the legacy of colonialism was never fully overcome. Early in 1948, Japanese 'abuse' became a political issue when Korean residents in Japan protested new requirements on local Korean schools (catering for about 53 000 children) to abandon Korean materials and institute Tokyo's standardised curriculum and texts. Kim Ku and Kim Kyusik took up the issue as a deliberate attack on Korean culture and, amid fears the Cold War would revive Japanese militarism, they organised the Anti-Japanese Fighting Committee in June 1948. Popular anger was directed not only against Japan and the United States (both for its leniency towards Japan and for overseeing the imminent election which would formalise the division of Korea), but also against President Rhee for drawing support from Korean businessmen, police and bureaucrats carried over from the colonial regime. Rhee, however, was always virulent in condemning Japan, and his immovable rejection of American pressure for a south Korean–Japanese rapprochement must be understood in the very real fear that Koreans had of their larger East Asian neighbour. The first postwar meeting of the two governments took place at United States urging in October 1951, one month after the signing of the San Francisco Treaty terminating the allied occupation of Japan. Predictably, the talks quickly degenerated into claims and counter-claims regarding Japanese colonialism, and no resolution was achieved.

South Korean–Japanese relations continued to stick through the 1950s on several issues. The most violent was that of fishery rights. South Korea established a unilateral boundary of about 95 kilometres from the Korean coast, known as the Rhee Line or Peace Line, and in which, between 1952 and 1964, over 200 Japanese fishing boats were seized. Discriminatory treatment of the Korean community in Japan was also a constant issue, not least because of north–south rivalries: Seoul made formal protestations to Tokyo, but tangible assistance to Koreans living in Japan was greatest from P'yongyang. The least tractable issue was a moral one: many Koreans expected Japan publicly to apologise, in the manner of Germany, for its military expansion. However, Japan never instituted the clinical eradication of racial groups in the manner of the Nazi regime and few would compare Nazi Germany with imperial Japan. Instead, Japanese politicians throughout the postwar period cited the benefits of Japan's colonialism, especially (albeit in an ill-informed fashion) regarding Korean education. In 1965, Foreign Minister Shiina Etsusaburo became the first Japanese official openly to regret Japan's annexation of Korea, and further apologies were given in the 1980s and 1990s by the Emperor Showa (Hirohito) and his successor Heisei (Akihito). However, south Koreans were unsatisfied by these politically calculated concessions, and many Japanese were openly unrepentant of the past. Chong-sik Lee has described south Korean–Japanese relations after 1945 as a clash of cultures: 'Korea's approach to Japan was spiritual, moral, holistic, and Oriental, whereas the Japanese approach was legalistic, pragmatic, piecemeal, and Western.'[4] As economic and strategic ties came to bind the two more closely, this cultural gap closed somewhat, but mutual attitudes remained as bad, if not worse, than between the English and Irish or the Russians and Poles.

Korea's image of the United States to 1945 had been largely remote and idealised: up to the 1930s, United States cultural and economic dynamism was the envy of the world (even in the Soviet Union), but when Koreans had appealed for direct United States support, in 1905, 1910 and 1919, they had felt themselves abandoned to a policy of realpolitik. Within Korea, contacts were limited to missionary education, a few commercial enterprises and perhaps the occasional movie. After 1945, south Korea had no choice in a polarised world but to seek United States assistance, even while (as noted above) remaining critical of its uninformed policies towards Korea and its undisguised concern with, firstly, Europe and then Japan. In the wake of the Korean War, however, there was a massive new American commitment to the ROK and, between 1945 and 1976, south Korea received approximately US$5.7 billion in economic and $6.8 billion in military assistance: at its height, between 1953 and 1961, United States aid financed over two-thirds of all south Korean imports and equalled about 80 per cent of total fixed capital formation.[5]

The other main areas of United States influence were in education and defence. From 1945–48, the United States had concentrated on building primary and secondary schools to spread basic skills and extend adult literacy beyond the current estimate of 22 per cent. The American system was introduced (six–three–three–four years at primary, middle, high school, and college or university), and by 1952 a quantum leap in primary enrolment had taken numbers up to about 2.37 million children, or more than 70 per cent above the figure for 1945. United States advisors hoped through education to instill the values of American-style democracy and responsibility. All schools became co-educational, and control was devolved (until restored by the republic after 1948) from central government to the township or county level. The school curriculum was completely revised, the Confucian classics abandoned in favour of han'gul texts on democracy and the individual and, in stark contrast to the respect for the traditional educator, students were encouraged to contest the teacher's authority (a lesson to be learnt all too well in later decades). All of this was similar to United States occupation policies in Japan.

Following the Korean War, United States priorities shifted to higher education and the need to supply a new generation of south Korean social leaders. In 1945, the only university had been Keijo Imperial (now south Korea's leading tertiary institution, Seoul National University). Following the establishment of the republic, however, there was a flood of universities with either new state or private institutions being founded, or existing colleges being upgraded to university status. Between 1950 and 1954 alone, eleven universities were established, including (using their own romanisation) Hankuk University for Foreign Studies, two women's universities — Dongduck and Duksung — and Sung Kyun Kwan University (i.e. Songgyun'gwan, upgraded in 1953), the historic centre of traditional Confucian study. During the 1950s, enrolment in higher education increased more than tenfold, with the United States providing finance, arranging educational missions to assist with instruction, curriculum and textbooks, and arranging institutional contracts with American universities. The largest of these was between Seoul National University and the University of Minnesota between 1954 and 1962, involving the exchange of professors and Minnesota staff advice on administration and teaching. Two of the south's other present-day élite institutions, Korea University (formerly Posong College) and the 1885 United States missionary-established Yonsei University, signed agreements with the Washington University of St Louis for training in business administration. The result was an initial Americanisation of south Korean universities and a flow of Korean overseas students, mostly heading to the United States.[6] In the 1970s and 1980s, however, there were indications of a cultural backlash against this American influence and some criticism of Koreans who left the homeland to obtain higher degrees from United States universities.

The most direct United States influence was on the ROK army. The sweetener for south Korean acquiescence, but not signature, to the 1953 Korean War armistice was a mutual defence treaty (effective from 1954), equipment and training for its forces, plus increased economic aid. South Korea's defence budget was paid largely by Washington, and its army, resurrected from the collapse of 1950 to about 600 000 men under Rhee, was trained and equipped to mesh with United States troops. Korean military academies were modelled on American institutions and many officers (over 35 000 by 1984) were sent to the United States for advanced education. A further result of the war was that a roughly 60 000-man United States force in Korea (USFK) remained in the peninsula. With rapid professionalisation of the ROK army, the USFK became militarily less important and increasingly symbolic. The symbolism, however, was two-fold: that of United States support against north Korean attack, but also that of United States wealth and power relative to the ROK. From the 1970s, and especially after the infamous Kwangju incident of 1980, these differing images were to become increasingly controversial, with the government in Seoul praising the USFK's externally oriented role, and domestic opposition groups attacking its internal alignment with what they considered a dictatorial regime.

Beyond its military and political implications, the presence in Korea of United States troops had far-reaching cultural effects. The American Forces in Korea Network (AFKN) began transmitting radio broadcasts to its troops in October 1950 and television broadcasts from September

1957. Seoul maintained tight control over its own media but was hard pressed to control Koreans listening in to the AFKN. One Korean army colonel told his American audience as late as 1987:

> The AFKN played a big role in producing new attitudes, hobbies, and a new way of expressing one's feelings, in addition to helping students learn English. It was good to learn to understand the United States but, at the same time, the new enthusiams had an adverse effect on the rehabilitation of Korean culture. The mixture of old and new cultures was frequently indigestible. It widened the gap between young and old. The question must be asked: is there any way to reduce the influence on Korean society of this broadcasting?[7]

United States bases provided jobs to many local people, though the prevalence of a 'camp-follower' economy of bars and prostitution caused social concern. In the early years, PX supplies were frequently leaked through blackmarketeers, spreading corruption and visible consumption: despite official attempts, the PX drip was still apparent into the 1970s. Significant contributions to the local economy began from 1955, when USFK began procuring locally rather than from the United States. This boosted employment, improved techniques of food sanitation and gave a start in construction work to present-day conglomerates such as Hyundai. The inevitable human contact between United States servicemen and Korean women, however, was less well received, while mixed-blood children were generally rejected in a Korean society notable for its racial homogeneity, and were even exempted from military service.[8]

Rhee's heavy-handed centralisation of power and commitment to armed expansion, military reunification and *laissez-faire* economics stultified the maturation of south Korea's polity and economy. By 1960, inflation and unemployment were on the rise while United States economic aid was in decline. Political corruption was rife and, despite the extraordinary increase in university graduates, prestige employment opportunities in government or leading corporations were minimal: this bred disaffection in the group least bound by social ties to the existing system. There was also growing unrest in the army. Rhee had used promotion to ensure officers owing him personal loyalty dominated senior command, and exploited units such as the Army Counter-Intelligence Corps to neutralise political opponents. The military received about 40 per cent of the national budget and, with government connivance, there were rich pickings to be had from illicit sale of arms and commercially valuable goods provided by the United States. In the face of this corruption and abuse of the army, junior officers and men subsisted on meagre pay and poor conditions with promotion stymied for those outside of Rhee's circle. In view of their social and ideological differences, however, the discontented among workers, students and soldiers were unlikely ever to unite. In the presidential elections of 1956 and 1960, Rhee literally outlived his rivals, who died of old age before the vote, but was himself increasingly outliving his political welcome. His obvious attempt at rigging the 1960 presidential election finally ignited mass demonstrations led by the urban students. The initial trigger, as it would be in future demonstrations, was the discovery of a young corpse, clearly killed by the authorities and dumped in Masan Bay. On 19 April 1960, students marching on the presidential palace were shot at by police and in riots across the country over a hundred protestors were killed. Martial law was announced, but the Korean army remained on the sidelines leaving Rhee politically naked. With the United States urging him to quit, Rhee finally resigned the presidency on 27 April and left for exile in Hawaii. He was to die there in 1965, having spent no more than half his life on Korean soil.

Student-led movement topples Syngman Rhee regime, April 1960, Seoul
Source: Zai Nichi Karkoku seinen domei (League of Korean Youth in Japan), *Shigatsu Kakumei* (April Revolution), Tokyo, 1976, p. 3.

The brief second republic was instituted under the Democratic Party's Chang Myon as prime minister. The constitution was again revised, enhancing prime ministerial and cabinet powers, and reducing the presidency to a ceremonial office. However, there was no one able to display control at the start of the new decade: industry declined and unemployment stood around 24 per cent, while prices were on the rise and the Democrats, who had long been split between the so-called Old and New factions, were occupied by internal squabbles. Students demonstrated ceaselessly for change — more than 500 major protests occurred at universities alone — and in the nine months of the Chang Myon cabinet, the thirteen ministries hosted a total of 74 incumbents as politicians flailed in search of answers. Chang's failure to purge the army's upper echelon as promised made junior officers resentful and afraid of retribution from their seniors. As the chaos continued, and fears of north Korean intervention mounted, these young officers finally mounted a bloodless coup d'état in May 1961. Their leader was the 44-year-old Major-General Park Chung Hee (Pak Chonghui).

Park had graduated in 1940 from the Japanese-run Manchukuo Military Academy and from the Military Academy in Tokyo four years later. His core of support, however, came from the 1949 graduates (eighth class) of the Korean Military Academy: these included his nephew by marriage, Lieutenant-Colonel Kim Jong Pil (Kim Chongp'il), and class affiliations, similar to traditional clan factions, were to play a key role in army politics over the following decades. After seizing power in 1961, the officers dissolved the National Assembly, banned all political activity, censored the press and prohibited student demonstrations. From a Military Revolutionary Committee, subsequently renamed the Supreme Council for National Reconstruction, they held absolute authority over the executive and legislature. However, in the process of modernisation, south Korean politics had become a matter for domestic and international debate — the dark spaces in which traditional politics had been conducted without reference to the people or foreign relations no longer existed in the same degree. Having taken control, therefore, the officers began preparing to legitimise their authority both at home and overseas.

The third and fourth republics, 1961–79: Dependent development, the military and the mobilisational state

The goal of the Park regime was to forge a united south Korean public behind rapid industrialisation and export development. This meant unprecedented official intervention in education and social mobilisation; overcoming the economic indifference of the past and asserting a strong central managerial role; and expanding diplomatic contacts in order to ensure foreign loans, investment and markets. While south Korea and its position in the world were thus being refashioned, relations with north Korea were temporarily placed in limbo.

To create the climate for rapid development, the government constructed new vehicles for mobilisation and expanded the machinery of state control. Just as the functions of the modern state became more visible, so too did the movements of individual citizens, and a Central Intelligence Agency (KCIA), headed by Kim Jong Pil, was set up to watch over all government ministries, the armed forces and society at large.

Elected local government was replaced by control from the home ministry; banks were nationalised, giving the state authority over institutional credit; labour was placed under a single umbrella union and manipulated by the KCIA; and other groups, such as doctors, teachers and the press, were controlled through centralised professional organisations.[9] A social clean-up was carried out, with mass imprisonment of suspected communists and the arrest of petty thieves or gangsters, who were paraded in the streets in a pre-modern display of justice literally being seen to be done. In March 1962, the *Political Activities Purification Law* forbade until 15 August 1968 (note the date) all political action by what Park derisively termed the 'old politicians' — over 4000 men of all shades of opinion were temporarily blacklisted. As the government's mouthpiece, Kim Jong Pil organised the Democratic Republican Party (DRP) with help from young educators, journalists and bureaucrats. Extensive constitutional revision restored a strong presidency, if with the limitation of two four-year terms, and deprived the cabinet of its power to decide important policies. A popular referendum added public approval to the changes.

In preparation for elections, officers of the Supreme Council retired from active military service and citizen Park led the DRP to presidential victory in October 1963. His success was aided by the failure of opposition parties, including Yi Pomsok's genially named People's Friends Party, to unite against him. Park also bent the electoral rules, employing unofficial support groups in his campaign: these included the military-based May Comrades Society, of which he was president to its 300 000 members, and militant youth corps such as the Korean Youth Society. Yet, despite access to finance from industry and control of public order (one military rival, Liberal Democratic Party candidate General Song Yoch'an, was imprisoned before voting commenced), Park received only 42.61 per cent of the total vote compared with 41.9 per cent for incumbent president Yun Poson. In addition, while Park carried the five southernmost provinces, including his home base in Kyongsang, Yun received the four northern provinces and the urban vote (65.1 per cent in the capital).[10] South Korea in 1963 was clearly a divided society, though still predominantly rural and with the countryside providing the core of the army. The new 'quasi-civilian' government, however, found that clothing itself in the trappings of democracy required electoral skills and money. These requirements tipped it towards the modern sector and reliance on former Rhee supporters in politics and industry. Moreover, Park's modernisation program was based on urban capitalist development. Ultimately this was to undermine his rural base and bring about his downfall.

In developing societies, the military is often the most modern and technically efficient group, and also the most ideologically cohesive. Under Park, former army officers dominated the government, filled important cabinet posts, commanded industrial planning in key areas such as transport, communications and construction, served as provincial governors, and sat on corporate boards. The military became an important avenue for upward mobility and the soldier became a role model for Korean society: through its civic action program, the army went to the people, helping in road and bridge construction (the Seoul–Pusan superhighway was largely built by the army), erecting schools, distributing radios, providing medical services and aiding farmers at harvest time. The military was portrayed as a revolutionary social force rather than the pillar of stability as under Rhee, and its values of competence, co-operation and national service were propagated as official ideals. In a 1962 work published under his name, *Our Nation's Path: Ideology of Social Reconstruction*, Park echoed the Independence Club or 1920s cultural nationalists in attacking Korea's tradition:

> We must reflect upon the evil legacies of our past history, slough away the factional contentiousness inherited from the Yi dynasty, and the slavish mentality resulting from the Japanese colonial rule, and firmly establish a sound national ethics. Without a human revolution, social reconstruction is impossible . . .

There was a precedent for change: the Tonghak revolution, as Park termed it, was in his view Korea's first popular revolution, formed in the peasantry and with the Koreanised democratic principle of 'Man is God' — a principle, he noted, owing nothing directly to any Western philosophy. Drawing a direct spiritual line of descent from the Tonghak through the Samil rising and the 1960 student movement to his 1961 coup, Park hailed its native progressive assertiveness as the basis for his planned reconstruction of Korean society:

> We must rebuild a sound democracy. Taking a lesson from the failure of the imported democracy to take root in the soil of Korea's realities, we have to strive to build the groundwork of a Koreanized form of welfare democracy. A nationwide movement must be begun to train the people in the sound ethics required by democratic citizens. The spirit of autonomy should be inculcated if the people are to be enabled to elect their deputies and practise democracy in this land in a proper way.[11]

This was to be autonomy not of the failed Western individual genus, but of the community, committed to national rather than personal goals, and under the supra-factional leadership of the army.

Soon after taking power, the military junta had arranged a National Reconstruction Movement at regional and occupational levels, with public rallies by women and students against communism, corruption, poverty and outmoded thinking. There were also drives to eradicate illiteracy, expand agricultural development through land reclamation, irrigation and flood control, and promote what were termed 'sisterhood' relations between towns and farm villages to reduce the growing economic imbalance and cultural division between them. Having dismissed the political old guard, Park looked to youth as the founders of new Korea. Morals textbooks were revised for the three school levels under the titles 'Correct Life', 'Democratic Life' and 'National Ethics', stressing the themes of social harmony, and of moral and physical health.

Reversing the American approach, the child was educated to value its position less as an individual than as a member of the family, school, society and nation. Indicating his personal commitment to the issue, and rather in the manner of Japan's 1890 imperial rescript on education, Park in 1968 introduced the National Education Charter. This exhorted young Koreans 'to establish the attitude of self-reliance and independence', and pledge to 'create a new history with the untiring effort and collective wisdom of the people, looking forward to the future when we will have a unified nation to hand over to our posterity'.[12] The future of history, as it were, became the responsibility of youth, but the government was rarely to accord its young any freedom to experiment with ideas. This contradiction between responsibility and restriction later drove idealistic youths towards a highly commited student opposition to those in power.

Discontent with Rhee had exploded not because of his political machinations, but because of inflation, industrial malaise and unemployment. Having created a garrison state, he failed to stock the larder. Park was closer to the people and knew they had little interest in politics as such. Far more important was a chance to improve their livelihood: as he said in 1962, 'In human life, economics precedes politics or culture'.[13] For this reason, he reinstated the colonial Japanese emphasis on production first with political freedoms to follow at an unspecified date.

South Korea's new developmentalism was couched in a succession of five-year economic plans beginning with that of 1962–66. An Economic Planning Board had been established in 1961, staffed by professional economists and headed by the deputy prime minister. Park and his technocrats took a direct interventionist stance, distributing resources to chosen clients, targeting certain areas for development, setting export goals and over-riding opposition. This was a style of centrally managed national development, with proven results in postwar Japan, although its roots, as Chalmers Johnson has noted, are in the Japanese wartime structure. The same sense of crisis amid a hostile world was used to motivate south Korea in the 1960s but, whereas the postwar Japanese bureaucracy moderated its authoritarianism, Seoul's domination of the economy was far heavier handed, and in the 1970s was to stifle business expansion and entrepreneurial initiative. However, the benefits of a coherent program in Park's first decade took overall economic growth to about 10 per cent annually, with exports rising approximately 40 per cent per annum. Government rationalisation of industry produced a small group of *chaebol*, massive corporations working intimately with officials and dominating the home economy in the manner of Japan's *zaibatsu*. However, the historical weakness of Korean market towns and the lure of existing communications, especially the Seoul–Pusan railway, confined major industrial development to the narrow corridor between Pusan and the capital. This by-passed agrarian regions such as Cholla whose residents considered themselves deliberately slighted by the Kyongsang-born president. The uneven spread of resources was to remain a thorny issue into the 1990s. Exacerbating the situation was the fact that landlords dispossessed of land in the 1950s had received virtually nothing by way of compensation and lacked the capital to start local industries. The overall impact of industrial development in south Korea, as elsewhere, was to widen economic divisions between towns and villages and accelerate migration from agriculture to industry.

At the production level, south Korea's economic success depended on keeping wages low and expanding its market share even if this meant renouncing profits for an extended period. The relative decline in rural incomes ensured a constant supply of excess labour in the 1960s, and this maintained the downward pressure on wages. Workers were muzzled by the lack of union representation, by government appeals to patriotism and by the fear of communist subversion from north Korea. The result was an extraordinarily hard-working but poorly paid workforce (though Park's own reputation for diligence and personal austerity may have mollified them in part), and one which, due to educational expansion and conscription, was responsive both to government directives and the technical needs of modern industry.

Foreign dependence

Park initially hoped for native financing to rebuild Korea's economy, but the level of capital accumulation relative to the task at hand made this a vain endeavour. His inclination was to reduce Korean reliance on the United States, not least because of the unhealthy attitude fostered by dependence, but also because the United States had been critical of the 1961 coup and the manner in which 'democracy' was restored. However, the logic of an export-oriented economy required stable foreign relations, and Park acknowledged that south Korea needed aid, investment and friendship from the two main economic powers in the region: the United States and Japan. Thus, for the first time in its history, Korea voluntarily looked east.

1965 was the turning point. In that year, south Korea finally restored treaty relations with Japan, and sent troops to assist the United States in Vietnam. Both actions were in part the result of constant United States pressure for improved stabilisation in the region, and both were to bring enormous financial reward to the ROK. A rapprochement with Japan had been mooted by Chang Myon in 1960, but at the time neither Seoul nor Tokyo had demonstrated the political will to tackle the inevitable controversy that would attend negotiations. Park's ability to move on this question was aided by his own force of character, the worsening situation in Asia (China became a nuclear power in 1964), and the ascension in Japan of conservative prime minister Sato Eisaku. The treaty which they agreed in June 1965 committed Japan to pay south Korea US$800 million ($300 million of this in non-repayable grants-in-aid), set mutual coastal fishing boundaries at 12 miles (20 kilometres), and guaranteed Koreans living in Japan residency rights and equal access to public education or welfare (although full social welfare benefits were actually not granted until the 1980s).

The resumption of treaty relations was vastly more controversial in Seoul than in Tokyo, and Korean students, professors and opposition politicians took to the streets, heatedly denouncing what they considered a humiliating and unequal agreement. Their approach to Japan, confirming the verdict of Chongsik Lee quoted earlier, was essentially moral: Park's reasoning, by contrast, was coldly rational in the manner of Yi Wanyong in 1905, telling his detractors, 'We can hardly wipe out our past rancour. But if so doing promotes our cause, will it not be more patriotic to become friends with our past enemy?'[14] This appeal to self-interest was unsuccessful and, abandoning attempts at persuasion, Park had the National Assembly ratify the treaty on 14 August 1965, despite the refusal of all opposition members to attend, and ordered the army to clear the streets.

Taking advantage of the opposition's absence, Park simultaneously had the National Assembly approve a commitment of 20 000 troops to the United States military effort in south Vietnam. A medical team and 2000-man 'logistical support unit' had earlier been sent, and a total of 340 000 south Korean troops were to serve there between 1966 and 1972. This gave the army combat experience, a general sense of pride in helping the weaker Vietnamese and, most importantly, a rush of funds in foreign exchange and United States assistance. The United States met all the costs of troop despatches to Vietnam, and updated south Korea's existing military equipment, domestic military communications, anti-infiltration measures and armaments production. The United States also helped south Korean contractors, technicians and workers gain access to the massive reconstruction projects underway in south Vietnam, and provided extra loans to boost Korean exports in Southeast Asia.[15]

During the Vietnam War, the United States gradually reduced its presence in Asia, allowing Japan to assume a more prominent political role in the area. Relations between south Korea and Japan began on a solid foundation: both were capitalist regimes in a region of communist heavyweights, and Japanese leaders accepted Park's argument that support for south Korean industry equalled support for regional security. There was something of a common language and understanding: in Japan, there were many officials or businessmen from colonial times, and in Korea there were many, not least Park himself, educated in the Japanese system. Pro-south Korean groups in Tokyo included the Korea–Japan Co-operation Committee headed by former Manchukuo bureaucrat and postwar prime minister Kishi Nobusuke, and the Parliamentarians League, a gathering of Korean and Japanese lawmakers organised in the wake of America's military pullback from Asia.

In the decade following the 1965 treaty, Japan invested more money and established more concerns in south Korea than any other foreign state. Japanese aid, credits and loans exceeded US$1.5 billion, and it was with Japanese money that initial construction of the massive Pohang

Steel Works in south-eastern Korea was completed.[16] In the successive five-year plans between 1962 and 1976, Japan contributed about 25 per cent of the total foreign capital requirement and mutual trade to 1975 expanded from US$210.6 million to US$3669. Japan also became vital to south Korea's technological development, supplying nearly 60 per cent of all foreign technology between 1962 and 1979: this was a role vital to Korea's continued growth in the 1990s and, due to Japan's unwillingness to meet south Korean requests, a constant source of friction between Seoul and Tokyo.[17] To attract foreign capital, Seoul established the free export zone concept (borrowed by communist China at a later stage) from which entirely foreign-owned companies using Korean labour could export their products free of tax. Korean workers in foreign-owned enterprises were forbidden to strike. Resentment at this colonial-style relationship was to erupt in the 1980s with demands that local Koreans in foreign employ receive extra wages and that some foreign companies, preparing to close their operations, repay all profits ever earned before being permitted to leave the country.

The lightning pace of modernisation in Korean industry from the 1960s was made possible by foreign capital, but there was a clear price to be paid. South Korean foreign borrowing jumped from total net indebtedness of just US$11.6 million in 1960 to $301.3 million in 1965 and $2.57 billion by 1970.[18] This was bearable, but only so long as economic growth was sustained. Any faltering in the economy could see south Korea collapse into Third World impoverishment — another element in the atmosphere of crisis impelling Koreans to ever greater efforts. Moreover, as became clear at the start of the 1970s, dependency on international markets (especially those of the United States and Japan) increasingly brought international pressures to bear on domestic politics.

For the United States, the cost of commitment to south Vietnam exposed the kind of 'imperial overstretch' popularised by historian Paul Kennedy. Upon taking office in 1969, United States President Richard Nixon immediately began devolving security responsibilities in Asia under the so-called Nixon doctrine. For south Korea, this meant the rapid phasing-out of economic aid and the withdrawal of one-third of United States troops from 1971; but also left unanswered questions as to whether the remaining 40 000 servicemen would stay, and if so, for how long. On a visit to Seoul in 1970, United States Vice President Spiro Agnew only confused matters by reaffirming United States support for south Korea, but also indicating that all troops would in fact be removed within a few years. Park, worried that any diminution in the United States presence might tempt north Korean adventurism, reluctantly accepted the initial troop withdrawal, if only to forestall further reductions in the future. Relations with the United States worsened, however, under Washington's trade protection. Nixon had identified massive United States imports of Japanese textiles as a threat to domestic employment and decided in 1971 to retaliate by the imposition of quotas, but these were also extended to south Korea, for whom textiles were the principal export. Once again, Seoul could do no more than bow to events beyond its reach, but from this point on there were moves towards building a professional lobby group in Washington DC (one consequence of which was to be the 1975 Koreagate scandal). The inauguration of President Carter in 1977 brought a new coldness to United States–ROK relations over public attacks on Park's abuse of human rights. If traditional Confucian government involved the setting of a moral example to one's own people, President Carter attempted the admirable, if impractical, task of setting an international (and therefore inter-cultural) moral standard. Carter's policies of retrenchment and tempering support for overseas despots brought the Nixon policy of troop reductions back to the table, but on this occasion creative accounting as to north Korea's military strength prevented any further United States withdrawal.

Relations with Japan also suffered in the 1970s. A corollary of the Nixon doctrine was to reopen China's contacts with the capitalist West, an aim partially achieved by Nixon's visit to Beijing in 1972. Japan had quietly traded with China throughout the 1960s and quickly followed Nixon's diplomatic lead, but when Chinese Foreign Minister Zhou Enlai refused business access to Japanese firms linked to Taiwan or south Korea, some companies abandoned operations in the Korean peninsula. Politicians in Tokyo also began to urge a more even-handed approach to the two Koreas, an approach adopted from 1974 by the new prime minister, Miki Takeo. This occurred at the nadir of post-1965 Korean–Japanese relations following the KCIA's two-fisted abduction of Park's leading political rival, Kim Dae Jung (Kim Taejung) from a Tokyo hotel in 1973. With United States aid coming to an end, and south Korea completely dependent on foreign oil and facing massive energy bills in the wake of the 1973 oil shock, Japanese credit was the esential glue to maintain the economic achievements to date. In recognition of this, Park sent an emissary with an apology to Tokyo for the Kim affair, but south Korea's reputation had clearly suffered. Mutual security kept the two states together — a north Korean military tunnel was discovered in the demilitarised zone in 1974, and the collapse of south Vietnam in the spring of 1975 heightened tension in East and Southeast Asia generally — but inter-governmental relations were stiff and uncomfortable until new leaders in Seoul and Tokyo took power in the 1980s.

Social pressures

Although the south Korean government propagated the values of rural community, simplicity and service, its economic policies promoted urban industrialisation, booming profits for a narrow capitalist élite, and a widening cultural and economic gap between town and country. At the start of the 1970s, Park belatedly turned to reducing this growing division at home and to easing rural discontent.

About 99 per cent of south Korean farmers in 1971 worked less than 3 hectares of land, and rice was still the principal crop. The average annual income for a farming household was US$735, compared with $991 for urban wage earners. Virtually all land was worked as a family concern; wage labour and inter-village contacts were minimal. Farmers lacked a strong political organisation and to that point had not challenged the government either in the manner of the nineteenth century Tonghak or at the ballot box. Relative to other countries in Asia, rapid urbanisation in south Korea had been attended by spin-offs to agriculture through rising urban demand and a degree of tariff protection. However, these benefits were outweighed by the equally attendant problems: food prices were kept artificially low to contain urban wages and production costs, and the appeal of higher urban incomes and a better standard of living bled rural youth from the countryside. The average age of villagers tilted towards the elderly, and those young men who remained behind found it increasingly difficult to obtain village wives.

Park's answer was the Saemaul (New Village) Movement, officially launched in 1971. His role in this rural mobilisation program was highly public: attending the annual conference of Saemaul leaders, awarding medals and citations to Saemaul achievers, and even composing the movement's song and lyrics. The goal was to modernise south Korean villages through electrification and up-to-date facilities, but also to erode what the government considered traditional village conservatism, indolence, wasteful rituals and ceremonies, all the unwanted elements of Korea's folk tradition. The first step had already been taken in the winter of 1970–71, with the state distributing free cement (cynics alleged a cement glut as the real motive) to nearly all of Korea's villages. The villagers were free to use this largesse as they wished and many applied it purposefully to erect roads and buildings. The electoral setback of 1971 and a rival program in north Korea spurred Park to take up the Saemaul campaign in earnest from 1972, and henceforth it took on a bureaucratic life of its own, with the government exploiting inter-village rivalry and rewarding those who met its expectations with greater resources. Contrasting with its over-interventionist approach to youth or industry, the government's basic approach at the outset was exactly right: it set broad goals and provided basic materials but left villagers to act for themselves. Village committees formulated their own development plans, and these were executed by village-elected male and female Saemaul leaders who co-ordinated matters with the authorities. Military service gave male Saemaul leaders a core of organisational ability, while there were women leaders with experience from the 1960s campaign on rural birth control. Although these positions were unpaid, Saemaul leaders were recompensed through better access to farming loans, educational scholarships for their children and potential employment in government organisations. Moreover, the authorities actively encouraged public respect for Saemaul leaders, and this incidentally helped to raise the status of rural women: it was often the level of their dynamism rather than that of the men which decided the success or failure of village projects.

Up to 1976, about US$1.78 billion had been invested in the Saemaul program, though only some 44 per cent of this came from government; the rest, principally in labour costs, came from the villagers themselves.[19] Increased education and information from radio or newspapers helped the people utilise government assistance, and the movement enjoyed considerable success where villages were socially and economically integrated. Land values jumped and the gap closed between rural and urban incomes. However, in villages with disparate income groups, the well-off or the very poor resented community pressure to contribute land, labour or savings. Moreover, despite the myriad benefits of electrification, the cost of electric lighting was many times that of kerosene. Also, the state failed to keep its distance, coming to view Saemaul in the same terms as economic growth and demand ever greater improvements: fundamentally an authoritarian regime, it did not shrink from coercion, ordering thatched roofs to be replaced by brightly coloured tiles, or destroying lower-yield rice beds even though consumers disliked the higher yield strain pushed by government. Such intrusions blunted village enthusiasm for Saemaul and, ironically in view of the original aims, some critics allege that rural compliance with official targets became heavily ritualised, and that reports were simply doctored to please the distant bureaucrats. Also working against the continuing success of Saemaul were the government's concurrent subsidies to producers and consumers alike, which resulted in severe inflation. The real official purchase price of rice, relative to inflation, began to decline from about 1976, and in that year the government, for the first time, allowed large imports of livestock products. International pressure was mounting to reduce farming subsidies still further, and the net effect of all this was to unleash another exodus of people from the countryside.

Despite the problems, the government was proud of its rural modernisation and expanded the concept to other areas. In the mid-1970s there was 'Factory Saemaul', 'School Saemaul', even Saemauls for government, business and religion. Saemaul units were created at all levels within public offices to improve performance and eradicate idleness. In a sense, village ideals were being brought back to the (largely rural in origin) city dwellers with the government's call to learn from the farmers. One scholar, Mick Moore, sees other echoes of Maoist-style ideology in the Saemaul's insistence on wise leadership, correct thought and collective striving as the way to improve the community as a whole.[20] As in Communist China, however, the farmers preferred to choose how and with whom they worked, and to resist collective goals.

Park's political fortunes began to turn about 1971. In the 1967 presidential election, he could point to many achievements: production was soaring; industrial employment had risen from 390 000 in 1962 to 1.3 million in 1967; urban and rural incomes were both improving; and south Korea's economic success was written in the stone of its modern cities. Yet he still received only 51.4 per cent of the valid votes (though improving his urban support to 50.4 per cent generally and to 46 per cent in Seoul) and, though taking the east coast, he lost the western provinces.[21] With factionalism mounting in his own Democratic Republican Party, Park subsequently amended the constitution to extend his term of office and so allow him to contest the April 1971 election. However, in the final counting, farmers contributed to a significant anti-government vote and he only narrowly defeated Kim Dae Jung, a youthful (45 in 1971) populist candidate with a clear regional base in Cholla. Kim was to continue nipping at the heels of militarism for the next twenty years, but in 1970 his nomination as the New Democratic Party candidate had only just been achieved over an even younger rival, Kim Young Sam (44 in 1971) from Kyongsang. The factionalism of the two Kims was also to recur at crucial points in succeeding decades, fatally weakening the political opposition.

While Park had no power over south Korea's external problems, he attempted to compensate by asserting his authority at home. In October 1972, he declared martial law and introduced a new constitution under the name Yusin or 'revitalisation' (i.e. Japanese *ishin*, the term used for the Meiji restoration). This removed presidential election from the public sphere, instead assigning that responsibility to an electoral college. It gave the incumbent president an enormous advantage in re-election by empowering him to appoint one-third of the National Assembly, enhanced the president's emergency powers and gave him the right to an unrestricted number of six-year terms. In effect, as some have noted, this created a legal dictatorship, and Park was ruthless in crushing any sign of opposition to the new constitution. However, there is no indication that he had become addicted to the trappings of power: there are no Herculean statues in his image, and no national treasures secreted to his private residence. Instead he retained his reputation for simplicity, hard work and commitment to Korea. Rather, as a soldier, he was trained to lead in times of crisis, and as the country's troubles deepened with the 1970s, so his determination increased not to relinquish control to lesser men or partisan interests. The corollary of this determination was a heightening of government repression and a rising number of political prisoners.

The internal troubles of the 1970s, however, had their origins in domestic policies. Affluence led to better living standards, but also heightened ostentation and official corruption. Government rational-isation of industry was efficient in terms of resource allocation and implementation of central directives, but it also created *chaebol* behemoths which dominated capital markets and choked smaller, and perhaps more dynamic, entrepreneurs, but left them unable to compete internationally without government support. Education had increased enormously but, once out of the bottle, the intellectual genii could not be returned; from poorly co-ordinated personality groups in 1960–61,

Korean students gradually organised themselves into a censorate of repression, the traditional role of the literati. Communications had developed enormously — by 1976, south Korea boasted 200 500 vehicles (compared with 92 000 in the north) running on modern freeways — but overseas travel was still denied the majority. Radio, television and cinema reached a mass audience — total film attendance in 1969 exceeded 173 million[22] — but all betrayed the hand of official censorship, and conversations were held in whispers as economic affluence also paid the wages of an expanded KCIA.

Industrialisation not only depopulated the villages, it also drained members of urban populations under 100 000 (especially in the southwest) and packed them in the major cities. Park had called for parochialism and indolence to be replaced by a society in motion, but the lure of government, industrial, educational and cultural activities in Seoul, to which all roads ultimately ran, produced immense congestion in the capital. By the mid-1960s, Seoul's resources were overstretched, social mores suffered, and the city appeared symbolic of all that was wrong in Korea. A saying from the 1950s warned: 'Close your eyes in Seoul and someone will steal your nose', and a constant theme in literature and films, such as Kim Suyong's *Girls Who Went to the City* (1979) and Im Kwont'aek's superb *Mandala* (1981), portrayed the metropolis as a kind of pre-1949 Shanghai in which innocent provincials were corrupted in a nightmare of Western-style urbanisation. Government plans for the capital in 1966 and 1970 aimed at a balance between humanity, nature and business by eliminating squatter areas caused by rural migrants, preserving the city centre for commerce and establishing a green belt to limit urban sprawl. Excess population was to be relocated to southern Seoul, to new satellite towns like Gwachon, to industrial dormitory towns, or to research centres such as Daedok in the central west, modelled on Japan's (mortuary-like) Tsukuba Science City. Ultimately, however, in such a centralised system, industries were reluctant to leave the capital, and Seoul remained a magnet for ambition: even those who were forced to live beyond its geographical limits either commuted into the city or sent their children to its colleges whenever possible.

Finally, there was the army. This formed the basis of Park's authority, but a new generation of officers, ambitious and opinionated, was coming of age. Park had copied Rhee's style, constantly shifting men to prevent any of them gaining a power base — even his relative, Kim Jong Pil, had been removed from the premiership — but this left him isolated at the top and the unprotected focus of discontent. In addition, the army's domination of central decision-making had resulted in obsequiousness at the periphery. No one challenged government orders and one faulty decision could have appalling consequences: the spread of high-yield rice plants, for example, was to lead to disastrous crop failure at the end of the 1970s. Moreover, after 1973, the Nixon doctrine left south Korea with a colossal bill for its defence and forced it to develop a domestic arms industry. The result was a national defence tax (10 per cent income and sales surcharge) and 'voluntary' contributions which fell heavily on the public pocket and dissipated support for the army.[23]

Table 4.1 Military expenditure in north and south Korea, 1971–1979 (US$ millions)		
	North Korea	South Korea
1971	758	719
1972	1030	822
1973	1080	764
1974	1370	1078
1975	1080	1461
1976	1310	2160
1977	1250	2577
1978	1310	3262
1979	1320	3385

Source: Young Whan Kihl, 1984, p. 146

The ROK forces were, of course, directed primarily at their brethren to the north. To reduce border tension and improve his standing within south Korea, Park turned his hand to peacemaking in the early 1970s. In July 1972, he set up a high-level North–South Co-ordinating Committee to consider reunification of the peninsula, and in 1973 had school textbooks rewritten to downplay the theme of anti-communism (as well as Western-style democracy) and instead promote Korean nationalism. However, negotiations between the two states at Panmunjom collapsed in 1973 and, during a conciliatory speech in August 1974 (in which Park proposed a mutual non-aggression pact, freedom of travel between north and south, and all-Korea elections), a north Korean assassin narrowly missed the president, instead murdering his widely respected wife.

Confronted by these various problems, Park responded not with political liberalisation but with added repression. In 1970, a popular young poet, Kim Chiha, had been gaoled for a scathing work on the south Korean élite which he titled 'The Five Thieves' (i.e. military generals, high bureaucrats, millionaire industrialists, cabinet members and, notably, National Assemblymen). This intolerance of poets was extended following the collapse of south Vietnam in May 1975, and Park clamped down on all dissent, even to the extent that criticism of the president became a criminal act. A particularly reactionary move was to reimprison those considered possible recidivists. Thus men who had years before served prison sentences for alleged anti-state activities in the Korean War were rounded up and reincarcerated in the newly built Chongju Preventive Detention Centre: some were still there in 1989.

South Korea's domestic pressures built to a crescendo late in 1979 as the economy rocked under a second oil shock. By then, students had developed a unified sub-culture, enjoying its own language, motifs and heroes, all in opposition to the president's despised Yusin system; members of the middle class had grown dissatisfied with the litany of economic growth without political freedoms; and unionised labour was becoming increasingly assertive under the influence of students and Christian activist groups.[24] When, in September 1979, Kim Young Sam of the New Democratic Party was quoted in the *New York Times* labelling Park a dictator, his penalty was expulsion from the National Assembly. This was the trigger for massive anti-government protests engineered by the students. The situation in Pusan was met by a declaration of martial law on 18 October, but this did not deter plans for nationwide demonstrations on the 29th. With a bloodbath widely anticipated, unexpected intervention came from Park's own KCIA chief, who tried to head off confrontation and assassinated the president on 26 October.

If Park had grievously answered for his faults, worse was to come. The legacy of eighteen years of military domination, the absence of a logical successor and the fragmented nature of both the DRP and the opposition left a vacuum into which only one force, the army, was ready — and all too willing — to step. On 12 December 1979, Major General Chun Doo Hwan (Chon Tuhwan), head of the Army Security Command, arrested the sitting martial law commander and effectively took control of government. Other powerful army commanders were also arrested and units in the capital opposing Chun's coup were silenced by force. Like Park, a native of Kyongsang, Chun was an able and ambitious soldier and, along with Major General Roh Tae Woo (No T'aeu) and others, was a leader of a secretive fraternity of Korean Military Academy graduates known as the Hanahoe (literally Society of One). Over several months, he consolidated his power, taking control of the KCIA and, in May 1980, massively extending the scope of martial law and arresting men from both the ruling and opposition parties. In so doing, Chun unleashed a blaze of public fury. Nowhere was this more vocal and militant than in Kwangju, a city of about 900 000 in Cholla province, the agrarian region most neglected under Rhee and Park, and the base of Kim Dae Jung. On 18 May 1980, Special Armed Forces entered the city to crush student demonstrations against martial law and the arrest of Kim. The brutality of the 'invading' soldiers, who murdered protestors and bystanders alike, produced an insurrection involving all social classes and requiring further government forces to suppress. When all was done, at least several hundred citizens (or, according to opposition figures, several thousand) had been killed or injured. This incident was the catharsis for a new era in student radicalism, and was to haunt Chun well beyond his retirement in 1988. At the time, the people of Kwangju could only explain the soldiers's inhumanity as due to their being 'enemies' from Kyongsang, and it is a bitter irony that south Korean troops, employed since the Korean War only in Vietnam, should be decorated for their 'service' here.[25]

Residents of Kwangju, and subsequently many other Koreans as well, believed the United States had supported the massacre. Since November 1978, the United Nations force in Korea had changed to a bilateral ROK–United States Combined Forces Command (CFC) headed by a four-star

United States general, and popular wisdom held that south Korean troops could not have been despatched to Kwangju without approval from the United States commander. This was incorrect. The CFC held authority over about half the ROK troops in peacetime, but south Korean generals were unilaterally able to move their forces so long as notice was given (even after the fact) to the joint commander. Moreover, although the second wave of forces sent to Kwangju was part of the CFC, the Special Forces initially sent into the city were solely under Korean orders. Documents released by Washington in 1989 showed the United States ambassador and CFC commander to be ill-informed and unprepared to deal with what was occurring in Kwangju, but also appalled by Chun's ruthlessness. Such evidence, however, did not mollify those Koreans who, rejecting a legalistic approach, condemned the United States on moral grounds. The unending chorus of reproach pushed one United States official into a blunt but accurate assessment that, 'What the south Koreans have never been able to face is that Kwangju was about Koreans killing Koreans'.[26]

The fifth republic, 1981–87: Society versus the state

Chun carried out an accelerated version of Park's own ascension to power, retiring from the army and using the indirect electoral system to become president in August 1980. Predictably, the constitution was again revised, this time instituting a single seven-year presidential term. Chun successfully contested the presidency under the new constitution in February 1981 but, if nothing else, he was to respect his own provision and in 1988 become the first president of south Korea peacefully to transfer power. However, Chun was the least legitimate of south Korea's presidents. Unlike Rhee, who commanded genuine respect, and Park, whose 1961 coup had been greeted with popular relief, Chun had created his own crisis out of Park's murder and shed Korean blood on his way to power. Moreover, in a time of public politics, his image was one of cold arrogance, and his relatives, in contrast to Park's family, were to be involved in repeated financial scandals. On the broader level, Chun's regime was to see renewed economic growth and some improvement in ties with the United States and Japan, but also growing international rancour over the imbalance of Korea's foreign trade. The Chun years are also characterised — indeed, decisively punctuated — by the expansion and intensification of popular protest.

The political opposition was muzzled at the outset, with the National Assembly dissolved and the three Kims, Kim Jong Pil of the DRP, Kim Young Sam and Kim Dae Jung, all deprived of their political rights and either gaoled or put under house arrest. On the charge of having incited the Kwangju uprising, Kim Dae Jung was initially sentenced to death, but action by United States President Ronald Reagan, and criticism from Tokyo helped commute the sentence to life imprisonment. To control the Assembly, Chun followed Park's example by organising the

Democratic Justice Party (DJP). He also copied Park's early social purification drive: thousands of bureaucrats, journalists and teachers were purged from office and, from early August 1980 to January 1982, the government secretly ran the Samchong program, a string of military re-education and forced labour camps for political prisoners and social misfits, including gamblers, prostitutes and beggars. About 40 000 people were rounded up and incarcerated in the gulags, about one-quarter of them in the first two weeks of August 1980.[27] This was a hackneyed ploy, lumping political dissenters with the socially ostracised and pretending society would be better without them all. To balance severity with benevolence, Chun did relax certain measures: in January 1982, he ended the midnight curfew, in place since 1945; in March that year, amnesty was granted to about 3000 prisoners; and students at middle and high school were released from the uncomfortable military-style uniforms carried over from colonial days. These, however, were surface changes and in no way cloaked the persistent repression.

Having rebuilt the structures of central authority, the government turned its attention to the economy. In 1980, with the world in recession, violent unrest at home and a catastrophic harvest due to overplanting of the weaker high-yield rice, south Korea's economy had declined for the first time since the Korean War. Chun's promise was to restore economic growth (and with it the perception of national health) by restructuring industry and further expanding exports. In this, he was aided by a group of radical reformers whose targets were the swollen *chaebol*. Heavy industry was remodelled, with some firms forced to shift or swap their interests in key areas such as automobile production. The government also used its control of credit to manipulate the *chaebol*, and pressured them for generous donations to organisations such as the Saemaul movement and Chun's pet project, the Ilhae Foundation: when one corporation, the Kukje Group (south Korea's seventh largest *chaebol*), failed to meet Chun's expectations, government banks quickly forced it into bankruptcy. The government also attempted from 1981 to readdress the problem of regional development and provide room for smaller to medium-sized industry. Earlier policies had merely shunted Seoul's overpopulation into surrounding bed-towns, thus failing either to reduce demands on capital transport and facilities or improve development in areas such as Cholla. The Second National Physical Land Development Plan (1982–91) was aimed at balanced regional growth, giving special emphasis to the south-west, and offering tax breaks and preferential loans to entice industrial estates into the countryside.

In the end, however, south Korea depended on international credit and the debt burden grew to over US$40 billion by the mid-1980s. Exports were over-committed to sales of transport equipment, electrical goods, footwear and textiles in the United States, and the ROK remained dependent on Japan for innovative technology. However, relations with both states were affected by the authoritarianism of Chun's domestic rule, and by the existing imbalances in mutual trade.

Table 4.2 South Korean imports/exports, 1960–1987 (US$ millions)					
	Total imports	Total exports	Imports from US	Exports to US	Imports from Japan	Exports to Japan
1960	344	33	133.8	3.6	70.4	20.2
1965	463	175	182.3	61.7	166.6	44.0
1970	1 984	835	584.8	395.2	809.3	234.3
1975	7 274	5 081	1 181.1	1 536.0	2 433.6	1 292.9
1980	22 292	17 505	4 890.0	4 606.0	5 857.8	3 039.4
1985	31 136	30 283	6 489.0	10 754.0	7 560.4	4 543.4
1987	41 000	47 300	8 758.0	18 311.0	13 656.6	8 436.8

Source: Steinberg, 1989, p. 142

From a relatively even balance in 1980, south Korea developed a rising trade surplus with the United States of $3 billion by 1984, reaching about $7 billion in 1986. Faced with its own problems, Washington was quick to attack Korean protectionism, especially in agricultural goods, and in 1985 took action to limit imports from Korea. This came as a tremendous shock to the Korean government and people: the authorities responded by announcing selective import liberalisation, reduction of state control of finance and the easing of foreign investment rules, but south Korea undeniably remained a controlled and protected economy. On a popular level, the United States trade restrictions were resented as self-centred policies against a much smaller and weaker state, and one which had long been a faithful ally: in effect, the United States was being condemned for its failure to meet a Korean image of strength and majesty which never existed in reality, and this turnaround in Korean public perception was added to existing criticism of the United States over Kwangju.

In response to trade difficulties, south Korean officials and business-men began taking their case directly to the American people. They hired former Republican officials and United States consultants to present a positive image, and the Korean Economic Institute of America, a direct copy of the Japanese Economic Institute of America, was established to shape United States public opinion. This was a perfectly legitimate move in the United States, which functions through competing information, but one which the United States had no chance of exploiting in Korea. The ROK was able to use its economic muscle and Korean investment or purchases were welcomed in states such as Alaska, Illinois and Georgia, with Korean money targetting those states such as Kansas with political heavyweights in the Congress or Senate.[28]

As for Korea's relations with Japan, which remained primarily economic in nature, these continued to be troubled by domestic politics in the respective capitals. Even though it is Japan's bureaucracy which sets policy, it still requires a competent prime minister to deal with foreign relations. Prime Minister Suzuki Zenko, however, was credited with no more intelligence than a Muppet and the scandal of Japanese textbook revision in 1982, downplaying the nature of Japanese prewar expansion, brought outraged protest from governments around Asia. It was not until 1983, when Prime Minister Nakasone Yasuhiro took office, that a new era of mature co-operation was instituted. Nakasone visited Seoul early in 1983 and Chun reciprocated with the first official visit to Japan by a Korean premier in September 1984. This was an historic occasion but, for south Korean purposes, one centred on the willingness of Japanese authorities to apologise for colonialisation of Korea. In view of Japanese domestic realities, Emperor Hirohito's reference on 6 September was brief and general, admitting that 'there was an unfortunate past between us for a period in this century and I believe that it should not be repeated again'. Prime Minister Nakasone, at a less formal meeting the following day, was more explicit:

> In the history of the interchange between Japan and Korea wherein we owe a great deal to your country, regrettably, the fact remains that there was a period in this century when Japan brought to bear great suffering upon your country and its people. I would like to state here that the government and people of Japan feel a deep regret for this error and are determined firmly to warn ourselves for the future.[29]

With honour temporarily satisfied, President Chun could tell his host, in the manner of Park in 1965, 'the memories of the bitter past remain' but we do not 'have the time to debate the past', and they moved quickly on to concrete issues: the vast trade imbalance in Japan's favour and the need for Japan to buy more south Korean goods, freer access for Korea to Japanese technology, regional security, and the anomalous status of the 700 000 Koreans resident in Japan. Of these issues, the most emotive was the 'lost tribe' of Korean residents, but the most important to Seoul remained trade and technology. Although little of substance was agreed at this time, south Korea was treated with respect — the one commodity perhaps even more important than trade — and its press generally hailed the visit as contributing to Korea's international stature.

While Chun took steps to affirm ties with the United States and Japan, relations with north Korea remained highly volatile. In 1980, P'yongyang discussed a meeting of the two premiers but, in October 1983, Chun and his officials were the victims of a north Korean assassination attempt whilst visiting Burma (Myanmar): seventeen south Korean officials were killed. The following year, however, P'yongyang displayed its humane face, sending gifts including food, cement and medical supplies to assist south Korean flood victims. Following this symbolic gesture, talks were resumed on economic links and the reunion of families divided since 1953; 50 families were duly reunited before the television cameras in 1985. Then, in November 1987, a north Korean agent planted a bomb on a Korean Air Lines passenger vessel, killing 115 people. In the mid-1980s, reunification was a growing emotional issue in south Korea, one loudly supported by students and Protestant groups, but also one rendered impractical by the topsy-turvy nature of P'yongyang actions. These may have been due to internal political manouevring as Kim Il

Sung entered his twilight years, and south Korean officials privately doubted that any real progress could be achieved until after his death. The collapse of the north Korean economy and its failure to honour international debts, meanwhile, left Seoul with the upper hand, especially as the Soviet Union and China turned away from hard-line communism and began strengthening links with the West. However, the unpredictability of P'yongyang roused fears of an outrage at the coming 1988 Seoul Olympics, and the television news portrayed a huge dam on the border as being readied to flood Seoul once the games commenced. Extensive talks with north Korea towards sharing part of the games proved futile, but ultimately the presence in Seoul of Soviet and Chinese Olympians, and the international prestige of the games for the Korean people as a whole prevented any disruption the north may once have considered.

Although Chun tried to recreate Park's policies of centralisation and control, he was confronted by the same, but growing, forces of social change. None was more intractable than the spread of organised student radicalism. By 1985, a full 23 per cent of the population fell in the 15–25 age group and, while Vincent Brandt has noted the correlation between a 'youth bulge' and socio-political instability, it was Chun's repressive policies on thought and action that radicalised south Korea's educated youth.[30] The rise in college enrolments between 1980 and 1985 was particularly acute.

Table 4.3 School enrolments in south Korea, 1945–1985 ('000s)

	1945	1952	1960	1965	1970	1975	1980	1985
Primary	1366.0	2369.9	3622.9	4941.3	5749.3	5599.1	5568.0	4856.8
Middle	*83.5	291.6	528.6	751.3	1318.8	2026.8	2472.0	2782.2
High	*	133.9	263.6	426.5	590.4	1123.0	1696.8	2152.8
College and university	7.8	34.1	101.0	141.6	193.6	296.6	597.9	1260.3

Note:*1945 figure combined for middle and high schools
Source: Hakchung Choo, 1990, p. 174

The radicals numbered less than 10 per cent of the total number of students, but their moral fervour and Spartan discipline influenced many others. A new era in student protest began with the formation in May 1985 of Sammintu (Struggle Committee for Minjung Democratisation). This led the way in street rallies and organised the sit-in occupation of the United States Information Service library in Seoul in May 1985. It was from this time that anti-Americanism became a leading part of radical student ideology. The core of their thought was *minjung*, or the masses, defined as all those who were exploited by or alienated from the existing system, a system dominated by the military and capitalists, but one created by the United States-engineered division of Korea in 1945. Consequently, *minjung* believers (and in its expression it was a religion as much as a philosophy) demanded the withdrawal of United States forces from the south, the destruction of the militarist–capitalist regime, and the unification of Korea to bring about freedom and an intrinsic nationalist democracy. In this, they looked to Kim Il Sung and his Chuche ideal as the embodiment of an independent Korean polity, preserving Korean traditional values and rejecting the materialism and dependency of the south.[31] This was clearly a naive, outdated utopianism, with all-night discussion of Marxist texts and manual farm labour to toughen up student spirits, but the passion of the student activists and their refusal to kneel before government repression won them qualified public sympathy. This was strengthened by the public's receptiveness to student accusations of United States 'hegemonism' in the wake of the Kwangju massacre and continuing trade friction.

As in the 1920s, the radical students could not contain their ideological differences. The resulting split led to formation in March 1986 of the Minmintu, based at Seoul National University (SNU) but with a relatively broad membership across other universities, espousing the policies of anti-imperialism, anti-fascism and democracy, and portraying students at the forefront of the coming social revolution. Its rival was the Chamintu, organised in April 1986, based mainly at SNU and Korea University, and with a more radical program of revolution centred on the toiling masses rather than on students. In a powerful demonstration of commitment, Chamintu supporters were prominent amongst those students burning themselves to death in protest at Chun's despotism. Both groups, however, criticised the established opposition parties as opportunists and, in the manner of communists under Japanese colonialism, fought a war of attrition from their own tight-knit underground organisations, shifting their demonstrations from the closed space of the campus to the more fluid arena of the streets. As evidence of the seriousness with which the government viewed this youth threat, when students did come together to form a mass front at Seoul's Kon'guk University in October 1986, they were met by an army of 19 000 riot police. The 1275 arrests which followed represented, as Wonmo Dong notes, the largest single arrest of student activists anywhere in the world.

The growing extremism in student action and ideology led moderate supporters of reform, such as Cardinal Stephen Kim, Catholic archbishop of Seoul, to urge young activists away from revolution and towards democracy in order to retain middle-class support. A loose coalition of students, church and middle-class society finally came together in the first half of 1987. The starting point, as in 1960, was the news of a SNU student tortured to death by police in January. In National Assembly elections the following month, the government was rejected in all five of south Korea's biggest cities. Educators, Christian clerics and women's community leaders were all publicly critical of the Chun regime, and when he attempted to gag promised debate on constitutional revision, a mass campaign evolved under the Reunification Democratic Party (RDP), established in May 1987 by Kim Young Sam and Kim Dae Jung. With Samil-like public demonstrations for constitutional revision involving all classes, and Protestant and Catholic clergy and nuns on hunger strikes, neither the Korean army nor the United States administration sanctioned confrontation. On 26 June 1987, a Grand Peace march in Seoul and other cities involved hundreds of thousands and served to convince Roh Tae Woo, Chun's chosen successor as president and head of the DJP, that he must defuse public anger through broad concessions. Three days later, Roh announced his acceptance of direct presidential election, liberalisation of politics and the release of political prisoners. With this, fears (and hopes) of a Filipino-style 'people's power' uprising were calmed, south Korea's civic majority was appeased, Chun was rapidly confined to history, and the constitution was revised as promised late in 1987.

The political drama of mid-1987 brought to a head the long-standing rivalry between Kim Young Sam and Kim Dae Jung. The point at issue was which of them should oppose Roh in the December presidential election. Both had long years of experience and a high public profile, but appealed to contrasting elements in society. Kim Young Sam was the moderate preference, while Kim Dae Jung enjoyed a hero's following among radicals; this status brought the latter a barely veiled threat from the army chief of staff not to stand for president. A National Association of University Student Representatives, known as Chondaehyop (established August 1987), warned the RDP not to let the people down or face a public revolt against it, but ultimately neither man agreed to stand aside. Their break in October was duplicated in the student movement, with the Sodaehyop supporting Kim Young Sam and the militant Chondaehyop backing Kim Dae Jung. Many students, however, also worked for Roh in the DJP's Youth Volunteer Service Corps. In the final vote, the opposition split proved crucial, with the two Kims receiving about 27 per cent each to Roh's 36.6 per cent, and Kim Jong Pil, now leading the New Democratic Republican Party, taking only about 8 per cent. Roh's greatest constituency was amongst farmers, forest and fishery workers, and housewives. White-collar voters were decidedly for the centrist Kim Young Sam, but significantly, blue-collar support was not wholly behind any candidate. In February 1988, Roh Tae Woo became the sixth president of the sixth republic.

Table 4.4 Vote distribution in the 1987 presidential election			
Occupation	Roh	Kim Young-Sam	Kim Dae Jung
Agriculture/forestry/fishery	46.9	17.7	25.6
Small business	33.3	29.3	30.5
Blue collar	29.2	28.8	33.7
White collar	22.2	45.4	24.4
Housewives	39.6	24.8	26.4
Students	6.1	43.1	34.3
Unemployed	35.9	31.7	27.1

Source: Wonmo Dong, 1988, p. 183

Chun had been an anachronism and the public took its revenge by an intense National Assembly and media campaign to make him apologise for his actions: in November 1988, they finally got a televised apology for the Kwangju incident, the Samchong camps, the political purges and the financial corruption of his officials and relatives. He then retired to a Buddhist temple in a traditional indication of breaking with the world of affairs.

The sixth republic: The meeting of centre and periphery

From 1988, the Republic of Korea entered a new phase in its political and social development. There were constitutional safeguards against despotism, relaxation of censorship and, following the success of the Seoul Olympics, a new sense of Korea's status in the world. Roh's concessions in June 1987 had won him popular goodwill, and his ability to extend the political centre by discussion rather than force was shown in May 1990 with the creation of the Democratic Liberal Party. This was a merger of the government's Democratic Justice Party with the forces of Kim Young Sam and Kim Jong Pil, thus positioning Kim Young Sam to succeed Roh as president in 1993 (for this opportunism, Kim was publicly criticised), but more importantly giving the government a National Assembly majority and with it the promise of new period of political stability. The move also forced Kim Dae Jung, in 1991, to seek a broader base and merge his Cholla supporters with a Kyongsang-based party to form a new Democratic Party. Thus south Korean politics finally, even if only temporarily, began to overcome the regional particularism which had dogged affairs of state for so long. An unprecedented political diversity, and one more in keeping with a working democracy, arrived with the dramatic creation in 1992 of the Unification National Party by Chung Ju Yung, founder of the Hyundai corporation. As a businessman only entering politics in his 76th year, Chung was a political maverick, but his appeal was precisely that of a man untainted by politics, and his party captured 10 per cent of the parliamentary seats in elections during March 1992. Chung's willingness to speak out on sensitive issues, even to accept a communist party in south Korea as demonstrating the ROK's commitment to freedom of speech, injected a new vitality into the political arena and prevented the ruling party from lapsing into complacency.

Where Chun had been aloof and confrontational, Roh was generally accessible. In December 1991 he made history by meeting with leaders of the left-wing Minjung Party, the first official presidential meeting with leftist figures since 1948. Founded in November 1990 by former student activists, the Minjung Party was committed to work within the constitutional system and was avowedly moderate in its views: it desired nationalisation of major industries, but supported private ownership of land and smaller industry and had no illusions about north Korea. With this meeting, Roh gave its leaders respect and for men previously imprisoned for their beliefs, that was visible progress.

To some, however, Roh was an uncertain quantity, either too flexible or too much a militarist. Critics attacked his civilian front, others feared a military coup against him, and some army officers publicly challenged his softness on radicalism. However, he proved an adept politician, quickly removing senior commanders too closely associated with Chun, and dealing immediately with four army officers accused in mid-1988 of stabbing the editor of *Chungang Economic Daily* following articles critical of the military. Despite lingering discontent at the new democracy, senior officers such as General Kim Jinyong, Capital Garrison Commander and leader of the increasingly powerful class 17 (1961) of the Korean Military Academy, openly pledged the army to a strictly non-political role.[32]

Student demonstrations, however, did not cease or even slacken. As one Korea University teacher admitted, 'We professors have little authority over students as it was they who carried the brunt of struggle for democracy.'[33] Such a revolutionary tradition could hardly be appeased by Roh's centrism, and a resurgence of radicalism early in 1989 assailed 'comprador capitalism', with its toadying to foreign powers, and 'revisionist' parliamentary democracy. In clashes with students at Pusan, six riot police were killed. Perhaps in reaction against this, the radical Chondaehyop was defeated in about half the student council elections at Korean universities in November 1989, including the most radical of all, Seoul National University. However, when the police beat a student to death in May 1991, thousands joined in some of the most violent demonstrations ever seen, lasting for several weeks throughout south Korea, and including the self-immolation of seven students. The fighting was most violent in Kwangju, where annual unrest perpetuated the memory of the 1980 rising. As in 1986–87, students denounced what they saw as Roh's murderous regime and its United States supporters. Anti-American sentiment was fuelled by the strident nationalist newspaper *Han'gyore Sinmun*, founded in the liberal climate of May 1988 and quickly reaching a daily circulation of about 375 000. Many *Han'gyore* journalists had been purged or imprisoned by Chun, and they scorned any who had 'collaborated' either then or under Roh. Indeed, the litmus test of purity for the students and their supporters was opposition and rejection. Hence there was little chance of student reconciliation with any regime of power, especially one despised as capitalist and dependent on foreign commerce. However, after graduation, as with radical Japanese students of the late 1960s, many did fit into the system, and students from the radical heartland, SNU, continued their near-absolute domination of recruitment for the government, judiciary and top corporations.

The changes brought by rapid economic development were plain to see in south Korea's streets. By the late 1980s, about 40.9 per cent of all south Koreans were resident in cities of more than a million people, while Seoul alone housed about 10 million, or roughly one-quarter of the entire populace. Congestion and rising incomes inflated the cost of all urban land, which increased by 30 per cent in 1989 alone, but this was peculiarly felt in the capital. In 1991, Seoul accounted for 52 per cent of the country's total land value, a total estimated at nearly four-fifths that of the United States (some 94 times larger).[34] The capital was not a garden city with the beauty of London or Berlin, but it still had far more greenery and far fewer vehicles than Tokyo (though the difference may not immediately strike the unfortunate pedestrian). The south Korean people as a whole were increasingly mobile, with easier access to international travel, and passenger cars almost doubling between 1986 and 1988 from 664 000 to 1.2 million. This was not an unmixed blessing: the 1991 road toll of some 13 000 deaths was appallingly high; to put it in some perspective, Spain, with a roughly comparable population (39 million in 1990), vastly more cars on the roads and an international reputation for high-risk driving, had a death toll for 1990 of slightly less than 6000. Yet, in psychological and literal terms, south Korea was, as Park had wished, a society on the move — in 1986, about 8.7 million people, or more than 21 per cent of the population, changed their place of residence.[35] The question troubling many south Koreans was where all this movement was to lead.

The demographic flood remained one-way. There was some growth in environmental and health awareness, with people looking to eat and live better, but there was no significant return to the countryside, and young men and women continued to abandon the villages. The rural population fell to about 18 per cent of the total in 1990, compared with 55 per cent in 1965. Nearly all villages had improved standards of living as a result of the Saemaul movement, but urban monthly wages in 1986 averaged about US$822.50 compared with about $684.40 for rural workers.[36] Rice was still a protected commodity despite international complaints, but import liberalisation of fruits, grains and cotton forced Korean farmers out of those areas and caused them to crowd into the protected markets. The result was a collapse in domestic prices and more rice than anyone (except north Korea) needed. In February 1989, about 10 000 farmers came together outside the National Assembly, but their protest ended in pitched battles with riot police. As changes in the law prohibited a repeat demonstration, the farmers were left with no choice but to improve their political organisation and agitate for continued protectionism. However, officials in Seoul, as in Tokyo (which faced the same problem), acknowledged that subsidies would ultimately be reduced and farmers would have to diversify or disappear.

The spread of communications and information reached Koreans in both town and village. Televisions, radios and videos became more common, while popular magazines catered for an enormous variety of interests and relayed trends in thought and fashion current in Japan or the West. Fitness became a general obsession in the shadow of the

Olympics, and the government sponsored a 'sport for all' campaign of opening up school and other facilities to urbanites (though this was not least to give discontented youth a chance to let off steam). In terms of diet, the average Korean teenager was considerably taller than those of 1965. Birth rates declined under government birth control programs, while better health and medicine improved the average life expectancy by 1984 to 64.5 years for men and 70.9 years for women. However, where there was little movement was in social and sexual roles. These were still largely frozen in the Confucian past: society remained a construction of clearly defined relationships and individualism was viewed, to quote one author, as 'the ultimate danger of modernization', a disease to be charted by the media with as much concern as the spread of drug abuse.[37] Men had legal ownership of children and divorced women were regarded with distaste. Young women were constantly pressed by their families into matrimony, but many Korean companies refused to employ married women. Women were paid less for doing the same job as men, and their political representation was minimal. Nine women candidates stood for the National Assembly in April 1988 but none was elected: this situation was only rectified with the March 1992 election.

The greatest degree of flux was in the ideas and values of youth. Roh allowed open discussion of Marxism, and the first complete translation of *Das Kapital* appeared in 1987. Some publishers made available reprint editions of works from P'yongyang, and universities began courses in north Korean studies.[38] The intellectual searching was keenest in native culture. Affluence and political freedom enabled Koreans in the 1980s to excavate the bones of tradition; archaeological exploration was at a height in the south and new museums and temple restorations proceeded apace. Historians in the Council for the Study of Korean History established twenty research themes, the majority of which, following the tradition of Ch'oe Namson and Sin Ch'aeho, dealt with ancient history and the quest for a purely Korean identity unsullied by contact with the outside world. Oral culture was also a key area of preservation: protest songs had been seen as integral to the anti-Chun resistance and, building on this, the *Han'gyore* newspaper sponsored Kim Mingi, south Korea's pioneer of protest music, to gather Korean folk songs at home and in the expatriate communities. Some music critics pursued an individual Korean sound, distinct from the phonic influences of China, Japan or the West, and this, in turn, led to the so-called unification music movement in which south Korean musicians sought exchanges with colleagues to the north and promoted an interest in the post-1945 music of north Korean socialist realism.[39]

While the modern student eschewed the traditional pen for urban activism, literature in south Korea still played an important social role. In contrast with the arts in advanced capitalist societies, oscillating between abstraction and entertainment, south Korean writers tended to be more 'engaged' and less 'pure' artists. Seoul National University professor Paik Nakchung is credited with leading the call for a class-specific literature in his 1969 essay, 'On citizens' literature'. In this, he demanded a literature for the common people, not the entrenched capitalist élite, and the guiding principle of all south Korean art through the 1980s was that it be relevant to the Korean masses. Under Roh, this evolved into a more openly Marxist literature, espousing the themes of worker-peasant suffering, and even criticising men such as Paik for being too academic and estranged from the people. Despite its echoes of the proletarian literary movement of the 1920s, Seong-Kon Kim explains that modern Korean writing concerned itself less with the universal proletariat, instead stressing characters, situations and a style which were intrinsically Korean.[40] Applying the test of purity, former literary heroes such as Yi Kwangsu were villified anew for 'collaborating' with colonial Japan, while those who had resisted oppression were granted new heroic status.

The recurrent motif both of literature and history, however, was to show the foreign-imposed division of Korea, the resulting exploitation of the *minjung* by native élites and the psychological impact of division on the Korean people. One of the most famous authors of the so-called 'literature of division' was Kim Won'il, whose novel *Winter Valley* explored the massacre by ROK forces of south Korean villagers at Koch'ang in February 1951. As with the other arts, the literature of division also sought a fuller understanding of contemporary north Korean writing.

This trend of aesthetic nationalism and political engagement was prominent in the other arts. Drama on Taehangno, Seoul's Broadway, tested the new freedoms with satires and experimental performance; traditional dance and folk theatre took on strident sociopolitical themes such as anti-Americanism, the Kwangju incident and labour misery; and painting was split between modernism and critical realism, the latter extolling *minjung* liberation. South Korean cinema flourished under looser government control and, although mainstream films prospered from the freedom to depict sex and violence in greater detail, there were underground films capturing new audiences, and a continuation of the anti-urban trend of the 1970s. Some directors worked as independents to investigate social issues or the daily lives of workers or peasants, while a group of feminist directors challenged the continuing patriarchy of south Korean society. These movements, whether of social realism, feminism or exposing the past corruption of government and élites, were largely the work of young Koreans, some of whom, like female director Kim Soyong, had studied in the United States.[41]

However, the intellectual revival and 'nationalisation' of folk arts missed the essential point — naturalness. Folk culture is a product of its environment, not the creation of intellectuals, and the demand for broader socio-political relevance threatened a kind of cultural colonisation from the centre. This was a danger inherent in the creation in 1990 of south Korea's first Ministry of Culture (as separate from the former Ministry of Culture and Information), charged with the task of 'managing' the nation's arts. South Korean intellectuals in the 1980s actively participated in the post-modernist debate with its deconstruction of the hidden structures underlying thought and action in existing capitalist systems, mainly of the West; indeed, post-modernism had much in sympathy with the 'anti-imperialism' of south Korean discourse and targeted the same culprits. However, in the rush of freedom after 1987, it was debatable whether Koreans were fully aware that nationalism may become a form of domestic imperialism. Moreover, post-modernism is essentially a negative approach, literally deconstructing the bases of earlier exploitative relations between states and within societies. The question remained whether south Korean intellectuals would continue to find a community with foreign thinkers in a post-postmodernist world.

As Park Chung Hee had suggested, it was the economy to which most south Koreans looked as the barometer of national well-being and, at the end of the 1980s, this showed an erratic and unpredictable progress. Announcing his policies for the early 1990s, President Roh indicated that the era of crisis had yet to pass:

> The birth pangs of the new order are causing anxiety and uncertainties, which, in turn, accelerate fierce competition among nations for a place in the sun, as well as the formation of regional blocs . . . Our capabilities for development are now being severely tested as long pent-up demands erupt as a corollary of democratization and as contradictions that have deepened in the shadow of rapid growth and industrialization rise to the surface.[42]

In 1989 economic growth stood at 6.5 per cent, with a current account surplus of US$5.1 billion; in1990, growth rose to 9.2 per cent, but there was the first current account deficit in five years at US$2.1 billion. Roh attacked management practices as outdated and over-reliant (compared with Japan) on family control. Worker morale had fallen, while wage expectations had exploded since late 1987, and unions had split between those seeking practical gains and those, under the influence of *minjung* radicalism, fighting an ideological contest. Higher wages lit the fuse of inflation, officially estimated at 8.6 per cent in 1990, and caused swelling production costs. The result was increasing offshore industrial relocation in Southeast Asia and, in the case of Hyundai's personal computer operations, a move to California (though this was also to gain better access to the immensely lucrative United States market).

For Roh, the weaknesses of Korea's economy were not the result of foreign influence, but of Korean society itself. His response was to go back to the patriotic enlightenment and cultural nationalist remedy of moral solutions, and plead for a social compact of unity, moderation and sacrifice. Of course, this was not (as it never had been) sufficient by itself. In 1990 the government eased Chun's restrictions on *chaebol* growth and access to cheap credit, and recommitted itself to export development as its first priority. Repeated campaigns against 'luxury' imports, however, failed to address the real problem, that of south Korea's crippling dependence on imported energy, with a bill in 1988 for US$4.3 billion on oil alone. To maintain public support into the 1990s, Roh promised to clean up society, act against large-scale tax evasion, improve the police and combat decadence, and also build extensive low-cost housing to ease the residential crush. He pledged to improve facilities for rural villages, establish massive development projects along the south-west coast in part to assist Cholla's economy, and to enhance local government, an ambitious mix of extending central resources while defending local autonomy. Education, not of expanding the individual's awareness but of reciting formulae and fielding exams, had long been the golden road to success, but university overcrowding produced an annual half-million youths missing out on tertiary education; these were potent recruits for social unrest, and Roh promised more vocational training, less emphasis on exams as the fulcrum of schooling, and a new style of education teaching the skills of debate and conciliation.

The thing most desired of the outside world, as it had been in the 1880s, was science and technology, and the new official goal for south Korea was to become one of the seven technological powers by the turn of the twenty-first century. By 1990, it was the world's sixth largest producer of electronics, and Samsung (south Korea's largest *chaebol* with annual sales in 1989 of US$32.6 billion), along with Hyundai, Lucky Goldstar and Daewoo, was investing heavily in advanced technology. Given the enormity of the project, and of the potential rewards, these plans served to reaffirm the intimate ties between south Korea's government and industry. The administration supplied cheap corporate finance, sponsored research facilities in semiconductors and robotics and, through the Education Ministry, arranged a rapid increase in university enrolment of engineering students. In a world in which military force no longer enjoyed the kudos of the nineteenth century, scientific advance became the standard of success; as Roh declared, 'To boost the country's technology to the highest level is to overcome the last barrier between us and our determined goal of joining the ranks of the world's advanced nations.'[43]

By the 1990s, south Korea was no longer the 'hermit nation' of Western mythology. It was recognised as a major economic player, a status which brought it respect and goodwill for its overseas investments, but also recrimination for its unbalanced trade from the United States, Japan and the EEC. However, beyond the simple fact of its production, there was no great Western advance in understanding; rare was a course in Western schools or universities on Korean language or history. Foreign visitors to south Korea in 1988, the year of the Seoul Olympics, totalled 2.34 million, but about half of these came from Japan (including many Korean residents visiting their homeland) and the rest mainly from Hong Kong or Taiwan. South Koreans were improving their understanding of the outside, expanding production into Europe and using their affluence either to travel or import more of foreign culture, but Western reciprocity was slow in coming.

The United States and Japan remained the two most vital foreign links. This is demonstrated by overall trade figures for 1990: total south Korean imports were valued at US$69 billion, of which Japan provided one-third and the United States 21 per cent; the figure for exports was US$64 billion, from which a massive 40 per cent went to the United States and a relatively small 15 per cent to Japan.[44] The national security of the ROK was still based on the defence relationship with the United States, and Seoul, whatever the public ambivalence, wanted American forces to stay for the time being: in its first ever defence policy paper in 1988, south Korea justified the continued United States military presence by exaggerating the north's capabilities and by emphasising north Korean chemical weapons development at Sinuiju and Hamhung (the centre of colonial Japan's chemical industry).[45] The United States could not say, as it said of Japan, that south Korea was not contributing sufficiently to its own defence, and a slight trade deficit with the United States in 1991 helped improve Seoul's reception in Washington. President Bush, however, facing his own crisis of recession and unemployment at home, continued to scale down United States forces and to call for greater liberalisation of Korean markets, with all the problems this portended for Korean farmers and the pampered *chaebol*. Bush's position fuelled the antipathy of south Korean radicals who continued to demand removal of all 'colonial' United States forces and reject the 'aggressive' United States trade demands. However, the heat of the United States–ROK relationship is seen by one south Korean scholar as a natural part of Korea's maturation and of America's position as the world's greatest power:

> Anti-Americanism in Korea is a product of Korea's history. It had to happen because the new generation seeks a more independent and assertive Korea. In short, anti-Americanism in South Korea is a kind of symbol of Korean nationalism calling for the Koreanization of answers to Korean problems.[46]

With Japan, the relation was no less tortured. In economic terms, Japan clearly held the upper hand and posted a trade surplus with south Korea in 1991 of US$8.8 billion. South Korea remained critically dependent on Japan for advanced technology, but domestic politics forced Roh to make the Korean community in Japan the determining issue for his visit to Tokyo in May 1990, and to seek further apologies for the colonial past from the new emperor, Akihito, and from Prime Minister Kaifu. When Kaifu returned the visit early in 1991, the accompanying Japanese press were noticeably impatient with the continued south Korean attacks plus grand claims on Japanese largesse, and the danger to south Korea was that a relentlessly moral stance towards Japan would ultimately damage its own interests. However, history, unlike old soldiers, refused even to fade away, and in the first days of 1992, further documents were made public on Japanese wartime recruitment of Korean women and girls as army prostitutes. The hapless Japanese prime minister, Miyazawa Kiichiro, was confronted by emotional demonstrations on his visit to Seoul that January, but his only response was to apologise repeatedly (eight times during the brief visit) to the Korean people and to suggest that Japanese textbooks should be more open on the colonial issue. The position of the Japanese Education Ministry, however, was unlikely to be sympathetic, and in the 1980s had even started to move towards a more positive depiction of Japanese imperialism.

While history dogged south Korea's two most important relations, ties with the old enemies were notably free of ideology. In the 1980s, dramatic improvement was made in trade with the Soviet Union and especially with China. As the communist giants looked for ways to develop their own economies, south Korea found itself unburdened by Japan's historical troubles with the Soviets over the northern islands dispute and with China over the 1930s invasion. Indirect two-way trade between China and south Korea accelerated from US$19 million in 1979 to $1.29 billion in 1985 and about $3.2 billion in 1989. Roughly half of south Korea's exports to China were electronic and electrical goods, and China's exports to Korea were mainly textiles, agricultural, marine or mineral products. Thus south Korea established with China something of the goods for materials relationship that Japan had with Korea in the late nineteenth century. However, the growth of Chinese textile and rubber footwear production hit Korean producers in Pusan, and the threat of a low-cost Chinese electronics industry pressured south Korean concerns to develop joint ventures in order to gain more assured access to China's domestic market. Among the leading south Korean investors were Daewoo Electronics, with US$10 million in compressor production at Fuzhou, and Goldstar's US$5 million colour television manufacturing at Zhouhai.[47]

South Korea's relations with China, especially in Manchuria, were helped by the presence of expatriate Koreans. In the 1980s, about 1.8 million Koreans lived in China, mostly in the Yanbian Korean Autonomous Region of what was formerly Manchuria's Jilin province. There they enjoyed relative affluence, the freedom to support Korean culture in print, art, dance and theatre, and bilingual media on radio and television. Until the Cultural Revolution, they had also benefited from the use of Korean as the principal language of instruction at Yanbian University, an institution whose student body remained overwhelmingly Korean. Relaxation of tensions between China and the outside world from the early 1970s permitted greater communication between the Koreans in Manchuria and south Korea. From 1988, tourism was allowed with south Korean visitors to Yanbian finding long-lost relatives, and visiting the Chinese side of Korea's sacred Mt Paektu, the birthsite of Tan'gun, the legendary founder of the Korean people.[48]

Trade with the Soviet Union developed slowly, from a paltry US$36 million in 1980 to about US$600 million in 1989 — double the figure of 1988, and expected to double again in 1990, but still small compared with south Korea's interests elsewhere. The Soviet economy was in dire need of foreign capital to develop its resources, especially in Siberia, where Japanese investors had been less than satisfied; Hyundai quickly set about arranging a joint forestry venture in the region. In June 1990, Roh engineered a meeting with Mikhail Gorbachev in San Francisco and at one stroke undermined the credibility of Soviet help for any north Korean aggression. Full diplomatic relations were established in September 1990. The replacement of the Soviet Union in December 1991 by the Commonwealth of Independent States, as with the breakup of East European communism, portended even more economic openings for Seoul.

At the end of the day, however, trade, defence, politics and culture all coalesced in the question of north Korea. In the 1980s, the north was looking for foreign investment, even talking of a free trade zone at Najin, the port developed by Japan in the 1930s on the east coast. The south had the money and was already buying up north Korean debts to foreign banks as they became available. In 1989, the head of Hyundai Business Group visited north Korea to discuss joint development of resort facilities on the beautiful central east coast of north Korea. Kim Il Sung, the previous year, had for the first time accepted the principle of co-existence with the south: this was followed by moves from Seoul to widen discussions, even towards military reduction, and to call for a historic summit between the two presidents. With both China and the Soviets distancing themselves from P'yongyang, Kim sent his premier on a landmark visit to Seoul in September 1990, a visit reciprocated by the south Korean prime minister in October 1990. In 1991 both states entered the United Nations and finally, on 13 December 1991, an agreement was signed to free up direct communications and trade and pave the way for a long-awaited peace agreement. On the last day of the year, this was supplemented by an agreement in principle to renounce the possession or use of nuclear weapons: with this, Seoul declared that the Team Spirit military exercise with the United States would not proceed, and it was already understood that United States nuclear weapons either had been, or were then in the process of being, removed from the peninsula. Early in 1992, the south Korean Education Ministry declared that school textbooks were to be rewritten from 1995 to stress peaceful co-existence between the Koreas. Thus the year started with greater cause for optimism than at any time since 1945.

North Korean officials still warned of decadent capitalist culture and its impact in earlier undermining East Germany, while in the south there was still unease about rumoured nuclear weapons development in the north and about the debt burden if the two states were to be reunited prematurely. These were problems to confront the new administration of Kim Young Sam, victor in the presidential election of December 1992 by nearly 2 million votes over his nearest rival, Kim Dae Jung. South Korean politics quickly reverted to an essentially two-party system as Chung Ju Yung, under intense government pressure, announced his decision to quit politics and return to business. However, change is integral to the modern world, and as international society (Western and capitalist to be sure) expanded still further with the collapse of European communism, even Chuche was being redefined, and as Kim Il Sung had told Japanese visitors in July 1991, 'We are one of the countries on this earth, and we will act in accordance with what happens in the world.'[49]

Notes

1 Oliver, 1978, p. 230
2 Oliver, 1978, pp. 109–11, Ben Limb to Syngman Rhee, 18 June 1947
3 Henderson, 1968, pp. 160–62
4 Chongsik Lee, 1985, pp. 24–25
5 Mason et al., 1980, pp. 182–85
6 Sungho Lee, 1989, pp. 238–44
7 Lee Suk Bok, 1987, p. 78
8 Lee Suk Bok, 1987, pp. 78–83
9 Steinberg, 1989, p. 130
10 Joungwon A. Kim, 1975, pp. 250–54
11 Park, 1962, pp..4–5; on the Tonghak, see pp. 103–05.
12 Quoted in Suh, 1988, p. 97
13 Mason et al., 1980, p. 251
14 Chong do Hah, 1967, p. 53
15 Joungwon A. Kim, 1975, p. 263
16 Hahn, 1980, p. 1091
17 Hyun-chin Lim, 1985, p. 66
18 Chung, 1983, p. 193
19 Man-Gap Lee, 1982, p. 247
20 Moore, 1984–85, p. 580
21 Joungwon A. Kim, 1975, p. 270
22 Lent, 1990, p. 128
23 Steinberg, 1989, pp. 114, 137
24 Lee, Eckert et al., 1990, pp. 368–69
25 Linda Lewis, 1988, pp. 22–23
26 *Far Eastern Economic Review*, 12 January 1989, p. 26
27 *Far Eastern Economic Review*, 20 October 1988, p. 23
28 Chungin Moon, 1988
29 Korean Overseas Information Service, *Opening a New Era in Korea–Japan Relations*, Seoul, 1984: Hirohito speech, pp. 28–29; Nakasone speech, pp. 42–43
30 Vincent Brandt, 1989, p. 81
31 Manwoo Lee, 1988, pp. 12–16
32 *Far Eastern Economic Review*, 24 November 1988, pp. 40–41
33 *Far Eastern Economic Review*, 27 April 1989, p. 11
34 *Far Eastern Economic Review*, 5 December 1991, p. 54
35 *Korea Annual 1988*, p. 196
36 *Korea Annual 1988*, p. 199
37 Michael Kalton, 1989, p. 123
38 Seong-Kon Kim, 1991, p. 97
39 ibid., pp. 99–101
40 ibid., p. 102
41 ibid., pp. 109–16
42 'A decade of hope and fruition', speech to Korean press, 10 January 1990, *Korea a Nation Transformed: Selected Speeches of President Roh Tae Woo*, Seoul, 1990, pp. 128–40
43 Quoted in *Far Eastern Economic Review*, 31 October 1991, p. 66

44 Figures from *The World Almanac and Book of Facts 1992*, NY, 1992
45 *Far Eastern Economic Review*, 26 January 1989, p. 34
46 Manwoo Lee, 1988, p. 27
47 Noh, 1989, p. 431
48 Chae-Jin Lee, 1986, 1989; *Far Eastern Economic Review*, 7 November 1991, pp. 40–42
49 *Far Eastern Economic Review*, 22 August 1991, p. 21

Like central Africa on the eve of Western colonial conquest in the
nineteenth century, north Korea towards the end of the twentieth
century remained a land largely beyond the world's ken, apparently
closed, forbidden, threatening and sunk in superstition and idolatry. Yet
it is also, at least on the surface, an urban, educated and industrial society
— in short, 'a modern industrial state' [1]

What is most remarkable about it is precisely the uniqueness of its
blend of tradition and modernity and the degree to which it has pursued
its own course of history while minimising contacts with the rest of the
world. Much that seems puzzling and paradoxical about the country
begins to be understood when the historical conditioning factors are
clarified. The predominant influences on north Korea have been
Confucian-bureaucratic, Japanese imperialist, and Stalinist–Maoist
communism; in perhaps no other country do liberalism, democracy and
'civil society' rest on thinner foundations, while few can match the
degree of destruction and violence from the Korean War and none has
confronted for so long the hostility of the world superpower, the United
States.

At the beginning of the 1990s, however, cracks began to appear in the
edifice of the north Korean state that was created in the late 1940s. The
dissolution of the Cold War structures within which it was born and
nurtured and the commencement of talks towards normalisation of
relations with Japan and the United States (following entry into the
United Nations in 1991) meant that the 'siege' mentality was gradually
yielding to one of more openness to the rest of the world.

The Kim family state

No state in modern (and few in ancient) times has constructed an
identity so closely identified with that of its ruler as has north Korea with
Kim Il Sung (b. 1912), whose inevitable decline and passing will
therefore also herald the passing of an age. For this reason, the history

of north Korea since the end of Japanese imperialism is marked by remarkable continuity and stability. The problem of power exercised at the centre by Kim Il Sung is therefore central to understanding the north Korean phenomenon. As Dae-Sook Suh puts it, 'the study of Kim and his rule is the study of north Korea'.[2]

The early career of Kim Il Sung, and his involvement in the Korean War, was covered in Chapter 3. Kim's career at the helm of the north Korean state over the span of nearly half a century is remarkable for longevity and for consistency of political purpose. As with most state leaders, however, his image owes as much to conscious construction as to spontaneous generation. His regime has been characterised by its stress on two things: nationalism and unity. The regime is represented as the crystallisation of the Korean essence, maintained against all external encroachments by preservation of strict internal unity, the avoidance of factions and the prevention of political opposition. The person (and the family) of Kim Il Sung became the embodiment of both virtues, and of virtue itself.

Yet the vehemence with which the guerrilla origins, nationalistic purity and monolithic unity of the regime are proclaimed is such as to raise doubts. In the official history that was gradually constructed after 1945, Kim Il Sung became the embodiment of the regime's legitimacy and symbol of its virtue. As a boy of 13, Kim is said to have commenced an exemplary political career by mastering Marxism–Leninism and forming a 'Down with Imperialism Union' among his classmates; at the age of 22 (in 1934) he founded a 'Korean People's Revolutionary Party' to organise and lead the struggle for Korean independence from Japan; he persisted in that struggle even against terrible adversity during the darkest times of Japanese repression which forced him to retreat with his closest followers to the mountain fastnesses of north-east Korea, but re-emerged with his unit intact in 1945 and joined Soviet forces in dealing death blows to Japanese imperialism and liberating his country.

None of this was true, although Kim Il Sung had a respectable and honorable early career. Like many other nationalist-minded young Koreans he left his Japanese-dominated homeland as a boy for education in China, and became a member of the Chinese Communist Party and an anti-Japanese guerrilla in north-east China (Manchuria) between 1932 and 1940. He then retreated under Japanese military pressure in 1940 to the Soviet Union, where he became member of a Soviet force until the end of the war in 1945. After the war he returned to Korea and was chosen by Soviet occupying authorities, and in due course by Stalin himself, to play a leading role in his liberated country. From the late 1980s a wealth of evidence became available from Chinese, Russian and various Korean sources which clearly showed the hollowness of the official myths.[3]

So far as unity, the other central dogma, is concerned, the record does indeed show remarkable continuity of political purpose and coherence of state power and direction, but this too has to be understood in the context of the means by which it was attained: periodic ruthless purges, merciless punishment of dissent, and intense and sustained ideological propaganda and control of information.

Nothing is more hostile to the pretensions of the north Korean propaganda machine than the harsh fact that Kim Il Sung was initially taken from a camp in the Soviet Far East, brought back to north Korea on a Soviet ship well after the end of the war against Japan, and imposed in power by Soviet writ, endorsed by a personal decision of Stalin the following year. During the early years of Soviet occupation, Kim was understandably fulsome in his praise for Stalin, the Red Army and the Soviet Union generally. The official foundation myths were only developed and propagated later, as his hold on power strengthened.

The central institution of power in north Korea has been the Korean Workers' Party, founded in August 1946 in north Korea and expanded in 1949 by incorporation of its south Korean equivalent. Though nominally a united front of communists and non-communists, in practice communist control was tight. Among the communists, sharp rivalry existed between four main factions: the so-called Kapsan or ex-guerrilla group from the north-east (most of whose members had long experience as members of Chinese and/or Soviet units in the 1930s and 1940s), dominated by Kim Il Sung; the southern communists, dominated by Pak Hon-yong, a founding member of the Korean Communist Party in 1925, who had spent nine years in prison under the Japanese and who in the early post-war years was much better known nationally than Kim Il Sung; the 'Soviet Koreans', or ethnic Koreans, who had been living in the Soviet Union for one or more generations and who often spoke Russian and were members of the Soviet Communist Party; and the returned Koreans from China, known as the 'Yanan (or Yenan) Group', many of whom were members of the Chinese Communist Party. Unity was not easily to be forged between men of such different backgrounds, many of whom had been out of the country for the formative years of their lives. Kim was unusually well placed from the start because of his strong Soviet connections (as later he was to benefit from his close Chinese connections), but it was the combination of this external support with his talent for meticulous organisation, manipulation of lesser threats in order to isolate and defeat the greater, and ruthlessness when necessary, which enabled him to win dominance in the Korean Workers' Party and ultimately in the country.

To do so he built a centralised party of iron discipline and gradually purged one after another of the other factions until his own, Kapsan, group was in unquestioned control. The process took a number of years and was only consolidated in the late 1950s. The first major phase of his rivalry with Pak Hon Yong was decided in July 1946, when both he and Pak were summoned secretly to Moscow by Stalin to decide which should become the focus of Soviet support. After interviewing both and considering their explanations of the Korean situation, Stalin chose Kim.[4] Pak served as Kim's subordinate and was only eliminated as a rival when purged in 1953 from his party and government positions. He was tried and executed in December 1955 as a 'spy', on the improbable charge of having served both the Japanese during the colonial period and the Americans during the Korean War.[5] The details of the case against him were never published, though it seems likely that he was eliminated both because of the potential threat he represented to Kim Il Sung's leadership and as a scapegoat for the failure of the masses in south Korea to rise up to welcome the Korean People's Army as a liberating force in 1950.

The late 1950s was a particularly intense period of struggle. Firstly, leading figures of the Yanan faction, who had been critical of the emerging 'cult' around the personality of the 'Great Leader', were purged.[6] They were followed by the 'Soviet-Koreans', who were influenced by Krushchevite notions of coexistence and detente. A decade later, even members of Kim's own partisan group were progressively removed from their posts, after the failure of the militant and confrontationist (with south Korea and the United States) policy pursued during that period.[7] After that, there were further sporadic inner party upheavals and rumours of violent purges. By the time of the Fifth Party Congress in 1970, anyone with the potential to rival Kim Il Sung had been removed and Kim was surrounded by technocratic functionaries who owed their positions to him.

In other words, north Korea's single and continuing Democratic People's Republic may seem to have been much more stable than the six consecutive republics of the south, but actually the political upheavals in the latter were matched in intensity, if not in scope, by the violent contests in P'yongyang over power and policy. The difference is that in the north these struggles were contained from spilling over into the public arena. In the 'merciless struggle' against 'impure elements'[8] to achieve party unity, absolute loyalty to Kim Il Sung came to be adopted as the touchstone of political purity, and the elements of what were to become known as the 'cult' of the 'Great Leader' were gradually put in place.

Faced with the legacy of political repression and the absence of liberal or democratic traditions, political instability in both south and north was scarcely surprising. Leader cults are one way of resolving the dilemmas and have been common enough in transitional phases of national development in many parts of the world, including Hitler's Germany and Stalin's Soviet Union. The ingredients differ, being drawn from traditional ideas of power and legitimacy on the one hand and modern state and industrial ideologies on the other. What is common, however, is the emphasis on unity, the suppression of dissent and general mobilisation for state building programs. It is the particular quality of the blend of tradition and modernity in north Korea, and its intensity, which is unprecedented.

The country's relatively small population (9.6 million in 1950 and 21 million in 1990) and degree of insulation from contacts with the outside world made possible social experimentation on a grand scale. By March 1948, 735 762 people were enrolled in the Korean Workers' Party, a figure which rose to 3 million (approximately 17 per cent of the population) by 1980. Virtually every adult was a member of one or other mass social or political organisation of women, youth, farmers, etc.[9] Both the party and the mass organisations were subordinate to the direction of the Political Committee of the Workers' Party. The state itself was controlled by the party in accordance with Leninist political doctrine. The choice of candidates for state office was carefully orchestrated and the chosen 'slate' of candidates commonly returned with 100 per cent ratification by the electorate. The achievement of 100 per cent of eligible voters casting ballots unanimously for the endorsed candidates was described after the 1962 elections as 'an epochal victory unprecedented in the entire history of elections',[10] which no doubt it was.

The charter of the ruling Korean Workers' Party enjoins party members to fight against:

> all antiparty and anti-revolutionary lines of capitalism, feudalistic Confucianism, revisionism, dogmatism, flunkeyism, factionalism, provincialism, and nepotism that are prejudicial to the unitary ideological system of the party

and to 'uphold the unity of the party based on the chuche ideology'.[11] The prerogative to define what all these things, including the correct line (and the definition of terms such as 'dogmatism', 'Confucianism' and 'nepotism'), is guarded by the 'Leader' and his closest associates.

The harsh reality of dictatorship is softened by the way it is represented symbolically. As in traditional Korean society, Kim's authority as ruler has been dressed as legitimate because it stems from his virtue and benevolence, and reinforced by attribution to him of the role of 'father' of the nation. He became, therefore, both just ruler and loving father. Under his rule, the structures and organisations of civil society, already enfeebled by long Japanese imperial rule, were reduced to insignificance.

Until the death of Stalin in March 1953, the elevation of Kim was somewhat constrained by the existence of one acknowledged to be *his* 'Leader'. After Stalin's death, that constraint was removed and the denunciation of those being purged was accompanied by panegyrics to the fount of true wisdom, to whom the term 'Suryong' or 'Great Leader' was thereafter unambiguously applied. As light shone through him, and love flowed from him, his warm bosom enveloping his people, nurturing and feeding them, his authority was placed beyond challenge.

His embrace, however, tended to suffocate, since all initiative and decision-making was reserved to him. Though known most commonly as 'The Great Leader', Kim was also known at times as wise creator and builder, genius of thought, lodestar of our times, ever victorious and wise general, supreme brain of the nation, leader of the Third World, hero of the twentieth century, sun of the world, greatest leader in 1000 years, whose 'tactics and strategy amaze even God'.[12] A typical expression of the phenomenon was the following poem, entitled 'We live in the bosom of the leader':[13]

His love is boundlessly warm
It is the brilliant sunshine
We live in the bosom of the leader
We boast of this happiness to the world
Oh, the heavenly leader Marshall Kim Il Sung
The people look up to him swearing allegiance

Though north Korea is usually described as 'communist' or 'socialist', such corporatist or organic representation of the relationship between ruler, state and people was actually part of the fascist political tradition. Significantly, the emphasis placed on 'Chuche' thought, or on 'Kimilsungism', grew stronger in north Korea as references to Marxism-Leninism diminished.

Monolithicity was the proud claim of this system.[14] There could be no debate on policy, or readiness to criticise past mistakes, since all decisions emanated from one who was supremely wise. In place of democratic consultation and involvement of ordinary people in the political process, north Korea practised a kind of direct encounter between its president and the ordinary people — farmers, workers, technicians, party cadres — described as 'on the spot guidance'. The word 'guidance' seems apt, since the context of the encounters, which by their nature were highly irregular, was ritualistic, deferential, even reverential. They had more in common with the ritual encounters between a benevolent despot of a pre-modern kingdom and his subjects than with modern citizen participation in the political process.

The paradox of equating absolute subservience, so that people 'will think and act the way the party wants them to, anytime and anywhere', with absolute freedom as 'masters of the revolution' was enshrined as the state ideology under the name of 'Chuche' (or 'Juche'). It is usually rendered into English as 'self-reliance', and has the strong connotation of autonomy and independence in opposition to 'Sadae' or reliance on the great powers (which is seen as the fault of all previous Korean regimes), but it was also defined by Kim Il Sung as 'iron discipline' and the 'solemn duty' to carry out the Party's decisions.[15] First proclaimed in 1955, when the purge of Soviet and other factions was in progress and nationalism the watchword, the content of Chuche gradually shifted so that uniformity and obedience was stressed, until ultimately it became a paradoxical term which meant *both* independence (of other countries) *and* dependence (of everyone on the Leader).[16]

The objects of the cult included not only Kim himself, but also his mother, father, grandfather, great-grandfather, former wife and, above all, his son, Kim Jong Il (b. 1942) — in short a pure revolutionary blood line.

By the early 1970s, major rivals had been purged and a distinctive political style solidly entrenched. The new 'socialist' constitution of 1972 codified the structures of the Kim-ist state. His thought, described in

Article 4 as 'a creative application of Marxism–Leninism', was substituted for communist ideology as that by which the state was to be 'guided', his family and its struggles ensconced as orthodox history (Articles 3 and 4), and his ideas on economic organisation (Articles 12 and 13) substituted for any recognition of the rights of workers. Kim himself assumed the role of president of the republic, under a four-year term which was subsequently repeatedly renewed without challenge. The 'working masses' were, by Article 27 of the Constitution, 'the makers of history'. They were described by Kim Il Sung as 'the masters of state and society', but within a 'monolithic ideological system' they were subordinate to 'the party's lines, policies, decisions, and institutions as an absolute truth'.[17] A very 'top-down' kind of mass line is implied: the experience of the masses, being fragmentary and untheorised, required the party, and the leader, to give it form and coherence, whereupon it would be returned to them as absolute truth. Chuche was a paradoxical principle, according to which people became 'masters' only to the extent to which they faithfully served their leader.

Despite formal protestations of state power being in the hands of the people (Articles 7, 17, 27), and the clauses on equality and the basic rights of freedom of speech, press, assembly, association, thought and religion (Articles 53 and 54), actually the power of the Korean Workers' Party (not mentioned in the constitution) remained supreme, and the brief clause enjoining on citizens the duty 'to strictly observe the socialist norm of life and the socialist rules of conduct' (Article 67) was in practice much more important than those supposedly enshrining their rights. The motive force in history in north Korea became the will of the leader rather than the struggle between classes rooted in antagonistic relationship to the forces of production. In place of critical and scientific thinking, the major intellectual thrust became elucidation of the truth as revealed in the works of the Leader, which by definition were beyond criticism.

Insofar as the word and will of the Leader carried more weight than law or constitution, and as personal fealty to the Leader and his family outweighed either bureaucratic function or generalised national or patriotic duty, north Korea had something in common with pre-modern, even 'feudal', regimes, despite the modernity of its industrial and urban infrastructure.

Expressions of adulation of the Leader were intense and continual. His image, whether in the form of statue (sometimes of colossal dimensions), photograph or badge (worn on the lapel of virtually everyone) was omnipresent. His birthplace at Mangyongdae became a national shrine (Korea's 'Bethlehem'), and other places associated with his career, from mountains where he is supposed once to have camped to chairs on which he once may have sat, served as mini-shrines. In schools, children gathered in special 'Kim Il Sung rooms' to recite elaborate pantomimes about the episodes of his life — which served, in effect, as their catechism. Music, the visual arts, theatre and literature all served the primary end of reinforcing the message. In factories and collective farms, everything was attributed to him. The history of Korea became the history of the glorious deeds of the Leader and his ancestors,[18] philosophy the elucidation of his wisdom as encapsulated in the Chuche idea, and his judgments on all manner of things were given priority over scientific or objective assessment. One estimate in the 1970s was that 65 per cent of 1300 class hours at Kim Il Sung University, the country's premier institution of advanced education, was devoted to teaching the principles of Chuche and the ideas of Kim Il Sung.[19] A typical expression was the launching of a university campaign, early in 1981, known as the 'Movement to Read 10 000 Pages', the object of which was to complete a course of core readings of the 'classic works of the Great Leader and his moral tracts', plus other items such as a twelve-volume collection of 'true' and 'personal' stories about him.[20] The full impact of the imposition of dogmatic, and demonstrably false or fantastic, beliefs — such as the birth of Kim Jong Il on Mt Paektu (when he was certainly born near Khabarovsk in the Soviet Union[21]), or the launching of a revolutionary career by Kim Il Sung at the age of 13 (as commemorated by a massive triumphal arch erected in P'yongyang in the 1980s) — on historians, journalists and citizens generally could only be guessed.

It is hard to avoid the impression that such an 'embrace', while no doubt warm, was also suffocating and debilitating of popular imagination, initiative and culture. Dominated by the family of the great patriarch, there was little room for deviance — or, indeed, spontaneity. The children in nurseries and kindergartens *seemed* cheerful and spontaneous, yet there was a strong underlying sense of constraint, or spontaneity carefully channelled, whether in the disciplined, organised and intense classrooms, in the well-orchestrated performances to which guests were treated, or in the bands of children marching and singing on their way to school or to the performance of some social task.

Officials of the regime boasted that pre-marital sex, divorce, prostitution, homosexuality, drunkenness and crime were unknown, that even blindness and deafness among children were unknown, being pre-revolutionary phenomena (according to the director of a kindergarten), that schools experienced no discipline or truancy problems (according to the principal of a girls' middle school), and that serious illnesses were unknown (according to the chairperson of a collective farm).[22] One visitor commented that in a country which was known to have suffered terrible war casualties, 'you never see a single person who is scarred, mutilated or disabled'. He asked: 'What have they done with them all?'[23]

The reverse side of the extraordinary public cult of the Leader and his family and the orthodoxy they represented was that of the suppression of non-conformity and dissidence. There is sufficient indication from public documentary references to 'impure and hostile elements' and to 'punishment', as well as to intellectuals who 'still suffer from obsolete ideas to a considerable extent and are also highly susceptible

.of bad ideas', to know that the ideological remoulding goals of the state had not been fully accomplished and that deviant thoughts occurred, and were punished. Information was less readily available about the scale on which they occurred and the severity with which they were punished. Independent sources such as Amnesty International believed there might well be widespread repression.[24] South Korean sources published details of a network of camps within which dissidents were said to be held, apparently under conditions of extreme privation.[25] There might be as many as 100 000 persons, including 23 000 Koreans who had emigrated from Japan at the end of the 1950s, held in these camps.[26] Korean sources connected with the nearly 100 000 Koreans who migrated to north Korea from Japan between 1959 and 1984 told appalling stories of the way some of them had been treated.[27] Their combination of south Korean family background and Japanese sojourn made them doubly suspect. Many were pronounced counter-revolutionary.[28]

The origin of the north Korean cult almost certainly owed a great deal to Stalinism in the Soviet Union, but it might even have exceeded it in depth and intensity, and perhaps also in efficacy. A standard work written in the early 1970s, though very critical, could nevertheless concede that the regime was 'able to command the allegiance of the great majority of the Korean people'.[29] However, while reliable information is scarce, reports from time to time of riots, with 'up to 500 workers' said to have been killed in clashes in June 1982,[30] the successive purges of large groups of civil and military officials, and the deteriorating economic conditions through the 1980s made it likely that that allegiance later wore thin.

One of the key institutions of the north Korean state has been the military, the Korean People's Army (KPA). Reliable information on it is scant, but its size (as of the beginning of the 1990s) was variously estimated at between 842 000 and 1 110 000.[31] Party control over the KPA is said to be stronger than in either China or the (former) Soviet Union, and there is no record of any dispute between party and army. Political education, comprising propaganda and training in the principles of Kim Il Sung-ism, is intense. While military commanders are said to play a 'paternal' role to their subordinates, the role of political officers is 'maternal'.[32] There is little evidence to suggest that technical modernisation within the KPA has yet been matched by any encroachment of 'modern' ideas or values. The minimising of the role of objective law or principle in both army and state in north Korea, in favour of 'pre-modern' and absolutist notions of loyalty and 'love', is unprecedented in a modern society.

The economic record

North Korea's economic record is impressive, despite the growing evidence of serious problems and the comparisons that are inevitably made with the achievement of south Korea. Assessment is complicated by the fact that the government published only selected figures, often those designed to impress rather than inform, and north Korean sources rarely refer to foreign aid, which particularly in the early decades was very substantial.[33] Still, sources with every reason to treat official claims with scepticism, such as the American CIA (see below), were very positive in their appraisals through the 1970s. Thereafter, however, problems began to mount in the north, while the south, especially since 1981, astonished the world with its performance.

Such industrialisation as was undertaken in Korea during the Japanese period tended to be concentrated in the north, where 65 per cent of the country's heavy industry (but only 37 per cent of its agriculture) was located and where the communications system was relatively well developed,[34] although that industrialisation was of problematic value after the Japanese empire of which it had been an integral part collapsed, leaving industry 'in a state of chaos and disrepair'.[35] After the initial confusion of the liberation, occupation and division of the country in 1945, however, and until the war brought devastation between 1950 and 1953, the spate of reforms and reorganisation of the economy achieved significant gains. Land reform was accomplished very briskly under a 5 March 1946 law, and the countryside was transformed, in the space of a few weeks and with apparently minimal violence or disorder, into a pattern of small peasant cultivator holdings similar to that adopted almost simultaneously in Japan. A *Labor Law* (24 June), *Sexual Equality Law* (30 July), and *Nationalisation of Industry, Transport, Communications and Banks Law* (10 August) combined to meet the general expectations of expropriation of Japanese properties and basic rights for women, workers and farmers in a new, national economy. North Korea's industrialisation policy then followed a basically Stalinist pattern, with emphasis on heavy industry and considerable assistance from the Soviet Union. A significant economic recovery had been accomplished before the outbreak of the war in 1950.[36]

The destruction achieved in the war was almost total, however, save for that industrial plant which had been moved into caves deep underground to escape the bombing. Power production in 1953 was only 26 per cent of what it had been in 1949, fuel 11 per cent, chemicals 22 per cent and metallurgy 10 per cent. Agriculture had been devastated, and the 1953 crops wiped out by bombing of the dykes and dams. The population is reported to have fallen by 11.76 per cent during the war years.[37]

After the war, north Korea pursued what was possibly the most centralised and planned economic development strategy of any country in the world. Even though other countries had abandoned or drastically modified reliance on central planning mechanisms by 1990, there was still no sign of change in P'yongyang. The regime also relied heavily on mobilisation campaigns, long after their abandonment in the Soviet Union and in China. From the late 1950s, production campaigns, dubbed 'Chollima' (after a legendary flying horse), encouraged workers to exceed (even double or treble) their quotas. As Suh pointed out, the New Communist, described in the constitution as 'knowledgeable, virtuous and healthy' (Article 39) was 'a superhuman working machine that owned nothing and worked constantly without complaint for minimum reward.'[38] The *Socialist Labor Law* guaranteed him/her an eight-hour day, but combined it with the obligation to study the thought of Kim Il Sung for a similar period.[39]

The reliance on the psychological and spiritual incentives to spur the workers to greater efforts at production, while offering minimal material incentives, clearly worked up to a point. Kim Il Sung devoted much of his time to personally visiting production sites to encourage greater effort. However, the quality of such work often left something to be desired, and the returns from such campaigns diminished over time, so that Kim had to berate factories and enterprises that 'dawdle away their time and produce little in the early and middle parts of the month but fulfil their monthly plans through rush work towards the end of the month'.[40] The longer coercion and overwork continued, the more likely it became that the quality of the work would diminish and the workers become exhausted and alienated.

Land was collectivised in stages between 1953 and 1958, a process simplified by the need to pool limited resources and labour in order simply to survive. Landlords had been eliminated either by the earlier reforms or by the war; consequently (so far as is known) resistance was minimal, and the process was accomplished with little violence or compulsion. Despite the urgency of the task of capital accumulation for industrialisation, the regime seems not to have squeezed the farmers too hard, allowing them to experience gradually rising living standards and reduced taxation levels, until the tax on the agricultural yield was eliminated entirely in 1966. Irrigation, terracing of hillsides, mechanisation (large-scale production and allocation of tractors) and chemicalisation (use of fertilisers) were promoted on a large scale.

The regime in P'yongyang claimed that, despite the harshness of the climate and the difficulty of the terrain, less than 20 per cent of which was suitable for agriculture, output rose by an average 10 per cent during the 1950s and 6.3 per cent during the 1960s. Self-sufficiency was apparently attained, and in the 1970s north Korea began to export rice. By 1979 it was claiming world record figures for rice yield per hectare. The United Nations Food and Agriculture Organization (FAO) accepted that north Korea was indeed number 1 in the world in terms of its yield of rice per hectare between 1979 and 1990. In all years, north Korea was ahead of other major producers such as Japan and south Korea (or smaller but very efficient producers such as Australia), and it was more than three times as efficient as Thailand and significantly better than the United States. In 1990 it produced an average of 8209 kilograms of paddy rice per hectare, or an estimated gross crop of 5.5 million tonnes.[41] In terms of calory intake, too, north Korea was reported by FAO in 1990 to have performed better for its people than south Korea, or other countries such as Finland and Sweden, throughout the decade of the 1980s, although FAO in 1991 revised its figures to give a superiority (though marginal) to south Korea.[42]

Extremely intensive farming was combined with ambitious projects to expand the area under agriculture, thus presumably further increasing overall output. Huge infrastructural projects under the 1978–84 Plan included the reclamation of 100 000 hectares of new land and the construction of 150 000–200 000 hectares of terraced fields, plus the reclamation of tidal land. In 1986 an 8 kilometre-long dam — the longest in the world — was completed on the Taedong River, after five years of construction and at an estimated cost of $4000 million, and the reclamation of a further 300 000 hectares of tidal land was undertaken in the 1987–93 Plan. In 1989, when there were aready 40 000 kilometres of waterways providing irrigation to about 70 per cent of the country's agricultural land, a new project to build a 400 kilometre long canal, which would divert the flow of the Taedong River along the west coast of the country and feed water to rural areas and newly reclaimed tidelands, was also undertaken.[43]

This enormous effort to increase agricultural (and fishery) productivity should have turned the self-sufficient north Korea of the 1960s into a major food exporter in the 1980s. Yet the fact is that, despite it, food shortages, rationing and hardship were widely reported. Unusually severe natural conditions may have played some part in causing this, and it is known that north Korea was for long exporting a significant proportion of its rice (to earn foreign exchange), while importing cheaper grains for domestic consumption.[44] The hillside terracing program is reported to have had some negative effects, such as erosion, silting of rivers and diminished hydroelectric power.[45] Even taking this into consideration, however, it is difficult to understand how the country recognised by the United Nations' FAO as the world's most efficient rice producer should in 1990 have found it necessary to begin importing rice (3000 tonnes from south Korea, with reportedly a million tonnes to come over the next two to three years),[46] and why food rationing could still be necessary, as was reliably reported. Shortages were so severe in 1991–92 that people were reportedly reduced to two meals a day.[47] Conditions in P'yongyang were described by the Pravda correspondent as being worse than in Moscow.[48] Not only was food rationed — and the proportion of rice to other, coarse grains such as millet, reduced to 30–40 per cent (much less outside P'yongyang), but it was increasingly available only on the black market. Meat rations were restricted to five days in the year which were national holidays, such as the birthdays of the leaders. Protein deficiency was becoming a widespread problem.[49] The possibility of a catastrophic decline in grain output in 1990, perhaps to a mere 2.9 million tonnes, was strong,[50] and food riots were reliably reported in June and July 1991.[51]

Kim Il Sung had promised as early as 1962 that once the 1963 targets were met, the working people of the country would be able to 'lead a rich life, living in tile-roofed houses, having rice and meat, and wearing fine clothes'. In 1970 he claimed that the food problem 'has been solved completely'. Similar claims have been made from time to time. The reiteration of the claim, however, points to the continuing importance of the problem, rather than its successful resolution.[52] Ominously, it was repeated in January 1992 as a 'long-cherished desire' of the people and a 'goal . . . in socialist construction' that people should be able to 'eat rice and meat soup regularly, wear silk clothes and live in a house with a tiled roof'.[53] In this area, as in nearly every other, hard information was at a premium. It is possible that north Korea might have done as its close ally, Romania, did under the Ceausescu family rule: fake the harvest figures[54] *and* deliberately export food (to pay off debts), regardless of the consequences to the people's livelihood.[55]

The transformation from agrarian to industrialised economy seems nevertheless to have been accomplished during the two decades following the Korean War. The urban proportion of the population, 17.7 per cent in 1953, was between 60 and 70 per cent by the early 1980s.[56] Experienced observers from the early 1970s were describing the society as the most industrialised in Asia, after Japan.[57] Industrial output grew by an estimated average of 23.5 per cent during the period from 1954 to 1970,[58] and at 16.3 per cent during the 1970s with the exception of the 'bad' year of 1977 (which recorded 'minus' growth figures of 3 per cent).[59] Such figures, while very high, would account for the CIA's 1978 assessment that, as of early 1976, the north Korean economy was out-producing the south in per capita terms in almost every sector, from agriculture through electric power generation, steel and cement, to machine tools and trucks (but not in televisions and automobiles). Electric power generation, for example, which may be taken as a good general index of overall industrialisation, was in per capita terms approximately double that of the south, and the figure for industrial growth over the years 1965–76 was given at 14 per cent.[60] The growth targets for the 1980s, if achieved, would have put north Korea's industrial output by 1990 on a par with that of the advanced countries of Western Europe and Japan at the end of the 1970s.[61]

However, whether they were in fact achieved is another matter. One authority has concluded, concerning the second Seven Year Plan (1978–84), that:

> It is highly unlikely that the total industrial output increased at an average rate of 12.2 per cent per annum, as claimed. The fact that another three years elapsed before the formulation of the next economic plan is another indicator of the failure of the 1978–84 Plan and of the severity of the problems that confronted north Korea in the mid-1980s.[62]

Between the (one-year delayed) completion in 1985 of the second Seven Year Plan and the commencement in 1987 of the third Seven Year Plan, another interval of a year elapsed. Even after that Plan commenced, no statistics were published.[63]

By the end of the decade, the problem had become even more serious. There were no wholly reliable statistics, but the best estimates were that industrial output might have grown at an average of about 6.3 per cent between 1985 and 1990, although crucial sectors like electric power were, in 1988, still below what had been claimed for them in 1984,[64] and wastage was probably at a high level. No increase had been claimed in agricultural output since 1984, with the gross output of 10 million tonnes only being announced each year.[65] However, the growth rate for the economy seems to have dropped from around 2 per cent in 1989 to −3 in 1990 and −5 per cent in 1991, making those the worst years since 1953. Although the official target for the third Seven Year Plan (1987–93) was for an average annual growth rate of 10 per cent,[66] there was serious trouble in most sectors of the economy and minus growth figures (−3.7 and −5.2 per cent respectively) were reported for 1990 and 1991.[67] Plan targets were, in effect, shelved.[68]

It is perhaps more remarkable that, with such a small population and against such odds, north Korea had been able to achieve so much in a few decades, than that it should have eventually landed in such trouble. Some economists looked on north Korea as evidence that it was possible to defy both capitalist linkages and economies of scale and 'socialist' integration (since north Korea declined to join the Soviet-dominated COMECON), and successfully pursue self-reliant economic policies. In a few decades north Korea had risen from nothing to be able to manufacture its own locomotives, tractors, bulldozers, 30 000 tonne ships, and indeed virtually everything else. Perhaps only Cambodia under Pol Pot in the 1970s had attempted to pursue such fiercely nationalistic policies.

However, the brilliance of the north Korean model quickly tarnished. It is now clear that the much-trumpeted 'self-reliance' of the development model concealed a high degree of reliance on Soviet aid. Most of the major industrial installations were built with Soviet technical assistance and financed by Soviet credit (never repaid). The constant drain of scarce resources into military-related industries over such a long period[69] produced some positive economic effects, with a burgeoning weapons export sector that accounted for up to one-third of exports in the 1980s, worth about $4 billion between 1981 and 1988. [70] But the incapacity to meet basic social needs became more and more serious. There was increasing reason to think that the north Korean economic locomotive in the 1980s had both run low on steam and headed up some ill-chosen tracks. The reliance on frenzied, Stakhanovite-style productivity campaigns (the 'speed of the eighties') brought ever-diminishing returns. The people grew tired; the machines began to wear out; and 'top-down' planning methods failed to develop mechanisms of flexibility and (consumer) feedback.

Attempts to recreate linkages with the capitalist world economy in the 1980s proved difficult and frustrating, both for the Koreans and for the countries and businesses that dealt with them. Early in the 1970s, following the relaxation of tensions in the Cold War, the United States rapprochement with China, and the north–south talks of 1972, P'yongyang began to purchase Western technology on credit, sometimes entire petrochemical plants from countries like Japan, Switzerland, West Germany and France. But at the very moment it moved to reassociate itself with the world capitalist economy, the fabric of the system was rent by the cumulative crises of the oil shocks, world recession and reduced demand and prices for its own export commodities (especially minerals such as tungsten, tin and zinc). In January 1976, north Korea defaulted on repayment of part of its debts. This problem of credit (and credibility) continued thereafter to plague its efforts to expand its role in world trade. Between 1984 and 1990, not even interest was paid on the sum of $900 owed to a syndicate of 140 Western banks. Other major debts included $700 million to Japan and $2.2 billion to the Soviet Union, with little prospect of repayments on any of them.[71]

The importance of re-establishing linkages with the world economy was stressed repeatedly in the 1980s, indicating recognition that the country was nearing the limits of self-sustained (or Soviet-aided) growth. The goal of a 4.2 times increase in foreign trade was announced in 1980; special overtures were made to try to attract Japanese technical co-operation and in July 1984 a *Joint Venture Law* was proclaimed. A renewed goal of 2.2 times increase in foreign trade was set for the 1987–93 Plan, and south Korean enterprises were also encouraged to enter joint ventures in the north. However, reiteration of the desire was itself an indication that the goals were not being met. As of 1990, three-quarters of the country's trade was still with China and the Soviet Union.[72] Joint ventures were few (most of them with north Korean-affiliated groups from Japan). Both China and the Soviet Union began in 1991 to charge 'market' rather than 'friendship' prices for their oil, and hard currency to buy necessary new technology was desperately short. While stagnation deepened in the north, the south continued its boom, the volume of its trade growing to be about 30 times greater than that of the north.[73]

The blockage was probably to be explained by continuing un-certainties in the political, strategic and diplomatic circumstances of north Korea. These in turn were only likely to be fully resolved when a state of normalisation was achieved with both the giants of the capitalist world, the United States and Japan, and the most dynamic region of the developing world, south Korea. As of the early 1990s, therefore, the best chance for the blockage to re-entry into the world economy being successfully negotiated lay in progress in the negotiations which were being pursued on all these fronts.

Apart from these external uncertainties, however, the political priorities imposed on economic decision-making by the megalomania of the leadership cult imposed serious strains on the economy. The cult was expensive. For decades a substantial industry was devoted exclusively to the production and promotion of hagiography devoted to Kim Il Sung in all the main languages of the world, and this process intensified during the 1980s. The landscape was punctuated with monuments — as many as 50 000 of them by one estimate,[74] often in marble or granite. Prominent among them are the Museum of the Korean Revolution (with 95 halls and 4.5 kilometres of exhibits showing the life and achievements of the Leader and his family), museums and statues built in various locations to both parents of Kim Il Sung and sundry other relatives, the

P'yongyang: Children marching, 1992
Source: *Korea Today*, P'yongyang, 1992

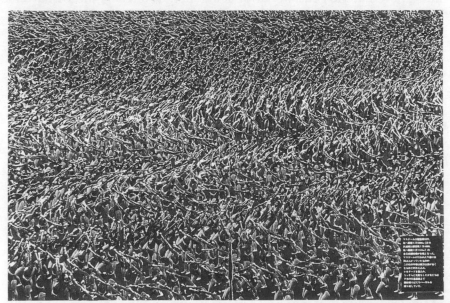

'Mass Games', P'yongyang, April 1992 (Birthday celebrations for Kim Il Sung's 80th birthday
Source: *Bart*, Tokyo, May 1992

museum built in the mountains of the north-east to house the 28 000 items presented to Kim Il Sung by foreign leaders from 146 countries (including items such as a large double bed),[75] the 25 metre bronze statue to him, the 170 metre Chuche Tower, and the 60 metre high Arch of Triumph, built (on the occasion of Kim Il Sung's 70th birthday in 1982) of 25 000 blocks of white granite, each symbolising days lived by Kim up to his 70th birthday, and slightly larger in scale than the one in Paris.

Grandiloquent gestures designed to impress a sceptical outside world proliferated, such as the 105-storey (3000-room) Yukyong Hotel, which had been under construction in P'yongyang so long that in 1992 its concrete facade was reported to be crumbling, although completion was still not in sight and the elevators and toilets were still to be installed,[76] and the various facilities prepared to house the 13th World Festival of Youth and Students in July 1989. These are estimated to have cost hundreds of millions (if not billions) of dollars.[77] Although designed to rival the successful Seoul Olympics of the previous year, they attracted little world attention save for astonishment at the lavish 'mass games' in which 50 000 people were mobilised in giant pantomimes designed to spell out revolutionary scenes or messages of loyalty and love for the Great Leader.[78] The April 1992 80th birthday celebration for the Great Leader cost an estimated $1 billion, and 100 000 people were mobilised for the celebratory mass games.[79] The new P'yongyang–Kaesong Expressway was opened, evidently an impressive engineering feat, although Western journalists reported seeing only four vehicles, two of them driving on the wrong side of the road, when they travelled on it.[80]

In short, north Korea, and especially its capital, was turned into a land of monuments, filled with the temples and shrines of the cult that constituted the state orthodoxy. The entire nation was caught up in the throes of a kind of mass quasi-religious movement. Even nature seemed to play its role, as the Great Leader had only to cast his line into the Daedong River to hook a remarkable 48 kilogram fish.[81] Visitors to P'yongyang described the city as an elaborate film set or a Disneyland. The primary call on public resources became the sustenance and promotion of the political system, and the satisfaction of Kim Il Sung's apparently 'insatiable craving for recognition and deference'.[82] These priorities gradually drained and exhausted both state and society.

By any standards, whether those of comparison with the rest of the developing world or with south Korea, and despite the unrelenting pressure deriving from confrontation with the United States, north Korea performed well, perhaps even brilliantly, through its early decades, until around the mid-1970s.[83] Some economists came to believe that north Korea's model of 'Chuche' autonomous industrialisation held important lessons for the Third World, while the capitalist world offered only the prospect of continuing dependence. North Korea seemed to be 'perhaps the world's sole example of industrialisation in a small country based primarily on indigenous resources and internal demand'.[84] In 1980, Kim Il Sung announced a per capita GNP of $1920, and some observers thought he could be close to the truth. By that time, however, international bodies such as the World Bank believed that the balance had shifted in the south's favour. Although both states were very close in indices such as per capita GNP, it estimated the figures for north and south at $1130 and $1500 respectively.[85] Thereafter, however, there is no question but that the growth rate of the north, while respectable by world standards, steadily fell behind that of the south.

By the end of the 1980s, few economists had any good to say of the north's version of autonomous development. What had been known as 'socialism' was in retreat around the world and P'yongyang itself was trying hard to re-link itself to the economies of the capitalist world. The best estimates were that in 1991 per capita GNP in the north was about one-sixth of that in the south ($1038 to $6498),[86] which would mean that there had been virtually no growth at all for a full decade. If Soviet sources (who had good reason to be well informed) were right, the estimates of the north's per capita GNP had to be even further slashed, to a mere $400. Industry was reckoned by the same sources to be operating at only 50 per cent capacity (perhaps as little as 30–40 per cent according to south Korean sources),[87] due to problems of supply of raw materials and transportation, electric power supply[88] and the decline of the industrial plant.[89]

By virtually all accounts, the north Korean economy in the early 1990s was in crisis. Both its closest allies, China and Russia, faced such problems that, even if they wanted to, they were in no position to 'help' their neighbour. Furthermore, both countries had opened large sections of their economies to market forces, and north Korea was alone in the world in proclaiming the superiority of the fully planned socialist economy.

P'yongyang in the early 1990s faced the problem of how to reconcile open engagement with the world (capitalist) economy with preservation of a closed political system. One formula it pursued with vigor was the creation of special zones, or enclaves to which foreign investment could be encouraged while also being confined and constrained from destabilising the social and political system. The area in the north-east of the country, along the Tumen River, and therefore bordering on China and Russia and facing Japan, was engaging public- and private-sector representatives from Russia, China, Mongolia, south Korea and Japan in ongoing discussions. The project was adopted by the United Nations Development Program in 1991, although the United Nations body estimated that development costs (over at least twenty years) would run to $30 billion.[90]

Succession

After being in effective control of north Korea for 45 years, when Kim Il Sung celebrated his eightieth birthday in 1982, he was in effect the world's senior statesman. He had witnessed the progress of glasnost and perestroika in the Soviet Union, the political upheavals leading to the declaration of the Communist Party as an illegal organisation, the collapse of the Soviet Union as a superpower and its disintegration as a state. He had seen the toppling of dictators, including many who had been his friends (and of their statues and memorials), across Eastern Europe and the rush to embrace capitalism that followed, and he had seen the inroads of the market in China and the waves of new thought that led to the Tiananmen massacre there in 1989. Above all, he had watched the succession of economic and diplomatic triumphs of south Korea, especially its burgeoning trade and wide-ranging contacts with both China and the Soviet Union. His reflections on these dramatic events may never be known, but the public record gave little reason to think that he was ready to begin in north Korea the sort of drastic reform that proceeded elsewhere.

From the early 1970s, Kim Jong Il gradually assumed a central role in north Korean affairs. In 1980 he was named as semi-official 'heir designate' to his father, with the title 'Dear and Beloved Leader' or simply 'Dear Leader', and in August 1984 was officially confirmed as successor to his father. Kim Jong Il's birth was described in terms suggestive of the virgin birth of Christ: he was 'the guiding star which rose on the Paektu ridge', whose rays are such that, once exposed to them, 'everything on earth will revive, youth will spring up and vigor will pour forth; the dead will rise, the elderly will grow young and the ignorant will awaken'.[91] The following passage expresses the relationship between son and father as like that of:

> the great sun and its warm sunbeams which, regardless of the ebb and flow of time, continuously make bloom in crimson hues the flowers of revolution and bring back to life withering flowers, enabling them to emit the deep fragrance of revolution eternally. That sun is none other than the respected and beloved leader Comrade Kim Il Sung and that sunbeam is none other than the Party Center (Kim Jong Il) [who] is making blossom the lofty intent of the great leader.[92]

The stress on 'the blood vein for the continuation of the revolution' has been a common theme in north Korean propaganda since Kim's son was chosen as his successor. Birthdays of both son (16 February) and father (15 April) were pronounced public holidays, with the two intervening months becoming, in the late 1980s, a time of frenzied sycophantic celebration. Kim Jong Il's role as son in interpreting the doctrine revealed by his father and thereby helping the masses to achieve salvation had strong religious overtones. 'The absolute position of the leader in history' was described as a 'unique, profound idea',[93] although no attempt was made to distinguish how, if at all, such a claim differed from those advanced in other cultures and at other times, by absolute monarchs or leaders such as the Fuhrer in Nazi Germany, the Duce in fascist Italy, or the Shah in Iran. Corporatist imagery became very common, such that the Leader ceased to be a mere individual, but became 'the brain of the working masses and the centre of unity and cohesion'.[94]

Kim Jong Il (b. 1942) was educated at élite schools in P'yongyang, at the Air Force Academy in East Germany, and in Romania. He graduated from Kim Il Sung University in 1964 with a thesis interpreting his father's thoughts on the socialist rural question. From graduation, he began to implement what he had learned. The 'Three Revolutions' (ideological, technical and cultural) that were enshrined in the 1972 constitution provided the framework for his public career and the 'Three Revolution Teams' that were organised from 1973 to carry out the 'Revolutions' became his major organisational base.[95] These are sometimes described as Korea's 'Red Guards', though they lack the spontaneity and anarchy of at least the early stages of the Chinese phenomenon. Under Kim Jong Il's direction, some 40 000 to 50 000 of these youths, mostly college students, were sent throughout the country to raise ideological awareness and technical expertise. Speed campaigns, ranging from the 'Seventy Day Battle' in the 1970s through various '100 Day Drives' to the two successive 'Two Hundred Day Struggles' in 1988, were his specialty. In 1980, he was appointed to positions as secretary of the Central Committee, member of the State Secretariat and the Military Commission, the three wings of state power. He became second only to his father.[96]

After nearly twenty years, the process of installing Kim Jong Il as successor remained still incomplete and uncertain, although he was appointed supreme commander of the army in December 1991 (despite the plain terms of Article 93 of the Constitution which vests such power in the country's president) and upon his 50th birthday in February 1992 the north Korean media began to refer to him as the country's 'Dear Father', while Kim Il Sung became the country's 'Grand-father'. In April 1992, Kim Il Sung became 'Taewonsu' (Generalissimo or Grand Marshall) and Kim Jong Il (who had not held any previous military appointment) became 'Wonsu' (marshall). These titles put the father on nominal par with luminaries such as Stalin, Mussolini and Hirohito; and for the son meant it was only a matter of time before the prefix 'Tae' would attach to him too.[97]

The major responsibility for the construction of monuments to his father and family and the rebuilding of the city of P'yongyang is attributed to him. He is said also to have taken a strong interest in culture, especially theatre and film, and to have been responsible for six plays and musicals during the 1970s, including 'Sea of Blood', 'True Daughter of the Party', and 'Flower Girl', all extravaganzas with a strong Chuche or Kimilsung-ist message.

His enthusiasm for film, and desire to boost the north Korean film industry, led him in 1978 to organise the abduction and involuntary co-operation for the eight years that followed of the famous south Korean film director and his actress wife, Shin Sangok and Choe U-Ni. The subsequent revelations published by Shin and Choe after their flight and return to Seoul are a valuable, if unflattering, insight into the mind of the 'Young Leader'.[98] The man they came to know was a pampered young aristocrat, accustomed to luxurious living in a chain of villas throughout the country, equipped with saunas and elaborate video facilities. He evidently has a complex about his shortness of stature (153 centimetres) that makes him wear high-heeled boots and refer to himself (laughingly) as 'like a long thick turd'.[99] His video collection comprised 1500 videos from around the world, mostly 'pirate' versions collected by north Korean diplomatic missions. The involvement of a P'yongyang United Nations delegation in Rome in 1984 in a clumsy attempt to purchase pornographic material on the account of the south Korean embassy was presumably at his behest.[100] A senior north Korean diplomat who defected in 1991 reported that another task of the country's diplomatic missions was 'to procure for Kim Jong Il supplies of Hennessy cognac in France, crabs in Norway, Black Sea caviar and even the livers of blue sharks fished off the Angolan coast'.[101]

Apart from the grandiloquence of his artistic, architectural and culinary tastes, and his fondness for mobilisation campaigns, there was little original or profound in his thought, and almost no trace of Marxism. Characteristic instead was the emphasis on unity, the role of the Leader, and the need for greater effort. He was as much his father's son in the dullness of his prose as in his dedication to the elevation of the family. Whether the mass meetings convened to discuss his works such as 'Young Men and Women, Be the Vanguard Unfailingly Loyal to the Party and Leader' really did see them as great and 'immortal' is impossible to know.[102] His message, that 'individualism' had to be overcome, since 'collectivism is the fundamental demand of human beings'[103] and that socialism required 'unified guidance and control in the political, economic, cultural and all other domains of social life',[104] ran counter to a very strong historical current at the beginning of the 1990s, and the 'single-hearted unity of the Leader, the Party and the masses' was sorely tested by domestic and international adversity as he and his father faced their 50th and 80th birthdays.

A former senior north Korean diplomat named Ko Yon Fan, whose role had included interpreting into French for Kim Il Sung, defected to south Korea in May 1991. He argues that the north Korean state system ceased to be socialist at the end of the 1960s, being gradually turned instead into a patrimonial Kim domain.[105] The protracted process of nearly twenty years of transfer of power to Kim's son, rather than achieving the stability it was supposedly designed to ensure, seems instead to have radically disrupted state and economy. In the 1970s, Kim

Jong Il's 'Three Revolutions Teams' concentrated the reins of power in the hands of inexperienced activists who promoted extreme forms of Chuche ideology and adventurous foreign and domestic policies. When Kim Jong Il was eventually installed in 1980 as the designated successor, he seems to have set aside the second Seven Year Plan agenda and pursued instead what became known as the Ten Great Objectives. Confusion resulted.[106] Even those objectives were then shelved as the reconstruction of P'yongyang as a monument to his family and a statement to the world of pomp and grandeur, culminating in the 1989 World Games, drew more and more resources away from the productive economy and plunged the country towards bankruptcy. Late in the 1980s, as succession became imminent and assured, and as the international situation facing north Korea worsened steadily, Kim Jong Il seems to have undertaken another major upheaval to restore power and influence to a revolutionary second (or even third) generation of technocrats, those with experience of study abroad and skilled diplomats, provided only that they are seen to be totally loyal to him.[107]

Loyalty to him opens the way to power and privilege, but must be constantly renewed by acts of self-denigration and pledges of fealty. Thus the film production company which in the 1980s worked directly under Kim Jong Il's sponsorship received from him a 1986 New Year present consisting of 50 roe deer, 400 pheasants, 200 geese and 200 cases of Japanese tangerines, which provided an occasion for weeping, dancing, celebration and, most importantly, renewal of loyalty pledges.[108] The grant of huge (30 to 50 per cent) wage and allowance increases to the country's workers, pensioners and students on the occasion of Kim Jong Il's 50th birthday in 1992 was prompted by similar considerations.[109]

It would scarcely be surprising, however, if those planners and technocrats on whom Kim Jong Il had to depend to steer the country out of the crisis it faced in the early 1990s were to conclude that the main blockage to the modern industrial transformation of the country lay precisely in the feudal and dynastic character of its politics. The rise of Kim Jong Il has been accomplished at great cost. The telephones of even his closest associates are said to be tapped;[110] lateral information flows within the government and the bureaucracy is deliberately constrained so that only the central leadership — the 'Leader' — is all-knowing. Throughout the society, initiative and energy are sapped by the primacy accorded to the structures of surveillance and control.

Erosion of the monolith

Whether or not the state built up by the Kim family survives, the society had been profoundly transformed. The levels of education were high, with about half the population in some form of educational institution. Eleven years of schooling became free and compulsory in 1972. There were about 60 000 kindergartens and creches to accommodate tiny infants from the age of several months. Public health facilities were comprehensive and free, housing adequate and cheap, and there seemed to be no slums. Food supplies, at least until the difficulties of the late 1980s, were generally adequate, without the constant bottlenecks and shortages of the Soviet Union. There was no unemployment, and the regime proudly declared that there was no taxation. The 'standard of living', by any Third World standards, was high. The existence of child-care facilities and maternity leave provisions made it possible for women to participate in the labour force, of which they comprised about 48 per cent.[111]

The same points, however, might be expressed in negative form. State indoctrination was pervasive and intensive, commencing shortly after birth. In a country where labour was in short supply, women were mobilised into factories and farms, while also being encouraged to maintain high rates of reproduction, and were denied access to birth control or abortion. Political, bureaucratic and military power, however, was almost exclusively male. Employment assignation, food rationing and travel constraints all helped maintain surveillance and control. Taxation is one, but by no means the only, means by which states appropriate to themselves the surplus produced by the labour of citizens; the north Korean state used other, equally effective means. The privileges enjoyed by cadres, and the Sybaritic lifestyle of the leadership, refuted in practice the egalitarianism proclaimed in principle. The physical shape of ordinary people contrasted with that of the privileged as 'bananas' to 'apples',[112] and the extravagance of the Kim family in the early 1990s bore the same sharp contrast to the privations of the people as had been revealed after the collapse in 1989 of the regimes of Eastern Europe.

Since institutions outside party and state control were not allowed, there was no refuge for independent, private or critical thought. The claim of 'monolithicity' was not an empty one. This was a regime which even monitored the virginity and sex life of its women citizens by periodic compulsory physical examinations conducted in workplaces and on changes of residence.[113] Foreign travel was not possible for ordinary people; indeed, they were not free even to travel to other cities without permits and there were no inter-city buses. Within cities, bicycles were not permitted; everyone depended on the same public transport system. Information was strictly controlled, so that listening to foreign broadcasts was forbidden and fixed tuning devices were attached to all radio and television sets. Books, including Marxist classics, were only available to readers in the 'Grand People's Study Hall' on presentation of a special permit. To the Seoul film director, Shin Sang-Ok, this denial of access to books made the P'yongyang regime worthy of comparison with the infamous 'First Emperor' of China, who once tried to burn all the books in the kingdom.[114]

The strength of such a system might ultimately prove to be its weakness. Autonomy had been sucked upwards in an irresistable vortex from the citizens to the Leader and his retinue; initiative and creativity were destroyed; and the possibility of reform being promoted within the system was slight.

The crisis faced by the north Korean state in the early 1990s stemmed from the closely interrelated 'double punches' of declining domestic economy and straitened international circumstance. In its degree of international isolation for more than four decades, north Korea remained the heir of the nineteenth century 'hermit kingdom'. But, as the then 'hermit kingdom' experienced a series of external shocks before the coherent order of the Yi dynasty collapsed in rebellion and external intervention, so in its fifth decade the system carefully constructed by another dynasty, the Kim family, was also shaken by external events.

In its establishment and through the crisis of the Korean War, north Korea was profoundly influenced and aided by the Soviet Union and China. In 1955, north Korea proclaimed its autonomy of foreign policy, under the general rubric of Chuche, but close relations with the two socialist powers (and with the various other socialist countries, especially of Eastern Europe) remained a cornerstone of policy. Kim's style and mass mobilisation techniques owed much to Stalin and Mao, and Soviet aid and technical co-operation were basic to his industrialisation. During the Sino-Soviet confrontation and during the Cultural Revolution in China, north Korea managed to avoid serious breach with either, while from the 1960s it pursued a vigorous diplomatic initiative towards the Third World as part of the Non-Aligned Nations movement.

North Korea had a good deal in common with the small and middle-sized industrialising countries of the Third World, and in the light of the common problems faced by such countries, its record was both relevant and impressive. However, instead of sharing experiences and distilling from them some general lessons of development, there was, for north Korea, only one lesson — the 'unique and profound idea' of 'the Absolute Position of the Leader in History'. While the particular pretensions of the Kim family were of little interest elsewhere, the message that the dynamic force in history is that the role of the Leader was generally welcome to other leaders, and the techniques of the cult were studied and adopted in various countries, especially in Africa and Eastern Europe (Romania in particular). Suh sums up this aspect of north Korean diplomacy, commenting that Kim:

> failed dismally in his foremost objective, projecting himself as leader of the Third World. Although he entertained lavishly, established Centers in remote African countries to study his ideas, and hosted elaborate conferences to disseminate his brand of socialist patriotism at great expense to the Korean people, he won few converts. Except for those he supported financially, none of the Third World leaders looked to him for inspiration.[115]

It is ironic that a regime which adopted Chuche (or independence) as its slogan should have devoted so much of its diplomatic effort abroad to the promotion of sycophancy and flunkeyism. The purple prose that emerges from various 'seminars' and conferences around the world in praise of the Leader and his family, like the texts of paid advertisements inserted in the world's press, was relayed back into Korea to reinforce the domestic importance of the cult. Vast resources were devoted to the effort to persuade the people that their leader was also recognised as world leader, genius, hero and statesman. One venture, typical of the whole, was the international essay competition sponsored by P'yongyang, with the following suggested theme:

> On the patriotic and revolutionary family of the respected and beloved leader President KIM IL SUNG (sic) and the epochal significance of his birth.[116]

The effect was to expose both the country and its leader to widespread ridicule, and to deepen its isolation. But, since flattery and exchange of leadership techniques were important, relations with many of the world's most brutal and infamous regimes were close. In May 1978, the 'emperor' Bokassa of Central Africa was feted in P'yongyang, where Kim Il Sung announced that the two countries enjoyed 'an identity of the aspirations for the building of an independent new society'.[117] Strong support was also given to the regimes of Mobutu in Zaire, Macias Nguema in Equatorial Guinea, Idi Amin in Uganda, Pol Pot in Cambodia, Gaddafi in Libya and Ceausescu in Romania. Ceausescu was a particularly close ally who was visited by north Korea's prime minister in November 1989, one month before his regime collapsed.

The international image of the regime was further tarnished by the involvement of its diplomats in black market and drug dealing in the 1970s (which led to its diplomats being expelled from Sweden, Norway, Finland and Denmark) and, according to the investigation conducted by the Government of Burma, to the bombing attack in Rangoon on 9 October 1983 which resulted in the deaths of seventeen high south Korean government officials including the Foreign Minister (with the President narrowly escaping), as well as, apparently, the terrorist attack on the KAL flight in December 1987, to which a young woman, Kim Hyun-Hee, subsequently confessed (directly implicating north Korea's 'Dear Leader').

Ultimately, the peculiarities of the regime were all rooted in the abnormal circumstances of the continuing militarised division and confrontation of the country, and the long-sustained hostile confrontation with the superpower of the United States. As Gregory Henderson noted in 1980, United States hostility towards north Korea even then was unprecedented in United States history, long outlasting that towards George III's England, the Kaiser's and Hitler's Germany, Ho Chi Minh's Vietminh, Stalin and Castro.[118] The pressure resulting from this confrontation, and the continuing fear of rewewed conflict, leading possibly to nuclear annihilation, helped to sustain the monolithic unity of the regime and state. A more normal internal political practice could only be expected after the achievement of normalcy in north Korea's relations with the United States, Japan and (above all) with south Korea.

Between north and south Korea, tension continued unbroken for most of the nearly four decades after the end of the war in 1953. For a long time there was no contact at all. The infiltration of armed commando groups across the border to attack the (Presidential) Blue House in Seoul in 1967 and the capture of the American intelligence ship, the *Pueblo*, later the same year marked high points in this tension. In 1972, during a period of Cold War detente and following the United States rapprochement with China, a series of north–south meetings took place, which led to the signing of a Joint Communiqué on the principles which should govern the process of reconciliation and reunification. Subsequent negotiations, however, progressed slowly, despite occasional gestures such as the south Korean acceptance of flood relief supplies from the north in 1984, the (brief) reunion of some of the peninsula's estimated 10 million divided families in 1985, and the tentative opening of trade relations from 1990 and the signing of a 'North–South Agreement' in December 1991. In 1991 there were still nearly 2 million armed men, out of a total population of 64 million, confronting each other across the so-called 'Demilitarised Line'.

However, in the negotiations of the early 1990s, the north was playing from a very weak hand. Its longest ally and close supporter, the Soviet Union, had virtually collapsed, though not before opening very warm diplomatic and economic relations with south Korea. The fear of ideologically 'incorrect' or 'dangerous' ideas flowing to north Korea from the Soviet Union led in November 1990 to the order for the return home of all Korean students. The whole of Eastern Europe, and also Mongolia, opened relations with Seoul. China, while striving to maintain its own hard-line regime politically, was pursuing a flourishing trade with south Korea and moving towards full recognition. To the consternation of P'yongyang, Chinese Comunist Party Secretary Jiang Zemin stated in October 1991 that, while China and north Korea were tied by 'strong affection' from having once fought together, they were not allies.[119] Even in the non-aligned world, north Korea had been eclipsed by the south, with left-inclining countries such as Algeria, Namibia and the Congo recognising Seoul in 1990 and others likely to follow.

If a settlement could be reached on peaceful co-existence with the south, as part of a preparatory phase leading to reunification, on normalisation with the United States (replacing the 1953 Armistice with a formal peace treaty) and with Japan (settling the claims arising from the colonial period), the way would be opened to the flow of technology and capital so much needed for the economic modernisation of the country, and, more importantly, for demilitarisation and political liberalisation.

The regime was caught in a dilemma: while realising the need to open the country to new technology, capital, ideas and trade, it was also afraid that such opening might also bring with it degenerate capitalist phenomena such as 'thieves, punks or pimps',[120] and thereby jeopardise the carefully constructed system of control and the prospects for long dynastic rule. The role of the Leaders, Great or Dear, would almost certainly diminish to the extent the country was opened and the people began to be able to penetrate the web of sycophancy, deceit, bombast and irrationality that had been spun around them, and to fulfil their destiny as 'masters of creation'.

To few rulers in history, and perhaps to none in the late twentieth century, could the words of Louis XIV, also known as the 'Sun King', be applied as they could to Kim Il Sung: 'L'etat: c'est moi'. Louis's son and successor, Louis XV, became known to posterity above all by the pungent and prescient phrase: 'Apres moi, le deluge'.

Whether such would also be the eventual epitaph for the Kim family regime, only time would tell.

Notes

1 Tai Sung An, *North Korea: A Political Handbook*, Wilmington, Delaware, 1983, p. 130
2 Dae-Sook Suh, *Kim Il Sung: The North Korean Leader*, New York, 1988, p. xii
3 See especially the analysis in Wada Haruki, *Kin Nissei to Manshu konichi senso* (Kim Il Sung and the Manchurian Anti-Japanese War), Heibonsha, 1992.
4 According to Soviet General Lebedev, formerly political commissar of the Soviet 25th Army which occupied North Korea, interviewed at the age of 90 by the Seoul newspaper *Chungang Ilbo*, Japanese translation in *This is Yomiuri*, February 1992, pp. 84–87
5 Suh, 1988, pp. 134ff.
6 For a detailed account, see Koon Woo Nam, *The North Korean Communist Leadership, 1945–1965*, Alabama, 1974.
7 Suh, 1988, pp. 238–48
8 Kim Il Sung's words, from a speech in August 1946, quoted in Scalapino and Lee, p. 360
9 Suck-Ho Lee, *Party-Military Relations in North Korea: A Comparative Analysis*, Seoul, 1989, p. 160
10 Scalapino and Lee, p. 593
11 Charter of the Korean Workers' Party, Point 4(a), reproduced in full in An, pp. 245–68
12 From *Nodong sinmun*, the daily newspaper, in 1975, quoted in *Far Eastern Economic Review*, 4 July 1975
13 *The Path of Great Love*, Pyongyang, 1977
14 '[T]he Workers' Party of Korea has completely got rid of sectarianism and flunkeyism which had done enormous harm historically and achieved the iron unity and solidarity of the whole Party on the basis of the monolithic idea, the Juche idea': *Juche Korea*, Pyongyang, 15 September 1976
15 Kim Il Sung, op cit, 1980
16 For a discussion of Chuche (or Juche), see Chong-Sik Lee, *Korean Workers Party: A Short History*, Stanford, California, 1978, pp. 96–97. Cumings says of it: 'The more one seeks to understand Juche, the more the meaning recedes. It is a state of mind, and one that is unavailable to the non-Korean.' (Cumings, *The Two Koreas*, New York, The Foreign Policy Association, 1984, p. 56)

17 Kim Il Sung, 'Report to the Sixth Congress of the Workers' Party of Korea on the Work of the Central Committee', 10 October 1980, Tokyo, 1980, pp. 27, 76, 98

18 Suh, 1988 (p. 311) notes that 'More than half of the new thirty-three-volume Korean history deals with only fifty years of Kim's revolutionary past and his rule in the North.'

19 Andrew C. Nahm, *North Korea Today: Her Past, Reality and Impression*, Kalamazoo, 1978, p. 86

20 *North Korea Quarterly*, no. 26-7, August–November 1981, pp. 29–30

21 For a recent Japanese account, including interviews with Russian families acquainted with the Kim family at the time of Kim Jong Il's birth, see Eya Osamu, 'Kin Nissei shogun no abakareta shinjitsu' (The truth about General Kim Il Sung exposed), *Bart* (Tokyo), vol. 1, no. 11, November 1991, pp. 42–45.

22 Comments made to this author during a May 1980 visit to North Korea. For a fuller account, see Gavan McCormack, 'North Korea: Kimilsungism — Path to Socialism?', *Bulletin of Concerned Asian Scholars*, vol. 13, no. 4, 1981, pp. 50–61.

23 Aidan Foster-Carter, 'Monumental Puzzle', *Far Eastern Economic Review*, 26 June 1986, p. 37. According to Tanaki (p. 172), physically handicapped people are not allowed to live in Pyongyang.

24 For one detailed study by a former foreign detainee, a Venezuelan communist poet employed in Pyongyang as a Spanish language consultant and held in solitary confinement for six years as a spy after a trial which Amnesty said was 'a parody of justice', see Ali Lameda, *Ali Lameda: A Personal Account of the Experience of a Prisoner of Conscience in the DPRK*, London, Amnesty International, 1979; see also regular Amnesty International publications.

25 *Concentration Camps in North Korea*, Seoul, March 1982. See also *New York Times*, 11 April 1982, and Chon Bu-Ok, *Kin Nissei no uso*, Tokyo, 1988, pp. 325-34.

26 'Korea — History', *The Far East and Australasia 1990*, London, 1989, p. 534

27 Chan Myon Su, 'Kita no mori ni kieta kikokusha tachi' (Returnees who disappeared in the forest), *Bart*, vol. 1, no. 11, November 1991, pp. 130–33; and Kim Won Jo, *Todo no kyowakoku* (Frozen Land Republic), Aki shobo, 1984

28 O Gi-Wan and Chan Myon-Su (the former in charge of reception of returnees in north Korea and the latter in charge of their despatch from Japan), 'Fuman bunshi ni ha tokubetsu keimusho ha matte-iru' (Special prison camps wait for the disaffected), *Gekkan Asahi*, March 1992, pp. 142–47.

29 Scalapino and Lee, op cit, p. 843

30 *The Far East and Australasia 1990*, p. 534

31 Far Eastern Economic Review, *Asia 1989 Yearbook*, p. 149, for the first figure, and International Institute of Strategic Studies (London), *The Military Balance, 1989-90*, for the second.

32 ibid., p. 216

33 Jon Halliday, 'The North Korean Model: Gaps and Questions', *World Development*, vol. 9, nos 9/10, 1981, p. 895 (hereafter Halliday, 1981)

34 Jon Halliday, 'The Economies of North and South Korea', in *Two Koreas — One Future?*, eds John Sullivan and Roberta Foss, University Press of America, 1987, p. 19 (hereafter Halliday, 1987)

35 Joseph Sanghoon Chung, *The North Korean Economy: Structure and Development*, Stanford, 1974, p. 57, For a very positive assessment of the Japanese legacy, see Tamaki Motoi, 'Nihon no tai-Kita-Chosen keizai kyoroku' (Japanese economic co-operation with North Korea), Nihon boeki shinkokai (Japan

External Trade Organization, or JETRO), *Kita Chosen no keizai to boeki no tembo* (Outlook for North Korea's Trade and Economy), Tokyo, December 1991, pp. 108–23, especially at pp. 108–9.(This annual volume is a valuable source of information and is cited hereafter simply as JETRO, with the year of the report.)

36 See table in Halliday,1987, p. 23.
37 ibid., p. 26
38 Suh, 1988, p. 166
39 Tamaki Motoi, *Kita Chosen Q & A 100* (100 Questions and Answers on North Korea), Aki Shobo, 1992, p. 24. This division of the day followed remarks made by Kim Il Sung in a 1963 speech. See Suh, 1988, p. 218.
40 *North Korea Quarterly*, op cit, p. 22
41 FAO, *Yearbook — Production*, vol. 43 — 1989, Rome, 1990, pp. 118–19
42 ibid., 1990, table 106 pp. 290–91; see revised article in 1991 vol., p. 238.
43 Details of all these projects conveniently resumed in Chung, 1989, p. 539.
44 One estimate was that as much as half of the rice harvest might be exported. Adrian Buzo, 'Agricultural Malaise', *Far Eastern Economic Review*, 7 May 1987.
45 *Far Eastern Economic Review*, 26 March 1992
46 Various reports in *Far Eastern Economic Review*, 22 August and 10 October 1991
47 JETRO, 1991, p. 20
48 Nicholas Kristof, 'In North Korea, Food is Scanty but Hatred of Regime is Plentiful', *International Herald Tribune*, 19 February 1992
49 JETRO, 1991, pp. 163–64; 'Zen rodosha no chingin "50% age" no nerai to genjitsu' (The objective of the '50 per cent rise' for all workers and the reality), *Shukan bunshun*, 27 February 1992, pp. 136–39, at p. 138.
50 *Far Eastern Economic Review*, 26 March 1992
51 Articles by Chon Pu-Ok and Shiozuka Tamotsu, *Seikai*, April 1992, pp. 29-49.
52 Scalapino and Lee, pp. 616, 655
53 Kim Il Sung's New Year address, quoted in *Pyongyang Times*, January 1992, no. 1
54 Rice output was apparently calculated on the basis of the number of bags consumed. Because of the imperative of meeting plan 'norms', these were often stuffed with straw and waste materials. Actual rice output might be as low as 765 000 tonnes. Yi U-Hong, *Donzoko no kyowakoku: kita Chosen fusaku no kozo* (Bottom depths republic: The structure of North Korean crop failure), Tokyo, Aki Shobo, 1989, p. 144.
55 John Sweeney, *The Life and Evil Times of Nicolae Ceausescu*, London, 1991, pp. 130, 160.
56 Halliday, 1987, p. 28
57 Harrison Salisbury, *To Peking and Beyond: A Report on the New Asia*, New York, 1973, p. 205.
58 McCormack, 1981, p. 53
59 JETRO, 1981, pp. 52–53
60 United States Central Intelligence Agency, National Foreign Assessment Center, *Korea: The Economic Race between the North and the South* (ER 78-100008), Washington DC, 1978. Table giving the CIA estimates is reproduced in Halliday, 1981, p. 38.
61 JETRO, 1981, op cit
62 Joseph S. Chung, 'Economy of North Korea', *The Far East and Australasia 1990*, London, 1989, p. 539
63 JETRO, 1991, p. 19
64 JETRO, 1990, pp. 26, 35
65 ibid., p. 26
66 *Far Eastern Economic Review Yearbook 1991*, Hong Kong, 1991, p. 6, and Shim Jae Hoon, 'The Inevitable Burden', *Far Eastern Economic Review*, 22 August 1991, pp. 21–23

67 Bank of Korea (Seoul), *Korea News Review*, 22 August 1992
68 'Kita Chosen keizai ibara no michi' (The thorny path of the North Korean economy), *Nihon keizai shinbun*, 2 December 1991. For the South Korean National Unification Board's estimates of north Korean achievement, measured against the 1978–84 and 1987–93 Plans, in electric power, coal, steel, cement and textiles, see *Far Eastern Economic Review*, 26 March 1992.
69 Chung notes, however, that the defence proportion of total spending fluctuated greatly, from 3.7 per cent in 1959 to about 19 per cent between 1960 and 1966, 30 per cent between 1967 and 1971, and 17 per cent in 1972, gradually declining to about 12 per cent by the late 1980s; ibid., p. 543. South Korean sources in 1990, however, estimated North Korean military spending at 40 per cent of GNP. (Quoted in *Shukan Bunshun*, 27 February 1992, p. 137.)
70 Murakami Kaoru, 'Donzoku keizai ni ochita Kita Chosen ha misairu de gaika o kasegu ka' (Is North Korea's bottom depths economy raising foreign currency by selling missiles?), *Seikai*, April 1992, pp. 34–37; see also Tamaki, pp. 72–73.
71 JETRO, 1990, p. 90. When a Japanese debt rescheduling mission visited Pyongyang in February 1991 (after fifteen years without payment of either principal or interest on the debt owing it), the North Korean side proposed a further 'grace' period of ten years, after which repayments might then be made over the subsequent period of fifteen years: JETRO, 1991, p. 103.
72 'Kita Chosen keizai ibara no michi' (The thorny path of the North Korean economy), *Nihon keizai shinbun*, 2 December 1991
73 $46 billion compared with $1.348 billion: *Asahi shinbun*, 17 September 1991, p. 13
74 Chon Pu-Ok, op cit, *Seikai*, April 1992, p. 42
75 Yun Hak-Jun, 'Naze waga doho — Zainichi Chosenjin ha kyogaku kenkin o kyosei sareru no ka (Why are our North Korean compatriots forced to contribute huge sums of money?), *Sapio*, 9 April 1992, pp. 17-20
76 *Asian Wall Street Journal*, 13 May 1992
77 Far Eastern Economic Review, *Asia 1990 Yearbook*, Hong Kong, 1990, p. 152. The Japanese scholar, Tamaki Motoi, gives the figure of 'a nominal $4.7 billion'. See JETRO, 1991, p. 118.
78 Sekikawa Natsuo, 'Kukyo naru shinden' (Empty Shrine), *Bart*, vol. 1, no. 11, 11 November 1991, pp. 26–27
79 For remarkable photographs (by Imaedo Koichi) of these 'Games', see *Bart*, May 1992, pp. 20-25.
80 *Far Eastern Economic Review*, 30 April 1992
81 Interview with Kim II Sung, *Asahi shinbun*, 2 April 1992
82 Suh, 1988, p. 319
83 Tai, 1983, p. 140
84 Foster-Carter, 1986, p. 36. And see Joan Robinson, 'Korean Miracle', *Monthly Review*, January 1965, pp. 544–49.
85 Tai, 1983, pp. 139–40
86 Bank of Korea estimate, *News Review* (Seoul) 22 August 1992, p. 15
87 Louise Do Rosario, 'Passing the Hat', *Far Eastern Economic Review*, 10 October 1991, p. 75
88 Seventy to 80 per cent of power generated was being lost in transmission along cables long ago planted underground as a security measure (*Seikai*, April 1992, p. 25).
89 *Asia 1991 Yearbook*, p. 141
90 For a good detailed discussion of this project, see JETRO, 1991, pp. 143–50.
91 Morgan E. Clippinger, 'King Chong-Il in the North Korean Mass Media: A Study of Semi-Esoteric Communication', *Asian Survey*, March 1981, p. 306
92 ibid.

93 Speeches by Li Jong Ryong, president of Kumsong Political University, and U Dal Ho, director of the Kim Il Sung Party Academy, Pyongyang, March 1982, in *People's Korea,* 17 April 1982, p. 5

94 ibid. For an analysis of this theme, see also Bruce Cumings, 'Corporatism in North Korea', *Journal of Korean Studies,* vol. 3, 1983.

95 Suh, 1988, p. 277

96 ibid., p. 281

97 Chon, *Seikai,* April 1992, pp. 44-45.

98 Choe U-Ni and Shin Sang-Ok, *Yami kara no kodama* (Echoes from the Darkness), Tokyo, 2 vols, 1988–89

99 ibid., vol. 1, p. 40

100 'Roma: diplomatici nordcoreani burloni in nome della FAO comprano film sexy e poi lasciano un buco di 170 milioni', *La Fiamma,* 26 July 1984

101 Ko Yong-hwan, quoted in Francis Deron, 'China's dilemma as North Korea holds out the begging bowl', *Le Monde,* 9 October 1991

102 *Pyongyang Times,* 7 September 1991

103 From *Nodong shinmun,* 27 August 1991, quoted in Shirai Hisaya, 'Shinka towareru "Kim Jong Il taisei"' (The real worth of the 'Kim Jong Il system' under question), *Asahi janaru,* 27 September 1991, p. 80

104 Kim Jung Il, speech of 3 January 1992, in *Korea and World Affairs,* Spring 1992, pp. 132–35

105 A long and revealing interview with Ko is contained in *This Is Yomiuri,* February 1992, pp. 58–65.

106 See the analysis of Kuni Akira, 'Kita Chosen no seiji, gaiko' (The politics and economy of North Korea), JETRO, 1991, pp. 153–80.

107 ibid., p. 157

108 Choe and Shin, vol. 2, p. 279

109 *Shukan Bunshun,* op cit

110 According to Ko Yon-Fan, op cit

111 Halliday, 1984, p. 898

112 Chung Ik-Woo, '"Kenko no tame ni ichinichi nishoku" "beruto ha hikishimeyo" dai undo no hisan' (The tragedy of the big movement to "have two meals a day for one's health" and to "tighten one's belt", *Sapio,* 9 April 1992, pp. 24-25

113 Choe and Shin, vol. 2, p. 268

114 ibid, vol. 2, p. 190

115 Suh, 1988, p. 250

116 Pyongyang news release, 1981

117 *Korea Daily News* (Pyongyang), 4 May 1978

118 Gregory Henderson, 'North Korea: a need for reappraisal', *Christian Science Monitor,* 7 April 1980

119 Quoted in JETRO, 1991, p. 174. This would seem to suggest that the 1961 Treaty of Friendship, Cooperation and Mutual Aid was not worth much.

120 Deputy Prime Minister Kim Dal-Hyon, quoted in Simon Darlin, 'North Korea opens cautiously to the West', *Asian Wall Street Journal,* 13 May 1992

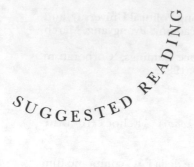

General

General histories are often a matter of personal taste. Andrew Nahm, *Korea: Tradition and Transformation, a History of the Korean People*, is both the most recent (at the time of writing) new history and the most comprehensively detailed. Ki-baik Lee, *A New History of Korea*, first published in South Korea in 1961 and revised on successive occasions, was first translated into English in 1984: in 1990, the English version was republished under the title *Korea Old and New: A History*. The major change was the inclusion of new chapters on the period 1864–1990 by Young Ick Lew and two excellent American scholars, Michael Robinson and Carter Eckert. Of the other general histories, Han Woo-keun, *A History of Korea* is perhaps the most accessible in style. On Korean historiography, one of South Korea's most eminent historians, Kang Man'gil, has written 'How History is Viewed in the North and in the South: Convergence and Divergence'; see also Doe Jin-soon, 'The Periodization of Modern and Contemporary History in North Korean Academic Circles'. A bold and provocative from the 1960s attempt to interpret Korean political culture is Gregory Henderson, *Korea, Politics of the Vortex*.

Women

The social and political role of women is briefly summarised in Bonnie Oh, 'From Three Obediences to Patriotism and Nationalism: Women's Status in Korea up to 1945'; fuller studies are mainly those by Kim Yung-Chung (ed.), *Women of Korea: A History from Ancient Times to 1945*, a straightforward narrative history, Sandra Mattielli (ed.), *Virtues in Conflict.: Tradition and the Korean Woman Today*, and Laurel Kendall and Mark Peterson (eds), *Korean Women: View from the Inner Room*.

Korean religion

An introduction to the history of religion, albeit one which has its critics, is James Huntley Grayson, *Korea, a Religious History*. A wide variety of religious topics, including ancestor worship, funerals, New Year's village rituals, rural women's rites, and the rise of new Buddhist movements, are discussed in Laurel Kendall and Griffin Dix (eds), *Religion and ritual in Korean society*, Berkeley, 1987.

Late Yi Korea

For the Korean polity on the eve of Japanese imperialism, the unrivalled study is James Palais, *Policy and Politics in Traditional Korea;* on the Taewon'gun's regency, see Ch'oe Ching Young, *The Rule of the Taewon'gun, 1864–1873: Restoration in Yi Korea*. The changing relationship with Japan and China is dealt with in an outstanding work by Martina Deuchler, *Confucian Gentlemen and Barbarian Envoys: The Opening of Korea, 1875–1885*, but see also Key-Hiuk Kim, *The Last Phase of the East Asian World Order: Korea, Japan, and the Chinese Empire, 1860–1882*. In detailing subsequent relations with Japan, Hilary Conroy, *The Japanese Seizure of Korea, 1868–1910* is still unsurpassed. Its interpretation of Japanese political 'realism', however, has been challenged (unsuccessfully in my view) by some historians in Korea. Broader, but very reliable, treatments of Korea's modern passage into the international world are C.I. Eugene Kim and Han-kyo Kim, *Korea and the Politics of Imperialism, 1876–1910*, and, extending into the colonial period, Chong-sik Lee, *The Politics of Korean Nationalism*. United States diplomatic records on Korea from the 1880s to 1905 are collected in three volumes, edited respectively by George McCune/John Harrison, Spencer Palmer and Scott Burnett. For early international trade, Cho Ki-jun, 'The impact of the opening of Korea on its commerce and industry' is concise and informative.

On specific events, Harold Cook, *Korea's 1884 Incident*, is both the only biography of Kim Okkyun in English and the clearest treatment of the Kapsin coup, but Shin Yong-Ha, 'The thought of the enlightenment movement' is a useful essay. Benjamin Weems, *Reform, Rebellion, and the Heavenly Way* is the standard treatment of the Tonghak and Ch'ondogyo. The Independence Club has attracted considerable attention: begin with Vipan Chandra's, *Imperialism, Resistance, and Reform in Late Nineteenth-Century Korea: Enlightenement and the Independence Club*, an excellent introduction to Korean society and politics late in the nineteenth century; also Shin Yong-Ha, 'Social philosophy of the Tongnip Hyophoe'; and Kenneth Wells, *New God New Nation: Protestants and Self-reconstruction Nationalism in Korea 1896–1937*, a thoughtful examination of Korean élite thinking late in the Yi and well into the colonial period.

The views of Westerners either resident in or visiting Korea at the turn of the century may be found in Homer Hulbert, *The Passing of Korea* (see also Clarence Weems (ed.), *Hulbert's History of Korea*, with a lengthy introduction by the editor on Hulbert's career); Isabella Bird Bishop, *Korea and Her Neighbours*, and William Sands, *Undiplomatic Memories* (Sands was a diplomatic advisor to the Korean government).

Colonial Korea

The colonial period as a whole is treated from various aspects in two volumes of papers: C.I. Eugene Kim and Dorothea Mortimore (eds), *Korea's Response to Japan: The Colonial Period, 1910–1945*, and Andrew Nahm (ed.), *Korea Under Japanese Colonial Rule*. Of these, Wonmo Dong, 'Assimilation and Social Mobilization in Korea' (Nahm) is an important paper on a highly emotive subject, while broad economic and social changes are deftly explained in Yunshik Chang, 'Planned Economic Transformation and Population Change' (Kim/Mortimore), much of which repeats his earlier 'Colonization as Planned Changed (sic): the Korean Case'. See also the papers on Korean education and agriculture in Ramon Myers and Mark Peattie (eds), *The Japanese Colonial Empire, 1895–1945*.

On the colonial economy as a whole, Sang-Chul Suh, *Growth and Structural Change in the Korean Economy, 1910–1940* is clear and concise. Carter Eckert, *Offspring of Empire*, and Dennis McNamara, *The Colonial Origins of Korean Enterprise* both portray the human side of Korean entrepreneurship and provide impressive explanations of the development of industrial capitalism in Korea and its intimate relationship with the Japanese authorities.

The most detailed and exhaustive study of Japan's rule in Korea, however, and its impact on the Korean people, remains Andrew Grajdanzev, *Modern Korea*, an extraordinary work given the time and circumstances in which it was written. Yoo Se-Hee's doctoral thesis, The Korean communist movement and the peasantry under Japanese rule, would have repaid publication, but there are authoritative works on the development of Korean communism: Dae-Sook Suh, *The Korean Communist Movement, 1918–1948*, and Robert Scalapino and Chong-sik Lee, *Communism in Korea*.

The thought and activities of intellectual nationalists, with a discussion of the writings of Yi Kwangsu, are provided in Michael Robinson, *Cultural Nationalism in Colonial Korea, 1920–25*. The campaign for a People's University is the subject of Abe Hiroshi, 'Higher Learning in Korea Under Japanese Colonial Rule'. A charming memoir by Japan's Princess Nashimoto, wife to the last of the Yi crown princes, is Yi Pangja, *The World is One* (in an ironic reversal of the bitterly hated policy of late Japanese colonialism, the princess prefers to use her Korean name). Richard Kim, *Lost Names*, is a beautifully written autobiographical novel of a young boy growing up under Japanese colonialism, and is especially evocative of Korean school life from the start of Japan's war with China (1937–45).

Post-1945 Korea

The literature on the Korean War and the two postwar republics is voluminous. Here we will mention only a few titles. A solid introduction on the two Koreas from 1945 to the early 1970s is Joungwon A. Kim,

Divided Korea. The best general introduction to South Korea is David I. Steinberg, *The Republic of Korea: Economic Transformation and Social Change*. An Tai-sung, *North Korea in Transition: From Dictatorship to Dynasty*, is useful.

Bruce Cumings, *The Origins of the Korean War*, is a two-volume magnum opus which carefully sets the stage of prewar Korea and then offers revelatory detail on the political developments within Korea between 1945 and 1950: John Merrill, *Korea: Peninsular Origins of the War*, is a shorter complementary study. A brief, profusely illustrated treatment of the same subject is Jon Halliday and Bruce Cumings, *Korea the Unknown War*. For the broader international picture, Peter Lowe, *The Origins of the Korean War* is a good, short and up-to-date introduction.

The leaders

Biographies of the Korean leaders are available in Robert Oliver, *Syngman Rhee: The Man Behind the Myth*, and Dae-Sook Suh, *Kim Il Sung*. The writings of Kim Il Sung are often to be found lying beside those of Mao Tse-tung in secondhand bookshops, while Park Chun Hee's beliefs are explained in his early work, *Our Nations' Path*. Michael Keon's *Korean Phoenix: A Nation From the Ashes*, is effectively a biography, largely in praise, of Park.

Economic development

The single fullest historical study of Korea's economy, replete with tables and statistics, is Hochin Choi, *The Economic History of Korea*. Postwar South Korean socio-economic development has been treated in a series of volumes from the Korea Development Institute, published by Harvard University Press: see the works by Roy Bahl, Ban Sung Hwan, David Cole, Leroy Jones, Kim Kwang-suk, Anne Kreuger, Noel McGinn and Edwin Mills. The volume by Edward Mason, *The Economic and Social Modernization of the Republic of Korea* summarises the main points from each of the previous publications in the series.

The military

The political roles of the Korean armies are analysed in Lee Suk-ho, *Party–Military Relations in North Korea*; and for South Korea, John Lovell, 'The Military in Korean Politics' and Jon Huer, *Marching Orders: The Role of the Military in South Korea's 'Economic Miracle' 1961–1971*.

Rural Korea

The Saemaul movement is discussed in Whang In-joung, *Management of Rural Change in Korea*, and critically assessed in Mick Moore, 'Mobilization and Disillusion in Rural Korea: The Saemaul Movement in Retrospect'. The impact of modernisation on South Korea's rural community is assessed by Vincent Brandt, *A Korean Village: Between Farm and Sea*, and more recently by Clark Sorenson, *Over the Mountains are Mountains*.

Chun Doo Hwan and student rebellion

The coming to power of Chun Doo Hwan and his early policies are examined from a government perspective by Harold Hinton, *Korea under New Leadership: the Fifth Republic* (which also contains key documents on Chun's takeover), while the Kwangju incident is explored from various angles in Donald Clark (ed.), *The Kwangju Uprising*. The radical student movement in South Korea is explained in Manwoo Lee, 'Anti-Americanism and South Korea's Changing Perception of America'.

Koreans overseas

The Korean diaspora is the subject of a number of books: Ivan Light and Edna Bonacich, *Immigrant Entrepreneurs: Koreans in Los Angeles 1965-1982*, examines what is perhaps the largest Korean community in the United States; the varied articles in Dae-Sook Suh (ed.), *Koreans in the Soviet Union* briefly cover Korean movements since the 1920s; Michael Weiner, *Origins of the Korean Community in Japan 1910–1923* (at the time of writing, Weiner also promised a study entitled *The Korean Minority in Wartime Japan*) and Richard Mitchell, *The Korean Minority in Japan* together provide a historical background to the sociological study of Korean residents in the 1970s by Changsoo Lee and George De Vos, *Koreans in Japan: Ethnic Conflict and Accommodation;* while Chae-Jin Lee, *China's Korean Minority: The Politics of Ethnic Education*, and Helen Hardacre, *The Religion of Japan's Korean Minority: The Preservation of Ethnic Identity*, as their titles indicate, deal with certain key aspects of overseas Korean ethnicity. A recent assessment of north and south Korea's foreign relations (albeit one outdated by events in the Soviet Union during 1991) is Michael Mazarr (ed.), *Korea 1991: The Road to Peace*.

Inside Korea

The essays in Chong-sik Lee (ed.), *Korea Briefing 1990* cover all major aspects of north and south Korean society, politics and economics: especially rewarding are Vincent Brandt, 'South Korean Society' and Kim Seong-Kon, 'On Native Grounds: Revolution and Renaissance in Art and Culture', the latter being a mine of information on nationalism in South Korea's arts in the 1980s. An insight into North Korean arts may be gleaned from Youngmin Kwon, 'Literature and Art in North Korea: theory and policy', and Park Myung-jin, 'Motion Pictures in North Korea'.

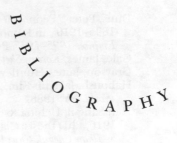

The Yi dynasty

Beasley, William, *Japanese Imperialism*, Oxford, 1987.

Bishop, Isabella Bird, *Korea and her Neighbors*, NY, 1898 (various reprints).

Burnett, Scott S. (ed.), *Korean–American relations: Documents Pertaining to the Far Eastern Diplomacy of the United States volume 3 — the period of diminishing influence, 1896–1905*, Honolulu, 1989.

Chandra, Vipan, *Imperialism, Resistance, and Reform in Late Nineteenth-century Korea: Enlightenment and the Independence Club*, Berkeley, 1988.

—— 'The Concept of Popular Sovereignty: The Case of So Chae-p'il and Yun Ch'i-ho', *Korea Journal*, vol. 24–1, April 1981, pp. 4–13.

Cho Ki-jun, 'The Impact of the Opening of Korea on its Commerce and Industry', *Korea Journal*, vol. 16–2, February 1976, pp. 27–44.

Ch'oe Ching-young, *The Rule of the Taewon'gun 1864-1873: Restoration in Yi Korea*, Cambridge, Mass, 1972.

Ch'oe Jae-hyon, 'Strategic groups of nationalism in nineteenth-century Korea', *Journal of Contemporary Asia*, vol. 16–2, 1986, pp. 223–36.

Ch'oe Yong-ho, 'Reinterpreting Traditional History in North Korea', *Journal of Asian Studies*, vol. xl, no. 3, May 1981, pp. 503–23.

Choi Hochin, *The Economic History of Korea*, Seoul, 1971.

Choi Sok-wu, 'Reception of Sohak (Western learning) in Korea', in Chun, Shin-yong (ed.), *Korean Thoughts*, Korean culture series, no. 10, Seoul, 1979.

Chun Hae-jong, 'Sino-Korean Tributary relations in the Ch'ing Period', in John K. Fairbank (ed.), *The Chinese World Order*, Cambridge, Mass, 1968.

Chung To-woong, 'The Opening of Korea and her Military Reform in the Late Nineteenth Century', *Revue International d'histoire Militaire*, no. 70, 1988, pp. 69–78.

Clark, Donald, *Christianity in Modern Korea*, NY, 1986.

Cook, Harold, *Pioneer American Businessman in Korea: The Life and Times of Walter David Townshend*, Seoul, 1981.

—— *Korea's 1884 Incident*, Seoul, 1972.

—— 'Pak Yong-hyo: Background and Early Years', *Journal of Social Sciences and Humanities*, no. 31, December 1969, pp. 11–24.

Conroy, Hilary, *The Japanese Seizure of Korea, 1868–1910*, Philadelphia, 1960.

Deuchler, Martina, *Confucian Gentlemen and Barbarian Envoys: The Opening of Korea 1875–1885*, Seattle, 1977.

Duus, Peter, 'Economic Dimensions of Meiji Imperialism: The Case of Korea 1895–1910', in Ramon Myers and Mark Peattie (eds), *The Japanese Colonial Empire, 1895–1945*, Princeton, 1984.

Gale, James, *Korean Sketches*, NY, 1898.

Grayson, James Huntley, *Korea a Religious History*, Oxford, 1989.

Haboush, JaHyun Kim, *A Heritage of Kings: One Man's Monarchy in the Confucian World*, NY, 1988.

Han Sang-il, Uchida Ryohei and Japanese continental expansionism 1874–1916, PhD thesis, Claremont Graduate School 1974, published in Korean as *Ilbon Cheguk Chui Ui Han Yongu*, Seoul, 1980, and in Japanese as *Nik-Kan Kindaishi no Kukan*, Tokyo, 1984.

Han Woo-keun, *The History of Korea*, Honolulu, 1970.

—— 'Perspective of Korean History', Chung/Ro, 1979.

Harrington, Fred Harvey, *God, Mammon, and the Japanese: Dr Horace N. Allen and Korean–American Relations, 1884–1905*, Madison, 1944.

Hatada, Takashi, *A History of Korea*, Santa Barbara, 1969.

Hulbert, Homer, *The Passing of Korea*, NY, 1909, rep. Seoul, 1969.

Hwang, I.K., *The Korean Reform Movement of the 1880s: A Study of the Transition in Intra-Asian Relations*, Camb, Mass, 1978.

Jeon Sang-woon, *Science and Technology of Korea: Traditional Instruments and Techniques*, Camb, Mass, 1974.

Kang Man-gil, 'How history is viewed in the North and in the South: convergence and divergence', *Korea Journal*, vol. 30–2, February 1990, pp. 4–19.

—— 'Reflections on the centenary of the opening of Korea', *Korea Journal*, vol. 16–2, February 1976, pp. 10–18.

Kim, C.I. Eugene and Kim Han-kyo, *Korea and the Politics of Imperialism 1876–1910*, Berkeley, 1968.

Kim Han-kyo, *Studies on Korea: A Scholar's Guide*, Honolulu, 1980.

Kim Key-Hiuk, *The Last Phase of the East Asian World Order: Korea, Japan, and the Chinese Empire, 1860–1882*, Berkeley, 1980.

Kim Yung-Chung (ed.), *Women of Korea: A History From Ancient Times to 1945*, Seoul, 1976.

Koh Sung Jae, *Stages of Industrial Development in Asia: A Comparative History of the Cotton Industry in Japan, India, China and Korea*, Philadelphia, 1966.

Korean National Commission for UNESCO (ed.), *Main Currents of Korean Thought*, Seoul, 1983.

Lee Chong-sik, *The Politics of Korean Nationalism*, Berkeley, 1965.

Lee Ki-baik, *A New History of Korea*, Camb, Mass, 1984.

Lee Ki-baik, Eckert, Carter and et al., *Korea Old and New: A History*, Camb, Mass, 1990.

Lee Kwang-rin, 'Korea's Responses to Social Darwinism', *Korea Journal*, vol. 18–4, April 1978, pp. 36–47, vol. 18–5, May 1978, pp. 42–48.

Lee Yur Bok, *West Goes East: Paul Georg von Mollendorff and Great Power Imperialism in Late Yi Korea*, Honolulu, 1988.

—— 'American Policy Towards Korea During the Sino-Japanese War of 1894–95', *Journal of Social Sciences and Humanities*, vol. 43, June 1976.

—— *Diplomatic Relations Between the United States and Korea, 1866–1887*, NY, 1970.

Lee Yur Bok and Patterson, Wayne (eds), *One Hundred Years of Korean–American Relations, 1882–1982*, Alabama, 1986.

Lensen, George Alexander, *Balance of Intrigue: International Rivalry in Korea and Manchuria, 1884–1899*, two vols., Tallahassee, 1982.

Lew Young Ick, 'Minister Inoue Kaoru and the Japanese Reform Attempts in Korea During the Sino-Japanese War, 1894–95', *Asea Yon'gu*, 27–2, July 1984.

—— 'American Advisers in Korea 1885-1894: Anatomy of Failure', in Andrew Nahm (ed.), *The United States and Korea: American–Korean Relations 1866–1976*, Kalamazoo, 1979.

—— 'An Analysis of the Reform Documents of the Kabo Reform Movement 1894', *Journal of Social Sciences and Humanities*, no. 4, December 1974.

Lone, Stewart, 'Of "Collaborators" and Kings: The Ilchinhoe, Korean Court, and Japanese Agricultural-Political Demands During the Russo-Japanese War 1904–05', *Papers on Far Eastern History*, no. 38, September 1988, pp. 103–24.

—— 'The Japanese Annexation of Korea 1910: The Failure of East Asian Co-prosperity', *Modern Asian Studies*, vol. 25–1, February 1991, pp. 143–73.

McCune, George and Harrison, John (eds), *Korean–American Relations, Documents Pertaining to the Far Eastern Diplomacy of the United States, Volume One, the Initial Period, 1883–1886*, Berkeley, 1951.

McKenzie, Frederick, *The Tragedy of Korea*, London, 1908.

—— *Korea's Fight for Freedom*, NY, 1920.

McNamara, Dennis, Imperial Japan and Nationalist Resistance: Japan and Korea 1876–1910, unpub. PhD thesis, Harvard University, 1983.

Michell, Tony, 'Jardine Matheson and Company in Korea 1883–1885', in International Centre for Economics and Related Disciplines, *Aspects of Anglo-Korean Relations*, Part 2, London, 1984.

Nahm, Andrew, *Korea: Tradition and Transformation, a History of the Korean People*, Seoul/Elizabeth NJ, 1988.

—— 'Korea and Tsarist Russia: Russian Interests, Policy, and Involvement in Korea, 1884–1904', *Korea Journal*, vol. 22–6, June 1982, pp. 4–19.

—— (ed.), *The United States and Korea: American-Korean Relations, 1866–1976*, Kalamazoo, 1979.

Oh, Bonnie B., 'From Three Obediences to Patriotism and Nationalism: Women's Status in Korea up to 1945', *Korea Journal*, vol. 22–7, July 1982, pp. 37–53.

Paik, George L., *The History of Protestant Missions in Korea, 1832–1910*, Seoul, 1971.

Pak Chong-hong, 'Historical Review of Korean Confucianism', Korean National Commission for UNESCO, Seoul, 1983.

Palais, James, *Policy and Politics in Traditional Korea*, Camb, Mass, 1975.

Palmer, Spencer (ed.), *Korean–American Relations: Documents Pertaining to the Far Eastern Diplomacy of the United States, Volume 2, the Period of Growing Influence, 1887–1895*, Berkeley, 1963.

Park Seong-rae, 'Introduction of Western Science in Korea, 1876–1910', *Korea Journal*, vol. 21–5, May 1981, pp. 29–38.

Patterson, Wayne, *The Korean Frontier in America: Immigration to Hawaii 1896–1910*, Honolulu, 1988.

Rees, David, *A Short History of Modern Korea*, Port Erin, 1988.

Sands, William, *Undiplomatic Memories*, NY, 1930.

Sato, Seizaburo, 'Response to the West: the Korean and Japanese patterns', in Albert M. Craig (ed.), *Japan: A Comparative View*, Princeton, 1979.

Shin Bok-ryong, 'A Study of Characteristics of the Donghak Revolution (1860–1894)', *Journal of Social Sciences and Humanities*, no. 39, June 1974, pp. 63–81.

Shin Il-chul, 'Shin Chae-ho and his Concept of Nationalism', in Chun Shin-yong (ed.), *Korean Thoughts* (Korean culture series no. 10), Seoul, 1979.

Shin, Susan, 'Tonghak Thought: The Roots of Revolution', *Korea Journal*, vol. 19–9, September 1979, pp. 11–19.

Shin Yong-Ha, 'The Thought of the Enlightenment Movement', *Korea Journal*, vol. 24–12, December 1984, pp. 4–21.

—— 'Social Philosophy of Tongnip Hyophoe', Korean National Commission for UNESCO, 1983.

Sohn Pow-Key, Kim Chol-Choon and Hong Yi-Sup, *The History of Korea*, Seoul, 1970.

Sugiyama, Shinya, 'Japan's Trade with Korea 1876–1895 as Reflected in British Sources', International Centre for Economics and Related Disciplines, *Aspects of Anglo-Korean Relations*, part 2, London, 1984.

Swartout, Robert Jr, *Mandarins, Gunboats and Power Politics*, Honolulu, 1980.

—— (ed.), *An American Adviser in Late Yi Korea: The Letters of Owen Nickerson Denny*, Alabama, 1984.

Synn Seung Kwon, *The Russo-Japanese Rivalry over Korea 1876-1904*, Seoul, 1981.

Wanne, J. Joe, *Traditional Korea: A Cultural History*, Seoul, 1972.

Weems, Benjamin, *Reform, Rebellion and the Heavenly Way*, Tucson, 1964.

Weems, Clarence (ed.), *Hulbert's History of Korea*, two vols, NY, 1962.

Wells, Kenneth, *New God New Nation: Protestants and Self-reconstruction Nationalism in Korea 1896–1937*, London/Sydney, 1990.

—— 'Yun Ch'i-ho and the Quest for National Integrity: The Formation of a Christian Approach to Nationalism at the End of the Choson Dynasty', *Korea Journal*, vol. 22–2, January 1982.

Yang Sung Chul, 'The Evolution of Korean Nationalism: A Historical Survey', *Korea and World Affairs*, vol. 11–3, Fall 1987, pp. 424–70.

Colonial Korea

Abe, Hiroshi, 'Higher Learning in Korea under Japanese Rule', *The Developing Economies*, vol. 9–2, June 1971, pp. 174–95.

Allen, Chizuko Takeuchi, 'Northeast Asia Centred Around Korea: Ch'oe Nam-son's View of History', *Journal of Asian Studies*, vol. 49–4, November 1990, pp. 787–806.

Brudnoy, David, 'Japan's Experiment in Korea', *Monumenta Nipponica*, vol. 25–1, 1970, pp. 155–95.

Brunner, Edmund, *Rural Korea: A Preliminary Survey of Economic, Social and Religious Conditions*, NY, 1928.

Chae Man-Sik, *Peace under Heaven*, NY, 1992.

Chang Yunshik, 'Planned Economic Transformation and Population Change', in C.I. Eugene Kim and Dorothea Mortimore (eds) *Korea's Response to Japan: The Colonial Period 1910–1945*, Kalamazoo, 1977.

—— 'Colonization as Planned Changed [sic]: The Korean Case', *Modern Asian Studies*, vol. 5–2, 1971, pp. 161–86.

Dong Wonmo, 'Assimilation and Social Mobilization in Korea', in Andrew Nahm (ed.), *Korea Under Japanese Colonial Rule*, Kalamazoo, 1973.

Drake, H.B., *Korea of the Japanese*, London, 1930.

Government-general of Tyosen, *Annual Report on Administration of Tyosen 1936–37*, Seoul, 1937.

Grajdanzev, Andrew, *Modern Korea*, NY, 1944.

The Japan Year Book

Jhin Dukyu, 'A Study of the Shaping of Nationalism in Colonial Korea with Special Attention to the Characteristics of Rightist Nationalism in the 1920s', *Korea and World Affairs*, vol. 11–3, Fall 1987, pp. 471–99.

Juhn, Daniel, 'Nationalism and Korean businessmen', in C.I. Eugene Kim and Dorothea Mortimore (eds), *Korea's Response to Japan: The Colonial Period 1910–1945*, Kalamazoo, 1977.

Kang Man-gil, 'Significance of the Shin'gan-hoe Society Movement in the History of the Korean National Movement', *Korea Journal*, vol. 27–9, September 1987, pp. 4–10.

Kang Wi Jo, 'Religion and Politics under Japanese rule', in C.I. Eugene Kim and Dorothea Mortimore (eds), *Korea's Response to Japan: The Colonial Period 1910–1945*, Kalamazoo, 1977.

Kang Young Hoon, 'Personal Reminiscences of my Japanese School Days', in C.I. Eugene Kim and Dorothea Mortimore (eds), *Korea's Response to Japan: The Colonial Period 1910–1945*, Kalamazoo, 1977.

Keidel, Albert, *Korean Regional Farm Product and Income: 1910–1975*, Seoul, 1981.

Kim, C.I. Eugene and Mortimore, Dorothea (eds), *Korea's Response to Japan: The Colonial Period 1910–1945*, Kalamazoo, 1977.

Kim Han-kyo, 'Japanese Colonialism in Korea', in Harry Wray and Hilary Conroy (eds), *Japan Examined*, Honolulu, 1983.

Kim, Richard, *Lost Names*, Seoul, 1970.

Kwon Ik Whan, 'Japanese Agricultural Policy on Korea 1910–1945', *Korean Quarterly*, vol. 7–3, Autumn 1965, pp. 96–112.

Lee See-Jae, 'A Study on Korean Rumors During Wartime Japanese Colonial Occupation', *Korea Journal*, vol. 27–8, August 1987, pp. 4–19.

McNamara, Dennis, *The Colonial Origins of Korean Enterprise*, Cambridge, 1990.

—— 'The Keisho and the Korean Business Elite', *Journal of Asian Studies*, vol. 48–2, May 1989, pp. 310–23.

—— 'Entrepreneurship in Colonial Korea: Kim Yon-su', *Modern Asian Studies*, vol. 22–1, 1988, pp. 165–77.

Moloney, Barbara, 'Noguchi Jun and Nitchitsu. Colonial Investment Strategy in a High-technology Enterprise', in William Wray (ed.), *Managing Industrial Enterprise: Cases From Japan's Prewar Experience*, Camb, Mass, 1989.

Myers, Ramon and Peattie, Mark (eds), *The Japanese Colonial Empire, 1895–1945*, Princeton, 1984.

Myers, Ramon and Yamada, Saburo, 'Agricultural Development in the Empire', Myers/Peattie 1984.

Nahm, Andrew (ed.), *Korea Under Japanese Colonial Rule*, Kalamazoo, 1973.

Oh Kon Cho, 'Resistance Theatres and Motion Pictures', in C.I. Eugene Kim and Dorothea Mortimore (eds), *Korea's Response to Japan: The Colonial Period 1910–1945*, Kalamazoo, 1977.

Park Soon Won, The Emergence of a Factory Labor Force in Colonial Korea: A Case Study of the Onoda Cement Factory, unpub. PhD thesis, Harvard University, 1985.

Park Yong-Ock, 'The Women's Modernization Movement in Korea', in Sandra Mattielli (ed.), *Virtues in Conflict: Tradition and the Korean Woman Today*, Seoul, 1977.

Rhee Ma-Ji, Moral Education in Korea under Japanese Colonialism During 1910–1945, unpub. PhD thesis, Rutgers, State University of New Jersey, New Brunswick 1989.

Robinson, Michael, *Cultural Nationalism in Colonial Korea, 1920–1925*, Seattle, 1988.

—— 'Ideological Schism in the Korean Nationalist Movement, 1920–1930; Cultural Nationalism and the Radical Critique', *The Journal of Korean Studies*, vol. 4, 1982–83.

—— 'National Identity and the Thought of Sin Ch'ae-ho: Sadaejuui and Chuch'e in History and Politics', *The Journal of Korean studies*, vol. 5, 1984, pp. 121–42.

Scalapino, Robert and Lee Chong-sik, *Communism in Korea*, two vols., Berkeley, 1972.

Shin Paull hobom, The Korean Colony in Chientao: A Study of Japanese Imperialism and Militant Korean Nationalism, 1905–1932, unpub. PhD thesis, University of Washington, 1980.

Song Seok Choong, 'Grammarians and Patriots: Han'gul Scholars' Struggles for the Preservation of their Linguistic Heritage', in C.I. Eugene Kim and Dorothea Mortimore (eds), *Korea's Response to Japan: The Colonial Period 1910–1945*, Kalamazoo, 1977.

Sorensen, Hendrik, 'Korean Buddhist Journals During Early Japanese Colonial Rule', *Korea Journal*, vol. 30–1, January 1990, pp. 17–27.

Suh Dae-Sook, *The Korean Communist Movement, 1918–1948*, Princeton, 1967.

—— (ed.), *Documents of Korean Communism 1918–1948*, Princeton, 1970.

Suh Sang Chul, *Growth and Structural Changes in the Korean Economy 1910–1940*, Camb, Mass, 1978.

Sung Hwan Ban, 'Agricultural Growth in Korea 1918–1971', Yujiro Hayami et al. (eds), *Agricultural Growth in Japan, Taiwan, Korea, and the Philippines*, Honolulu, 1979.

(Allen) Takeuchi, Chizuko, Ch'oe nam-son: History and Nationalism in Modern Korea, unpub. PhD thesis, University of Hawaii, 1988.

Tsurumi, E. Patricia, 'Colonial Education in Korea and Taiwan', in Ramon Myers and Mark Peattie (eds), *The Japanese Colonial Empire, 1895–1945*, Princeton, 1984.

United States State Department, Records of the Department of State Relating to Internal Affairs of Korea, Scholarly Resources Microfilm.

Vacante, Russell, Japanese Colonial Education in Korea 1910–1945: An Oral History, unpublished PhD thesis, State University of New York at Buffalo, 1987.

Wada, Haruki, 'Koreans in the Soviet Far East, 1917–1937', in Suh Dae-sook (ed.), *Koreans in the Soviet Union*, Honolulu, 1987.

Wells, Kenneth, 'Between the Devil and the Deep: Nonpolitical Nationalism and "Passive Collaboration" in Korea During the 1920s', *Papers on Far Eastern History*, no. 37, March 1988, pp. 125–47.

—— 'The Rationale of Korean Economic Nationalism under Japanese Colonial Rule, 1922–32: The Case of Cho Man-sik's Products Promotion Society', *Modern Asian Studies*, 19–4, 1985, pp. 823–59.

Weiner, Michael, *The Origins of the Korean Community in Japan, 1910–1923*, Manchester, 1989.

Yi Pangja, *The World is One*, Seoul, 1973.

Yoo Se Hee, The Korean Communist Movement and the Peasantry Under Japanese Rule, unpub. PhD thesis, Columbia University, 1974.

The Korean War

Cotton, James and Neavy, Ian (eds) *The Korean War in History*, Manchester, 1989.

Cumings, Bruce (ed.), *Child of Conflict: The Korean–American Relationship, 1943–1953*, Seattle, 1983.

—— *The Origins of the Korean War Volume 2: The Roaring of the Cataract 1947–1950*, Princeton, 1990.

—— *The Origins of the Korean War: Liberation and the Emergence of Separate Regimes 1945–1947*, Princeton, 1981.

Foot, Rosemary, *A Substitute for Victory: The Politics of Peacemaking at the Korean Armistice Talks*, Ithaca, 1990.

—— *The Wrong War: American Policy and the Dimensions of the Korean Conflict, 1950–1953*, Ithaca, 1985.

Gayn, Mark, *Japan Diary*, Tokyo, 1981.

Grey, Jeffrey, *The Commonwealth Armies and the Korean War*, Manchester, 1988.

Kim Chum-kon, *The Korean War*, Seoul, 1973.

Kim, Richard, *The Martyred*, Seoul, 1969.

Knox, Donald, *The Korean War: An Oral History*, NY, 1985.

Lowe, Peter, *The Origins of the Korean War*, London, 1986.
Matray, James (ed.), *Historical Dictionary of the Korean War*, Westport, 1991.
McCormack, Gavan, *Cold War Hot War: An Australian Perspective on the Korean War*, Sydney, 1983.
—— 'Korea: Wilfred Burchett's Thirty Years' War' in *Burchett: Reporting the Other Side of the World*, ed. Ben Kiernan, London, 1986.
McCune, George, *Korea Today*, NY, 1950.
MacDonald, Callum, *Britain and the Korean War*, Oxford, 1990.
McFarland, Keith D., *The Korean War: An Annotated Bibliography*, NY, 1986.
Meade, E. Grant, *American Military Government in Korea*, NY, 1951.
Merrill, John, 'Internal Warfare in Korea, 1948–1950: The Local Setting of the Korean War', in Bruce Cumings (ed.), *Child of Conflict: The Korean–American Relationship, 1943–1953*, Seattle, 1983.
—— *Korea: The Peninsular Origins of the War*, Newark, 1989.
Nagai, Yonosuke and Iriye, Akira (eds), *Origins of the Cold War in Asia*, Tokyo, 1977.
O'Neill, Robert, *Australia in the Korean War*, two vols, Canberra, 1981–87.
Ra Jong Yil, 'Political Crisis in Korea 1952: The Administration, Legislature, Military and Foreign Powers', *Journal of Contemporary History*, vol. 27–2, April 1992, pp. 301–318.
Rees, David, *Korea the Limited War*, London, 1964.
Riley, John and Schramm, Wilbur, *The Reds Take a City: The Communist Occupation of Seoul, with Eyewitness Accounts*, New Brunswick, 1951.
Simmons, Robert R., *The Strained Alliance: Peking, P'yongyang, Moscow and the Politics of the Korean Civil War*, NY, 1975.
Song Kwang-sung, The impact of US military occupation on the social development of decolonized South Korea, 1945–1949, unpub. PhD thesis, University of California, Los Angeles 1989.
Stone, I.F., *The Hidden History of the Korean War*, NY, 1952.
Stueck, William Whitney, *The Road to Confrontation: American Policy Toward China and Korea, 1947–1950*, Chapel Hill, 1981.

The Republic of Korea (south Korea)

Amsden, Alice, *Asia's Next Giant: South Korea and Late Industrialization*, NY, 1989.
Bae Chang-Ho, 'Seoul in Korean Cinema', *East-West Film Journal*, vol. 3–1, December 1988.
Bahl, Roy, *Public Finances During the Korean Modernization Process*, Camb, Mass, 1986.
Baldwin, Frank, *Without Parallel: the American–Korean Relationship Since 1945*, NY, 1974.
Ban Sung Hwan, Moon Pal Yong and Perkins, Dwight H., *Rural Development*, Camb, Mass, 1980.
Bartz, Patricia, *South Korea*, Oxford, 1972.
Brandt, Vincent, 'South Korean Society', in Lee Chong-sik, *Korea Briefing 1990*, Boulder, Col, 1991.
—— *A Korean Village: Between Farm and Sea*, Cambridge, Mass, 1971.
Chang Yunshik, 'The personalist ethic and the market in Korea', *Comparative Studies in Society and History*, vol. 33–1, January 1991, pp. 106–29.
Cheong Sung-hwa, *The Politics of Anti-Japanese Sentiment in Korea: Japanese–South Korean Relations Under American Occupation, 1945–1952*, NY, 1991.
—— Japanese–South Korean Relations under American Occupation, 1945–1952: The Politics of Anti-Japanese Sentiment in Korea and the Failure of Diplomacy, PhD thesis, University of Iowa, 1988.

Cho Hung-youn, 'The Characteristics of Korean Minjung Culture', *Korea Journal*, vol. 27–11, November 1987, pp. 4–17.

Chung Chin-wee et al. (eds), *Korea and Japan in World Politics*, Seoul, 1985.

Chung Chong-Shik and Ro Jae-Bong (eds), *Nationalism in Korea*, Seoul, 1979.

Chung Un-chan, 'The Development of the South Korean Economy and the Role of the United States', in Gerald Curtis and Sung-joo Han (eds), *The U.S.–South Korean Alliance*, Lexington, 1983.

Clark, Donald N. (ed.), *The Kwangju Uprising: Shadows over the Regime in South Korea*, Boulder, Col, 1988.

Cole, David, *Financial Development in Korea, 1945–1978*, Camb, Mass, 1983.

Cotton, James (ed.), *Korea Under Roe Tae-Woo: Democratisation, Northern Policy and Inter-Korean Relations*, Sydney, 1993.

Cumings, Bruce, 'Korean–American Relations: A Century of Conflict and Thirty-five Years of Intimacy', in Warren Cohen (ed.), *New Frontiers in American–East Asian Relations*, NY, 1983.

—— 'The Abortive Abertura: South Korea in the Light of Latin American Experience', *New Left Review*, no. 173, Jan/Feb 1989, pp. 5–32.

Curtis, Gerald and Han, Sung-joo (eds), *The U.S.–South Korean alliance*, Lexington, 1983.

Doherty, Thomas, 'Creating a National Cinema: The South Korean Experience', *Asian Survey*, vol. 24–8, August 1984, pp. 840–51.

Dong Wonmo, 'Student Activism and the Presidential Politics of 1987 in South Korea', in Kim Ilpyong and Kihl Young Whan (eds), *Political Change in South Korea*, NY, 1988.

Dredge, C. Paul, 'Korean Funerals: Ritual as Process', in Laurel Kendall and Griffin Dix (eds), *Religion and Ritual in Korean Society*, Berkeley, 1987.

The Economist, 'A Survey of South Korea', 18 August 1990.

The Far East and Australasia (annual publication).

Hah Chong-do, 'National Image and the Japanese–Korean Conflict, 1951–1965', in Sidney D. Brown (ed.), *Studies on Asia 1967*, Lincoln, 1967, pp. 33–69.

Hahn Bae-ho, 'Korea–Japan Relations in the 1970s', *Asian Survey*, vol. 20, no. 11, November 1980, pp. 1087–97.

Halliday, Jon, 'The Economies of North and South Korea', in John Sullivan and Roberta Foss (eds), *Two Koreas — One Future?*, Lanham, 1987.

Han Sung-joo, 'The Experiment in Democracy',in Lee, Chong-sik, *Korea Briefing 1990*, Boulder, 1991.

Hardacre, Helen, *The Religion of Japan's Korean Minority: The Preservation of Ethnic Identity*, Berkeley, 1984.

Henderson, Gregory, *Korea: The Politics of the Vortex*, Camb, Mass, 1968.

—— 'Constitutional Changes from the First to the Sixth Republics: 1948–1987' in Kim and Kihl, 1988.

Hinton, Harold, *Korea Under New Leadership: The Fifth Republic*, NY, 1983.

Huer, Jon, *Marching Orders: The Role of the Military in South Korea's 'Economic Miracle' 1961–1971*, NY, 1989.

Im Hon-yong, 'The Meaning of the City in Korean Literature', *Korea Journal*, vol. 27–5, May 1987.

Janelli, Roger and Dawnhee, *Ancestor Worship and Korean Society*, Palo Alto, Cal, 1982.

Jones, Leroy and Il Sakong, *Government, Business, and Entrepreneurship in Economic Development: the Korean Case*, Camb, Mass, 1980.

Kalton, Michael, 'Korean Modernity: Change and Continuity' in Lee Chong-sik (ed.), *Korea Briefing 1990*, Boulder, 1991.

Kendall, Laurel and Dix, Griffin (eds), *Religion and Ritual in Korean Society*, Berkeley, 1987.

Kendall, Laurel and Peterson, Mark (eds), *Korean Women: View From the Inner Room*, New Haven, 1983.

Keon, Michael, *Korean Phoenix: A Nation From the Ashes*, Englewood Cliffs, NJ, 1977.

Kihl Young Whan, *Politics and Policies in Divided Korea: Regimes in Contest*, Boulder, Col, 1984.

Kim, C.I. Eugene, 'The Impact of U.S. Military Presence on the Republic of Korea', in Joe C. Dixon (ed.), *The American Military and the Far East*, Washington DC, 1981, p. 220–31.

Kim, Choong S., *Faithful Endurance: An Ethnography of Korean Family Dispersal*, Tucson, 1988.

Kim, Joungwon A., *Divided Korea: The Politics of Development 1945–1972*, Camb, Mass, 1975.

Kim Kwanbong, *The Korea–Japan Treaty Crisis and the Instability of the Korean Political System*, NY, 1971.

Kim Kwang Suk and Roemer, Michael, *Growth and Structural Transformation*, Camb, Mass, 1979.

Kim Quee Young, *The Fall of Syngman Rhee*, Berkeley, 1983.

Kim Se-Jin, *The Politics of Military Revolution in Korea*, Chapel Hill, 1971.

Kim Seong-Kon, 'On Native Grounds: Revolution and Renaissance in Art and Culture', in Lee Chong-sik (ed.), *Korea Briefing 1990*, Boulder, 1991.

Koh Byung Chul, *The Foreign Policy Systems of North and South Korea*, Berkeley, 1984.

Korea Annual, (Yonhap News Agency publication).

Krueger, Anne, *The Developmental Role of the Foreign Sector and Aid*, Camb, Mass, 1979.

Kuznets, Paul W., *Economic Growth and Structure in the Republic of Korea*, New Haven, 1977.

Lee Chae-Jin, 'The Koreans in China: Identity and Adaptation', *Korea and World Affairs*, vol. 13–3, Fall 1989, pp. 503–18.

—— *China's Korean Minority: The Politics of Ethnic Education*, Boulder, 1986.

Lee Chae-Jin and Suh Dae-Sook (eds), *Political Leadership in Korea*, Seattle, 1975.

Lee Changsoo and De Vos, George, *Koreans in Japan: Ethnic Conflict and Accommodation*, Berkeley, 1981.

Lee Chong-sik, 'North and South Korea: From Confrontation to Negotiation', in *Korea Briefing 1990*, Boulder, 1991.

—— (ed.) *Korea Briefing 1990*, Boulder, 1991.

—— *Japan and Korea: The Political Dimension*, Stanford, 1985.

Lee Chung H. and Yamazawa, Ippei (eds), *The Economic Development of Japan and Korea: A Parallel with Lessons*, NY, 1990.

Lee Eun Ho and Yim Yong Soon, *Politics of Military Civic Action: The Case of South Korean and South Vietnamese Forces in the Vietnamese War*, Hong Kong, 1980.

Lee Man-Gap, *Sociology and Social Change in Korea*, Seoul, 1982.

Lee Manwoo, 'Anti-Americanism and South Korea's Changing Perception of America', Lee Manwoo et al. (eds), *Alliance under Tension: The Evolution of South Korean–U.S. Relations*, Seoul 1988, pp. 7–27.

Lee, Peter H.(ed.), *Flowers of Fire: Twentieth Century Korean Stories*, Honolulu, 1974.

Lee Suk Bok, *The Impact of US forces in Korea*, Washington DC, 1987.

Lee Sungho, 'The Emergence of the Modern University in Korea', in P. Altbach and V. Selvaratnam (eds), *From Dependence to Autonomy*, Dordrecht, 1989.

Lee Young-il, *The History of Korean Cinema*, Seoul, 1988.

Lent, John, *The Asian Film Industry*, London, 1990.

Lewis, Linda, 'The "Kwangju Incident" Observed: An Anthropological Perspective on Civil Uprisings', in Donald N. Clark (ed.), *The Kwangju*

Uprising: Shadows over the Regime in South Korea, Boulder, Col, 1988, pp. 15–27.

Light, Ivan and Bonacich, Edna, *Immigrant Entrepreneurs: Koreans in Los Angeles, 1965–1982*, Berkeley, 1988.

Lovell, John, 'The Military and Politics in Postwar Korea', in Edward Reynolds Wright (ed.), *Korean Politics in Transition*, Seattle, 1975.

Macdonald, Donald, *The Koreans: Contemporary Politics and Society*, Boulder, 1988. 2nd edn, 1990.

Mason, Edward S. et al., *The Economic and Social Modernization of the Republic of Korea*, Camb, Mass, 1980.

Mattielli, Sandra (ed.), *Virtues in Conflict: Tradition and the Korean Woman Today*, Seoul, 1977.

Mazarr, Michael et al. (eds), *Korea 1991: The Road to Peace*, Boulder, 1991.

McCormack, Gavan and Selden, Mark (eds), *Korea North and South: The Contemporary Crisis*, NY, 1978.

McGinn, Noel F. et al., *Education and Development in Korea*, Camb, Mass, 1980.

McNamara, Dennis, 'State and Concentration in Korea's First Republic, 1948–60', *Modern Asian Studies*, vol. 26–4, October 1992, pp. 701–18.

Mills, Edwin S. and Song, Byung-nak, *Urbanization and Urban Problems*, Camb, Mass, 1979.

Mitchell, Richard, *The Korean Minority in Japan*, Berkeley, 1967.

Moore, Mick, 'Mobilization and Disillusion in Rural Korea: The Saemaul Movement in Retrospect', *Pacific Affairs*, vol. 57–4, Winter 1984–85, pp. 577–98.

Nam Joo-Hong, *America's Commitment to South Korea: The First Decade of the Nixon Doctrine*, Cambridge, 1986.

Nam Koon Woo, *South Korean Politics: The Search for Political Concensus and Stability*, Lanham, 1989.

Noh Hee Mock, 'The Development of Korean Trade and Investment in the PRC', *Korea in World Affairs*, vol. 13–3, Fall 1989, pp. 421–39.

Oh, John Kie-chang, *Korea: Democracy on Trial*, Ithaca, 1968.

Oliver, Robert, *Syngman Rhee and American Involvement in Korea, 1942–1960: A Personal Narrative*, Seoul, 1978.

Park Chung Hee, *Our Nation's Path: Ideology of Social Reconstruction*, Seoul, 1962.

Roh Tae Woo, *Korea a Nation Transformed: Selected Speeches of President Roh Tae Woo*, Seoul, 1990.

Rutt, Richard, *Korean Works and Days*, Seoul, 1964.

Sorensen, Clark. W., *Over the Mountains are Mountains: Korean Peasant Households and their Adaptation to Rapid Industrialisation*, Seattle, 1988.

Steers, Richard, Shin, Yoo Keun and Ungson, Gerardo, *The Chaebol: Korea's New Industrial Might*, NY, 1989.

Steinberg, David I., *The Republic of Korea: Economic Transformation and Social Change*, Boulder, 1989.

Suh Dae-sook, 'Korean Nationalism: Communism and Democracy', *Korea and World Affairs*, vol. 11–3, Fall 1987, pp. 401–15.

—— (ed.), *Koreans in the Soviet Union*, Honolulu, 1987.

Whang In-joung, *Management of Rural Change in Korea: The Saemaul Undong*, Seoul, 1981.

Wright, Edward Reynolds (ed.), *Korean Politics in Transition*, Seattle, 1975.

North Korea — the DPRK

An Tai Sung *North Korea in Transition: From Dictatorship to Dynasty*, Westport, 1983.

—— *North Korea: A Political Handbook*, Wilmington, 1983.

Chey Youn-Cha Shin, 'Soviet Koreans and Their Culture in the USSR', in Suh
   Dae-Sook (ed.), *Koreans in the Soviet Union*, Honolulu, 1987.
Chung Chong-Shik and Ro Jae-Bong (eds), *Nationalism in Korea*, Seoul, 1979.
Chung, Joseph Sang-hoon, *The North Korean Economy: Structure and Development*,
   Stanford, 1974.
Clippinger, Morgan E., 'Kim Chong-il in the North Korean Mass Media: A
   Study of Semi-esoteric Communication', *Asian Survey*, March 1981.
Cumings, Bruce, 'Corporatism in North Korea', *Journal of Korean Studies*, vol. 3,
   1983.
The Far East and Australasia (annual publication).
Halliday, Jon, 'The Economies of North and South Korea', in John Sullivan
   and Roberta Foss (eds), *Two Koreas — One Future?*, Lanham, 1987.
Hardacre, Helen, *The Religion of Japan's Korean Minority: The Preservation of
   Ethnic Identity*, Berkeley, 1984.
Kihl Young Whan, *Politics and Policies in Divided Korea: Regimes in Contest*,
   Boulder, 1984.
Kim Il Sung, *On Juche in Our Revolution*, Pyongyang, 1975.
Kim Joungwon A., *Divided Korea: The Politics of Development 1945–1972*, Camb,
   Mass, 1975.
Koh Byung Chul, *The Foreign Policy Systems of North and South Korea*, Berkeley,
   1984.
Korea Annual, (Yonhap News Agency publication).
Kwon Youngmin, 'Literature and Art in North Korea: Theory and Policy',
   Korea Journal, vol. 31–2, Summer 1991, pp. 56–70.
Lee Chae-Jin, 'The Koreans in China: Identity and Adaptation', *Korea and
   World Affairs*, vol. 13–3, Fall 1989, pp. 503–18.
—— *China's Korean Minority: The Politics of Ethnic Education*, Boulder, 1986.
Lee Chae-Jin and Suh, Dae-Sook (eds), *Political Leadership in Korea*, Seattle,
   1975.
Lee Chong-sik, 'North and South Korea: From Confrontation to Negotiation',
   in *Korea Briefing 1990*, Boulder, 1991.
—— *Korean Workers Party: A Short History*, Stanford, 1978.
Lee Suk-ho, *Party–Military Relations in North Korea: A Comparative Analysis*,
   Seoul, 1989.
Mazarr, Michael et al. (eds), *Korea 1991: The Road to Peace*, Boulder, 1991.
McCormack, Gavan and Selden, Mark (eds), *Korea North and South: The
   Contemporary Crisis*, NY, 1978.
—— 'North Korea': Kimilsungism — Path to Socialism', *Bulletin of Concerned
   Asian Scholars*, vol. 13, no. 4, 1981, pp. 50–61.
—— 'Kim Country: Hard Times in North Korea', *New Left Review*, no. 198,
   March–April 1993, pp. 15–43.
Mitchell, Richard, *The Korean Minority in Japan*, Berkeley, 1967.
Nahm, Andrew, *North Korea Today: Her Past, Reality, and Impression*, Kalamazoo,
   1978.
Nam Koon Woo, *The North Korean Communist Leadership, 1945–1965*, Alabama,
   1974.
Park Myung-jin, 'Motion Pictures in North Korea', *Korea Journal*, vol. 31–3,
   Autumn 1991, pp. 95–103.
Soon Doe-jin, 'The Periodization of Modern and Contemporary History in
   North Korean Academic Circles', *Korea Journal*, vol. 31–2, Summer 1991,
   pp. 41–55.
Suh Dae-sook, 'Korean Nationalism: Communism and Democracy', *Korea and
   World Affairs*, vol. 11–3, Fall 1987, pp. 401–15.
—— (ed.), *Koreans in the Soviet Union*, Honolulu, 1987.
Suh Dae-sook and Shultz, Edward J. (eds), *Koreans in China*, Honolulu, 1990.